WHO'S ON FIRST?

EVERYTHING A
BASEBALL PARENT
NEEDS TO KNOW

BOBBY BRAMHALL & NATE HEADLEY
with
TED WHITMER & HERMAN DEMMINK

DESIGN: Kathy Mitchell, kathymitchelldesign.com
COVER DESIGN: Danielle Myers
EDITOR: Donald Weise

Bobby Bramhall Nathan Headley Who's On First?
Everything a Baseball Parent Needs to Know / Who's On
First LLC. Printed in the United States of America

ISBN: 979-8-9856386-0-8 (hardback)
ISBN: 979-8-9856386-2 -2 (paperback)
ISBN: 979-8-9856386-1-5 (ebook)
ISBN: 979-8-9856386-3-9 (audiobook)

DEDICATION

BRAMHALL

This book was made possible from the years of dedication, wisdom, sacrifice, and support throughout my career from my parents, J.P. and Belle Bramhall, and my sister, Kaci Anderson. The information and experiences in this career guide were gathered either directly from our challenges and accomplishments, or because of the opportunities and support they provided to make my way. I am forever grateful.

HEADLEY

I must first dedicate this book to my parents, Jane and Kim Headley, who ingrained in me at a young age to never be outworked nor settle for the norm. Thank you both for helping Chase and me navigate our baseball careers before there was ever a guide available like this book. I must also thank my younger brother Chase Headley who was a major part of baseball being a family passion and career path for us both. The memories and hours we spent on the field together and in the backyard training and developing our passion for the game is something I hold near and dear to my heart.

To my wife, Lori Headley, your patience and understanding have allowed me to pursue my goals and dreams of providing opportunities for so many others in this game. I cannot thank you enough for your selflessness in allowing me to travel all over the country and work ridiculous hours in order to create opportunities for young athletes. Finally, I dedicate this book to the thousands upon thousands of athletes and parents who have trusted me in any small way in the development of their game and career whether through on-field coaching or lessons in the cages. You are the ones who have fueled my passion to write this book and share the information we have learned together along the way. My only hope is that this book will help open doors and provide some structure and peace of mind to parents and athletes who do not have the resources available or guidance needed to navigate this process.

TABLE OF CONTENTS

PART II: FOUNDATIONAL ESSENTIALS

PART III: PERFORMANCE AND WELLNESS

AUTHOR BIOS

BOBBY BRAMHALL *is the President and Co-Founder of Athlete Licensing Company ("ALC"), a former NCAA Division I Assistant Athletics Director, and former professional baseball player. After receiving 2nd Team All-American honors at Rice University as a left-handed pitcher and appearing in back-to-back College World Series, he was drafted by the Milwaukee Brewers in the 18th round of the 2007 MLB Draft following his junior year. He went on to play with 4 MLB organizations over 7 seasons in the United States, and in Puerto Rico with the Gigantes de Carolina of La Liga de Béisbol Profesional Roberto Clemente (LBPRC), before attending law school at the University of Tennessee. He is licensed to practice law in Tennessee and currently resides in Nashville, TN.*

NATE HEADLEY *is a former collegiate athlete, former NCAA Division I Baseball Coach and Director of Baseball Operations, and current owner and operator of RBI Baseball & Softball in Knoxville, TN. He is also a professional hitting consultant for amateur, MiLB, and MLB players and teams, and a coach for the nationally ranked prospect team, the Home Plate Chili Dogs. Under his watch, his prospect-age athletes have a 98% scholarship rate at the collegiate level. Nate earned a Bachelor's Degree in Business Accounting from Colorado State University and a Master's Degree in Sports Management from the University of Tennessee. Nate and his wife, Lori, reside in Knoxville, TN.*

AUTHOR'S NOTE

Our individual journeys have spanned from the Little League days of local competitive youth sports all the way to the national arenas of the College World Series and professional competition with Major League Baseball organizations. In addition to the priceless playing experiences, we have coached all levels from youth sports to Division I collegiate baseball, provided skill instruction to developing ballplayers, and counseled parents along every step of that journey for the last twenty years.

Parents, guardians, and mentors of athletes frequently want answers to the many questions that naturally come with this specific path of talent development. In this book, we have compiled for your benefit, all of the knowledge and information we have learned and passed on to others over the years. It is geared toward parents, guardians, and mentors, but can be read by athletes as well because much of the information can only be communicated by speaking directly to them.

We have found that organizational psychologist, Adam Grant, was right when he said, "The most meaningful way to succeed is to help others succeed."[1] With our help, you will gain a meaningful understanding of everything required for the success of your athlete's baseball career, which could begin as young as seven years old. In addition to innate ability and genetic makeup, success is largely determined by what a player is privileged to know or learn through key coaches and mentors along the way. This is the first comprehensive guide in book form, available to all, to lead parents and their athlete(s) from youth baseball all the way to "The Bigs." The information you receive will empower you to direct your focus, invest wisely, and reap the rewards. You matter to the ultimate success of your athlete more than you probably realize. The windows of opportunity narrow as competition increases, and you must be prepared.

Accordingly, the best action you can take is to educate yourself on the various aspects of this industry. This book provides the most effective and efficient way to gain credible insight into the many elite levels of the game; understand how to navigate the relationships between coaches, parents, players, scouts and agents; understand how the talent level of rising athletes is evaluated, which affects future opportunities; gain insight regarding the interaction between a college coach and major league scout about a prospect; know what to expect on Signing Day; discover the best skill training resources; gain insight about nutrition and strength and conditioning; understand baseball injuries; and much more.

Without firsthand experience or a conversation with a professional, this information was previously difficult to obtain. As a result, many athletes have missed out on the opportunities and information needed to succeed. Let's be proactive with the aspects of this game that we can control far in advance.

This is not a book about baseball technique, mechanics, or any other specific skill, for that matter. The baseball industry already has an abundance of skill trainers and experts, many of whom we reference and endorse in the following chapters. This book is the ultimate baseball career advisor. It is a guide to success for you and your athlete in a sport that has many moving parts, both on and off the field.

Depending on what you do with this information, these moving parts can translate to the success or failure of your rising baseball star(s). Don't worry, it won't take you long to understand the bigger picture. We are here to clarify and provide you with an immense amount of credible information to help you see through the muddied waters of the rapidly changing industry in order to understand the lead measures you actually have an influence over. You will then be able to track and observe the variables that yield the results you and your athlete are striving to achieve, and make informed decisions.

The lessons shared in this book are often only available through the first-hand experiences of trial and error, success and painful failure. Luckily for you, you now have the opportunity to learn directly from some of the few who have successfully journeyed to the most elite levels of baseball, the 1%. We will show you the path cleared by those who have gone before us and provide insight for your decisions as parents. The more you know, the better off you and your ballplayer will be.

Here are the most frequently asked questions we receive from parents that we will answer in the chapters to follow:

1. Who are the best private baseball instructors and what do they teach?

2. Can you share the most impactful books on technique?

3. What should my expectations be as my athlete progresses to the next level?

4. How do I navigate the travel baseball circuit?

5. How does the industry look from the coach, agent/advisor, and scout perspectives?

6. What are coaches and scouts searching for when evaluating talent?

7. What options does my athlete have to play competitively after high school?

8. How do we navigate the recruiting process at prospect age?

9. Teach me about parent etiquette.

10. Who are agents and advisors and what do they do? Do we need one? If so, when?

11. What is Name, Image, and Likeness (NIL)?

12. How can I prepare for the political landscape of each level?

13. How can I invest wisely in nutrition, training, and injury prevention for my son/daughter?

14 Can you share your firsthand high school, college, and professional baseball experiences?

15 What are the most common injuries and how does an athlete manage the rehabilitation process following an injury?

16 What are the best resources to improve performance?

This book follows a natural baseball career progression and can be read chronologically for an overall "big picture" knowledge of the industry as your ballplayer develops. You may also use it to focus on the current phase of your athlete's career by referencing the Table of Contents and choosing the relevant section.

Don't be afraid to skip around to different chapters to learn about and verify what others are saying about particular topics. Search for and find what your ballplayer, or you as a parent, currently need for their and your mental and physical toolkit. As your ballplayer continues to develop, each phase passes seemingly more quickly than the previous. Understanding the process and making the best choices moment by moment, gives them the greatest opportunity to maximize their potential.

Trust this guide to accompany you through the hours of practice, private lessons, and road trips that your athlete's journey will take you on. With our help, the decisions you make off the field will be more effective and economical, ensuring results on the field. Give your ballplayer the opportunity to maximize their potential.

We thank you in advance for trusting us and our guidance. We look forward to hearing the many success stories in the future that are made possible by the information provided.

BOBBY BRAMHALL AND NATE HEADLEY

OVERVIEW

Navigating the performance and political landscape of one of the most popular and competitive American sports requires not only willpower and skill development to meet the challenges of the game but also the ability to exercise sound judgment, develop talent, and understand the industry. We divided this career guide into three distinct parts to allow you to focus independently and process all the information you will need for each phase of the journey. Ultimately, this career guide will:

1 Educate you on all aspects of the game off the field, and

2 Help develop a specific plan for artful execution on the field.

PART I: Development and Competition. This part covers everything you need to know about private baseball instruction, recreation and travel leagues, camps and showcases, middle school, high school, Junior College, NCAA Division I, II, III, NAIA, and all levels of professional baseball, including the recruitment process, agent and advisor representation, scouting, and parent etiquette. This section contains contributions from current and former big league players who reached the pinnacle of this career journey. The personal stories shared in this section are what bring meaning to the game, humanizing even the stars, and providing an inside perspective from players who progressed through each level.

PART II: Foundational Essentials. Regardless of what you think you know as a parent, pursuing the right development path is crucial as your ballplayer develops their career-determining playing habits and skill sets. For parents already in the middle of the journey, evaluate your current learning processes, coaching options, and development choices with the information we share to understand the aspects you should be aware of with respect to training.

With insights into the necessities of failure and advice on developing athleticism prior to specializing in baseball, you will gain a foundational understanding of how best to engage with and direct your ballplayer to make long-term improvements. The Throwing Insider and Hitting Insider chapters that follow provide the most credible resources in the game to maximize the time and effort you and your athlete will invest in this journey.

PART III: Performance and Wellness. This section will undoubtedly be part of your athlete's future, whether the journey ends before high school or at the Major League level. Building the foundation for success starts early. We first dive into baseball nutrition, strength, conditioning, and recovery, to build explosive, injury-free power, as well as prime the mental practices that separate the winners from the losers.

Next, we provide industry-leading insight regarding common injuries, injury prevention, and injury rehabilitation. We include the latest medical practices and research on recovery remedies with surgical and non-surgical considerations. Trust this section to answer your questions, address common misconceptions, and provide relevant information when making decisions on general wellness, performance tools or injury prevention and recovery.

Finally, Part III concludes with industry-leading insight regarding performance aides and state-of-the-art evaluation technologies, such as launch monitors, that will give your athlete the best chance at a long and prosperous journey.

OUR ANTHEM

"To fight the good fight is one of the bravest and noblest of life's experiences. Not the bloodshed and the battle of man with man, but the grappling with mental and spiritual adversaries that determines the inner caliber of the contestant. It is the quality of the struggle put forth by a man that proclaims to the world what manner of man he is, far more than may be by the termination of the battle.

It matters not nearly so much to a man that he succeeds in winning some long-sought prize as it does that he has worked for it honestly and unfalteringly with all the force and energy there is in him. It is in the effort that the soul grows and asserts itself to the fullest extent of its possibilities, and he that has worked will, persevering in the face of all opposition and apparent failure, fairly and squarely endeavoring to perform his part to the utmost extent of his capabilities, may well look back upon his labor regardless of any seeming defeat in its result and say, 'I have fought a good fight.'

As you throw the weight of your influence on the side of the good, the true and the beautiful, your life will achieve an endless splendor. It will continue in the lives of others, higher, finer, nobler than you can even contemplate."

HUGH B. BROWN

PART ONE

DEVELOPMENT AND COMPETITION

INTRODUCTION

Part I provides realistic and transparent information from the industry professionals who understand the big picture and how to succeed at each level. As your ballplayer's personal playing journey unfolds, they will come to many crossroads, and it is important that you and your athlete are educated on each level of competitive baseball by credible sources. Our goal is to guide you and your athlete in your decision-making processes to help you understand the landscape and opportunities that you both will encounter each step along the way.

To put things in perspective, 7.3% of high school players will reach NCAA Division I, II, or III. Of those who play at the college level, a mere 9.8% (0.71% overall) will be drafted from a four-year college baseball program to a professional baseball organization. Of those professional baseball players, only 82 per year will make a big league debut. From 2011 to 2018, 17.6% of all players who were drafted and signed with an MLB organization made it to the Major Leagues. Analyzed differently, there is a .0296% chance of a Little League baseball player making a Major League debut.[2]

Part of why we wrote this book is that in addition to the incredible odds to overcome and fortunate breaks necessary to reach the pinnacle, players with previous knowledge of the industry, skill development resources, a network, and good genes have a higher likelihood of realizing this dream. Although the playing field will never be completely level, we want to share valuable information to allow talent and competition to be the deciding factor, rather than an athlete having a disadvantage from being uninformed.

It is also important to realize that in team sports, there are many factors outside of the individual player's control. This is different than in individual sports, such as tennis or golf, where success is determined by the athlete alone. Objectively winning a match, tournament, or championship guarantees advancement, prize money, and/or recognition. For a golfer or tennis player, they must win the qualifier and place high in the subsequent tournament to move on and receive future invitations. Rankings are entirely dependent on individual wins, losses, and results.

In these sports, the athlete is in complete control of their outcome, win or lose. For example, a situation never occurs where a tennis player wins each match without any disqualification in a tournament and is not awarded the championship purse and trophy. Yet, baseball career success, especially at the higher levels, is largely dependent on a combination of network, projectability, market value, draft status, and measurable performance. In baseball, many subjective decisions are made on the athlete's future, and the athlete is forced to accept their fate in another decision maker's hands. Different from individual sports, politics are equally as impactful as performance.

In baseball, most of the players who are promoted or who ultimately reach the highest level are there because they are simply the best. Think about Mike Trout, Mookie Betts, and Carlos Correa here. These players have the most talent and are head and shoulders above the competition, and it shows. However, there is another group of players that does not exist in individual sports where winning is all that determines

Establishing trust is a key component to building psychological safety in teams.

and ensures career longevity. These players may not accomplish or contribute more than their peers on the baseball field. But because of prior investment, projected future value, or a fortunate window of opportunity, they may be promoted and given more opportunity.

This combination of team and individual aspects in baseball has the potential to be incredibly fulfilling and rewarding in the life of your athlete, regardless of the ultimate level achieved. As you and your athlete make decisions to invest in their future by joining competitive organizations from youth to the professional ranks, it is vitally important to join organizations that act with integrity and where their best interests are prioritized.

Red Auerbach, former sixteen-time NBA Champion Boston Celtics coach (including eight-straight) believed that a high level of trust in the organization leads to stability and commitment from the players. "Where players find themselves in a situation where management has a great deal of integrity, and they can depend on the word of the organization, they feel secure. And if players feel secure, they don't want to leave, and if they don't want to leave, they will do everything they can . . . to stay," said Auerbach.[3] Establishing trust is a key component to building psychological safety in teams. Google agrees. In fact, the company found that psychological safety was the top factor in high performing teams within their organization.[4]

In addition to evaluating and selecting teams and organizations in this section, we will discuss many other key components, and the nuances and challenges at each level. While you absorb the insights, our overarching message to you is this: enjoy baseball, compete hard, and control what you are able to while maintaining a realistic perspective. Remember that each successive opportunity is a gift that others may not reach, therefore, cherish your athlete's journey.

PRIVATE BASEBALL INSTRUCTION

"It is the things done when no fans are around that turn ordinary players into champions."

♦ WARREN MORRIS

"There is no limit on 'better.' Talent is distributed unfairly, but there is no limit on how much we can improve what we start with."

♦ KEVIN KELLY

INTRODUCTION

This chapter will provide you with the information necessary to: **1** evaluate whether private baseball instruction is beneficial; and **2** determine if the investment is worthwhile.

Most elite players likely had the benefit of a family member or private instructor they consistently worked with throughout their career, especially during the critical youth developmental years. As baseball evolves and players become more refined, it is exceedingly rare to encounter a professional athlete who did not utilize private baseball instruction in addition to team practices and/or self-instruction. Plainly stated, team practice is simply not enough.

A knowledgeable coach/instructor is crucial when it comes to demonstrating the right technique, developing mental fortitude, and addressing poor habits as they arise. Many private instructors are often owners of prospect age travel baseball teams, which will help your athlete's opportunities beyond private instruction due to their exposure to weekly team competition. These instructors have a vast network to connect players with teams, and understand the importance and intricacies of the recruiting process and the evolution of ever-changing performance philosophies. They make it their life's work to improve the abilities of the athletes they coach to compete at the highest level possible.

Private instructors are not all created equal. It is important to find one who utilizes the most current information available about the game. Poor instruction can lead to inefficient movements and poor habits. Once developed, poor habits are both difficult to change and developmentally oppressive because of the time and effort it takes to unlearn a sequence of movements after weeks, months, or years of dedicated practice. Physical ability should dictate a player's ceiling, not poor habits or lack of understanding arising from the philosophies of an uninformed instructor.

Therefore, it is crucial to invest in an instructor who understands what each individual needs to succeed and who supplements physical skill development with the psychology of success. Raw tools or potential, while necessary, do not translate to success in baseball without an understanding of how to efficiently and diligently work towards a mentally and physically polished product. Be careful of quick fixes, and trust the process!

HOW TO IDENTIFY QUALITY INSTRUCTION

We understand how difficult it is for you to know which drills or instructors are most beneficial. In fact, that's probably why you are reading this book. Many drills are not necessarily designed to address an athlete's specific skill set or mechanical inefficiencies. However, finding an instructor who can direct the athlete's development and relate to their specific needs is essential. A quality instructor will communicate well and individually prescribe specific drills and programming for each player's specific mechanical and psychological needs. Furthermore, a good instructor will build trust and confidence with the athlete. This only comes when the instructor is credible. An athlete's self-confidence and confidence in their instructor is important!

Private instructors charge more for their time due to sheer level of experience and expertise in a one-on-one setting, which allows for a custom program defined by each athlete's specific needs, deficiencies, and goals. If participation, rather than focused development, is your athlete's end goal, recreational day camp is probably a better and more affordable choice.

Whether your athlete takes a lesson with a Cy Young Award winner or your dad's former high school baseball coach, the key is to find an instructor who understands the best way to apply advanced subject matter on an individual player-by-player basis. It is one thing to be able to successfully perform a movement at a professional level and another to effectively teach the fundamentals to equip aspiring athletes with the proper tools to reach such a level.

Never allow an instructor to change natural aspects of a player's mechanics or limit their freedom of movement or athleticism. Individual technique instruction is never a cookie cutter, one-size-fits-all situation. It is most important for an instructor to understand how the athlete learns, whether through visual or auditory cues, and diagnose the individual's mechanics to properly move forward. Does the athlete learn by repetition at full-speed or slow motion? Will they benefit more from constant audible feedback, video review,

> **A quality instructor will communicate well and individually prescribe specific drills and programming for each player's specific mechanical and psychological needs.**

or working in front of a mirror? These are the questions a proper instructor will consider.

One pitcher may have trouble generating rhythm on the mound while another may have difficulty repeating a release point. One hitter may be off balance while another simply needs to swing with intent. If a specific instructor's drills and information are not tailored to address an athlete's specific challenge or desired output, that instructor is not doing an adequate job, and your money is better spent elsewhere.

There are countless collegiate and professional players, current and former, who are teaching the "right stuff." By maximizing the time period of an individual lesson by custom-tailoring it to the needs of each individual athlete, these instructors are able to passionately and effectively imbue invaluable knowledge and expertise to young ballplayers. You can trust word of mouth reviews from others, direct communication with the instructor, and social media content to ensure the philosophies taught by the instructor are a good fit for your athlete. Remember, each player has unique tools that require different adjustments. You wouldn't build a treehouse with drywall screws.

Ultimately, the instructor must figure out the right tools and fixes for each player. This is the most important first step for any pitcher, hitter, or defensive player. The ideal instructor will understand the areas needing improvement, have the expertise to fix these issues, and assist your athlete with appropriate skill development to stay on target towards their specific goals. Find the proper instructor to make long-lasting, positive change.

We encourage you to also research the articles, individual instructors, and information provided in Part II to improve your understanding of the importance of athlete-specific philosophies and quality instruction. Success in technical skill sports, like baseball, depends on much more than genetics or natural gifts because of the commitment required to refine and repeat difficult movements or conceptualize many different aspects of the game. As your overall awareness and perspective of the game improves, you will more easily identify and locate the best possible private instruction for your athlete.

HOW TO MAXIMIZE EFFICIENCY OF INSTRUCTION

An instructor's overall job is to share knowledge and train technique in such a way that the hitter, pitcher, or defensive player improves their unique abilities. The purpose is not to exhaust the player with repetition but to create awareness and develop muscle memory for prime athletic maturation.

As we've said before, the learning curve becomes exponentially steeper at each progressive level of the game. That said, a universal, one-size-fits-all lesson approach is not conducive to individual adaptation and development. It is imperative the athlete gains ground each lesson to create an environment where they both retain the information and understand its inherent value. Be aware of time-wasting methods utilized by some instructors. You want to maximize the benefits of a lesson rather than unwisely spending precious minutes on needless drills. These may include: an extended warm-up time that should be performed prior to the instruction session, inefficient transition from one drill to the next, and longer than necessary teaching monologues.

With respect to stretching and warming up, it is important to know where your athlete stands with regard to age, mobility, and experience. Discuss this with your instructor to determine whether they need direction in the areas of stretching and warming up. Many young athletes will. After this conversation, you and your athlete can establish a proper stretch and warm-up routine prior to the private lesson to permit the athlete to enter the instruction period loose and ready to work on skill development. This will also help to prevent injury. Trusting an instructor to independently make sure the player's arms, legs, core rotational muscles and joints are primed and ready is not a good approach because each individual athlete's warm-up needs are different and the short time available is used quickly.[5]

Spend your money and time on expert mechanical and psychological baseball development. Prior to the first lesson and on occasion thereafter, discuss the skills your athlete wishes to improve during private instruction. Find out what you and your athlete can do outside of the instruction period to maximize continued skill development. Remember, the instructor works for you. As a purveyor of a service, the instructor must modify routine and practice areas to earn your continued business. The needs of your athlete must always come first. Therefore, if proper attention is not provided or no improvement is made long-term, explore other options for private instruction.

THE MARKET PRICE

The current market for private lessons ranges from $30.00-$75.00 per thirty-minute instruction session, or $50.00-$120.00 per hour. Larger cities typically have higher rates due to costs of living, demand, notoriety, and/or facility expenses. However, price should not be the deciding factor. When searching for a private instructor, focus on the depth of information they have to share with your athlete. In private instruction, the phrase "you get what you pay for" doesn't always apply.

EASY WAYS TO SAVE MONEY:

1. Ask about bulk lesson packages at discounted rates;

2. Offer to schedule several lessons in advance; and/or

3. Consider group instructional sessions.

As you seek to hire a potential instructor, keep in mind that these professionals would prefer a busy schedule full of repeat customers.

By becoming a regular client or consistently attending group sessions, you will avoid the high premium of a one-time lesson and allow the instructor to build a better relationship with your athlete. Simply put, the better the communication, the more reliable the feedback. The three most important factors for a successful athlete-instructor relationship are:

1. communication

2. clear expectations

3. reciprocal growth

A healthy example of successful communication is if the instructor says: "This is the information I want you to know and apply because I see this potential in you." The player says: "This is the way I learn best; these are the questions that I have; and, these actions will show that I am absorbing the information you've given me." An ongoing relationship enhances habits and individual aspects of a player's physical and mental approach in ways a one-time lesson cannot.

Do not let price deter you from appreciating the full value of credible instruction. Remember to schedule in advance, work in group sessions, and utilize bulk package rates. Whether the accomplishment is making the local team at the next level or getting drafted professionally, when possible, don't let a dollar figure dictate your athlete's next priceless achievement. The lessons they learn on the field will prepare them for any career path, athletic or otherwise. Valuable baseball instruction will pay dividends in the short-term and long-term by instilling values that persist even after the baseball-playing days are over.

LESSON BLUEPRINT

This is the format for a proper lesson. Depending on where the athlete is in their development, the order may vary slightly.

1 Introduction and a general overview of the lesson. Parents are encouraged to participate in this portion to understand and discuss areas of focus with the player after instruction. Clear communication keeps everyone on the same page and allows the parent to reinforce the philosophies and practices taught by the instructor.

2 Review of concepts learned in previous lessons and/or an overview of the current session. This allows the player to get their mind in the right place to firmly establish which issues they will address going forward. This is a great time for video review to diagnose any issues or outcomes from previous practices or games. If the parent has live game footage, the instructor can use it to further tailor an athlete's individual instruction.

3 Engaged instruction. Remember, quality practice repetitions are more important than the total quantity of repetitions. Learning new skills requires both quality and quantity, however, sacrificing quality for quantity is an obvious cause of poor habit development. The best approach will depend on the age and ability of the player. The instructor will evaluate which movements to emphasize and how to achieve target goals.

4 Conclusion. The instructor should conclude the lesson by reinforcing the most important takeaways and reminding the athlete of the areas needing further improvement. The athlete should be given specific things to focus on between lessons that are unique to their needs. Examples may include performing a specific drill in a mirror or improving hand-eye coordination. Seek progress. These drills and individually-tailored approaches will accelerate improvement and inspire your athlete to dedicate personal time to development outside of private instruction. This will ensure they reach maximum improvement from week to week.

PITCHING LESSONS:

Each throwing drill should address arm path, body position and sequencing, ball spin/rotation, and release point. Playing catch should focus on throwing at a target, with particular attention to ball spin and balanced mechanics. Performing gimmicky drills week after week, without purpose or intent for improvement, is ultimately detrimental. Ensure each throw or pitch is for a purpose to maximize the benefit of a lesson.

HITTING LESSONS:

An instructor should provide feedback and take advantage of teaching moments to explain terms, ensure understanding, and/or supply constructive criticism for positive reinforcement between sets of full-speed swings. If an instructor is not allowing a hitter adequate time to rest, the hitter will surely develop bad habits. Fatigue may be the most detrimental factor working against the improvement of a baseball swing.

Fatigue may be the most detrimental factor working against the improvement of a baseball swing.

Each throw, pitch, and swing should be executed with intention. By keeping a player engaged and creating awareness using drills designed to encourage the retention of information, this will ensure your athlete performs the proper movements consistently in competitive environments. From time to time, the instructor should also let the player provide feedback. Self-awareness is important for any athlete.

Most importantly, identifying an outcome and working backwards to pinpoint the cause of a positive or negative result is key to fostering awareness of necessary adjustments for continued improvement. For example, discussing an at-bat from a previous game and reviewing the pitch sequence pitch-by-pitch reminds the player which particular decision or movement pattern produced the ultimate outcome. This process prevents the athlete from viewing the whole game or at-bat as a failure or success, but rather identifies cause and effect.

PARENT PARTICIPATION AND ETIQUETTE

If you are in a facility or your athlete is working with an instructor who permits you to be present for the lesson:

1 Listen and stay attentive, but allow the paid professionals to do their jobs.

2 If permissible, film instructors as they are using a certain drill, analogy, or teaching moment. Filming swings and pitches, both good and bad, provides invaluable understanding to the athlete for review during the processing and integration period after the practice session.

3 If you are in a situation where you cannot be present due to rules of the facility, discuss what the athlete learned from each lesson and what they should be working on before the next session.

The more you know about the environment of a private lesson, and how to interact with the instructor, the better your athlete's results will be. You should be an asset to the instruction process, not a hindrance. That said, as a parent, you absolutely have the right to ask questions and be a part of the process. After all, you are investing your time and money into your athlete's development. We have some tips to ensure that your involvement supports the process.

Initially, an instructor will work to build trust with the athlete while discerning how the athlete learns and applies the information from the lesson. Allowing this relationship to mature organically will create a safe environment for the athlete to openly and honestly discuss on- and off-the-field matters. Since you ultimately know the athlete better than anyone, the best thing you can do to help is to initiate a post-lesson discussion to understand how they are absorbing the information. If you have any lingering questions, have a conversation with the instructor before the next training session.

During training sessions, there are appropriate moments to ask the instructor to clarify a teaching point. The best moments for these conversations are in-between rounds while your athlete is picking up baseballs or moving equipment for the next drill. Moreover, it is also okay to ask questions to clarify information for yourself. This will help you to understand how/why your athlete should practice specific drills outside of the lesson to build muscle memory and accelerate improvement. In reality, the most significant developments occur outside of the lesson period. You should view the lesson as the "classroom." However, permanent integration occurs during at-home practice and individual training with daily repetition.

We've all heard of helicopter parenting. These parents are overprotective or over involved in the lives of their children. Not surprisingly, helicopter parents can become a detrimental hindrance to development when providing feedback during a lesson that is not directly from the coach/instructor or part of the training session. From the athlete's perspective, the parent is inherently a priority over the instructor. So, when a parent's feedback drowns out the instructor during a drill, it takes the athlete's attention away from the content of the lesson.

This is especially problematic when a parent, with the best of intentions, attempts to help by repeating a technique reminder such as "stay back," while the athlete is learning a new drill. The failure is teaching the athlete to adapt to the challenge, yet, their attention will naturally be constrained by your feedback. Moreover, at some point, your athlete will reach a maturity level that enables them to ask the proper questions and make adjustments without your involvement.

Provide opportunities for your athlete's development while also recognizing the many pressures and challenges that exist outside of training and competition. Figuratively speaking, feed your athlete when they are hungry but do not force them to eat. Do your best to provide opportunities for development when your athlete wants to practice, but recognize when they need a break. Despite the purity of your intentions, transferring your agenda onto your athlete may negatively impact their passion for the game, as well as the desire to continue training.

Most importantly, you must not become emotionally attached to the outcome of your athlete's performance and training. The best training inevitably results in failure because it exposes the limits of performance at that time and sparks growth and understanding for future performance. This type of failure does not mean your athlete is failing. Understand that the parent-athlete relationship involves more emotional baggage than that of the instructor-athlete relationship. Learning how to maintain a positive relationship with your athlete will strengthen your relationship going forward.

GROUP SESSIONS

If you cannot afford private lessons, group training sessions spread the cost of an instructor's time amongst several athletes. Frequent one-on-one sessions can be costly. Group sessions are a cost-effective alternative for high-level instruction and allow for many additional benefits for the athlete to train with their peers.

Further, group sessions create a competitive environment where multiple athletes are simultaneously working on similar skills. The environment challenges individual athletes to compete with one another as they are able to observe the results of their peers. This type of competition enhances the focus and accountability of the athletes, thereby maximizing the outcome of the training session. The intensity of the group atmosphere also encourages higher content retention. This is because information flows freely through all avenues of learning instead of being limited to the isolated channel of instructor to athlete.

In a one-on-one session, one of the most difficult hurdles for an instructor to overcome is facilitating a comfortable discussion of failure. In a healthy group session environment, athletes feel comfortable to freely discuss personal performance issues. These types of conversations benefit all athletes in the group as they develop the confidence to contribute their own experiences to the conversation. In group settings amongst peers, athletes are typically more comfortable sharing failures and performance obstacles.

FACILITIES

There are an overwhelming number of baseball training facilities across the country. When deciding on a facility, the most important considerations are: **1** what is best for your athlete in the current stage of their career; and, **2** where they are currently positioned in relation to the development of their peers.

When selecting a facility, it is imperative that you understand exactly what the athlete needs. Some facilities focus on specific skill development while others focus primarily on building high-level teams of prospects for recruiting exposure. At times, it may be difficult to find facilities that excel at both. Keep this in mind when determining whether your athlete would benefit more from one facility or another. Do they need skill development or recruiting exposure? It may also be necessary to send your athlete to one facility for skill development and another for recruiting exposure.

It is important to note that fame and/or marketing do not create a great facility. Knowledgeable baseball players often keep their focus on the game, while using word-of-mouth or Google reviews secondarily. Find the instructors and facilities that are providing credible, high-level pitching, hitting, or defensive instruction. Find the people and places that are passionate about passing along the best information to the upcoming generation of athletes.

Facilities purely specializing in exposure can be just as valuable as those primarily focused on credible, high-level instruction. These types of facilities are typically well-connected

 PRO TIP ——————

Driveline Baseball is an example of a facility you should use to compare instruction philosophies, the latest technology, and athlete development, especially in pitching.

with tournaments and showcases, in addition to benefiting from automatic bids into the most highly scouted and recruited showcase tournaments in the world. These are the types of facilities college and professional scouts rely upon to locate the best prospects. Find a facility that promises to develop your athlete for performing at any level of the game.

ONLINE TRAINING AND EVALUATION

Online video analysis and remote training can be useful for those in smaller cities who are not able to locate convenient, reputable instruction. These days, a large number of high-level instructors also offer virtual instruction. Do yourselves a favor and utilize the social media accounts of the credible instructors referenced herein. This will help you isolate the philosophies and theories you believe to be most beneficial to your athlete. Video instruction and feedback have both long-and short-term benefits, in addition to being an efficient use of time and money.

Nevertheless, there are a few negative aspects you should be aware of when utilizing online training:

1 The instructor is only able to diagnose and provide feedback based on the repetitions that are recorded and submitted. Some of the good and bad reps are missed, which serve as teaching moments during in-person instruction.

2 The suggested drills and mechanical work are limited to those capable of being performed on equipment already available in the athlete's practice environment. At a state-of-the-art facility, the athlete has access to more and diverse equipment/technology.

3 The instructor is not able to oversee the drills the athlete is performing to ensure proper understanding and execution. It is more beneficial to receive simultaneous instruction during practice sessions rather than after the athlete has already developed poor habits through improper repetition.

4 There could be a time delay in feedback as the instructor most likely prioritizes on-site training over online video analysis.

5 During online training, the athlete typically does not have the benefit of asking questions and receiving instant feedback. For example, body-awareness and understanding of swing or pitch sequencing can be difficult to correct/address without real-time interaction.

6 Online instruction may be more effective for the athletes who are further along in development, comfortable with swing patterns and pitching mechanics, and can make adjustments without real-time feedback or hands-on instruction.

Despite the challenges, credible online instruction is certainly still more beneficial than poor on-site instruction.

Finally, if at all possible, consider traveling on occasion to your preferred online instructor's facility for in-person training to supplement the online instruction. Even a single one-on-one session can make a huge difference in the athlete's long-term success. The instructor will be able to clarify terminology and proper drill instruction to ensure repetitions that will lead to proper development. On-site training will also enhance the instructor-athlete relationship by allowing the instructor to personally connect with the athlete, and fully understand how the athlete receives and retains information.

NAVIGATING THE TRAVEL BASEBALL CIRCUIT

INTRODUCTION

Travel or "select" baseball is understood to be the most serious and competitive version of youth baseball. The players competing in travel or select tournament baseball will be the best players, if not the only players, to make the middle school and high school teams. This means that competing in the travel baseball circuit before and during high school is necessary for your athlete's development and future if they hope to compete for school-affiliated programs. Our travel baseball circuit roadmap will keep you focused on the critical areas of involvement with accurate information about the best opportunities to provide advantages for your athlete.

WHEN TO PURSUE TRAVEL BASEBALL

Once an athlete has surpassed the talent level in the recreational leagues, or desires to be more athletic, talented, and committed to the game beyond what a recreational league can offer, travel baseball is the next step. A player desiring a greater challenge should be given the opportunity to develop the skills to chase that passion. The recreational leagues serve an important community purpose of involving kids in team activities that are enjoyable and lead to friendships and involvement in sports. However, there are players who will outgrow the less intense competition levels and require a greater challenge.

Currently, travel baseball begins as early as 7 and 8 years old (7U & 8U) and ends at 18 years old (18U). Pursuing travel baseball at an age when the athlete is ready may create more opportunities for the athlete and avoid loss of confidence or passion for playing. Starting too soon could backfire unless they are ready. Understanding the performance level and interests of your athlete should dictate when you seek to join a travel ball team.

A clear comparison of the difference between recreational and travel baseball is best understood by comparing them with "club" and "varsity" collegiate sports teams. Both teams consist of members who are interested in the sport, and both have skill, interest, and enjoyment in participation. However, one plays for championships, notoriety, and future opportunities, while the other's involvement is strictly for participation and entertainment and is not considered highly competitive. On the travel and varsity teams, the competitive players who are selected advance in commitment and skill development. If baseball is one of your athlete's highest passions, it is necessary for them to be around equally or more talented peers and adapt to the increasing skill and competition levels of the other athletes in their age group.

If baseball is one of your athlete's highest passions, it is necessary for them to be around equally or more talented peers and adapt to the increasing skill and competition levels of the other athletes in their age group.

TRAVEL BASEBALL AND SCHOLASTIC BASEBALL TEAMS

Scholastic baseball teams, which are affiliated with schools, can be enjoyable and contribute to long lasting friendships and fond memories. Competing for a school rallies the local community, especially in the playoffs, and is a proud experience for players and parents alike. Although a valuable aspect of overall development, scholastic baseball is not what ultimately elevates your athlete to the next level. Immersion in travel baseball is what creates the necessary development required for the most serious levels of competition nationwide.

One reason is that high school baseball coaches tend to pursue long-term careers in the school systems as teachers or athletic directors. They are often involved in many other sports or athletic responsibilities in addition to their full-time teaching duties. Due to the time constraints and availability, individual technical skill development may be limited. As a result, coaches' jobs are focused on team management and winning baseball games for the school program. What helps a middle school or high school program win games is not necessarily what elevates an individual player's game or provides opportunities for advancement to the next level.

Another reason is that many coaches have a knowledge and love for the game, but are primarily interested in impacting kids through leadership and involvement through school sponsored sports programs. The rapidly evolving research of the game and crucial individual athlete development aspects can be missed due to these varying priorities. While there are a number of scholastic programs and coaches around the country that develop players at a high level, the system, as a whole, is not designed for individual development and placement at the next level of competition.

Unfortunately, many public school systems require that a head or assistant baseball coach be employed by the school system primarily as an educator. This requirement limits involvement and impact by highly-qualified individuals and independent businessmen, who are often baseball experts. The result is a disservice to the athletic enhancement portion of our scholastic sports programs because proper screening and qualification assessments could be performed to allow employment by coaches unaffiliated with the education system to positively impact the programs, individual player development, and increase the competitive value of scholastic competition.

Finally, immersion in travel ball is necessary because a deeper talent pool exists by playing with and against the top players from each school, rather than with and against a handful of good players at only one school. Larger talent pools, regionally and nationally, improve competition and athletic development. Highly concentrated talent pools also attract college and professional scouts to one location to evaluate talent from several quality teams, rather than isolated single games with limited talent between two local teams. Thus, involvement in travel ball, in conjunction with scholastic programs, becomes an important aspect for optimizing and exposing the athlete's playing career.

IDENTIFYING AND SELECTING A TRAVEL BALL TEAM

Regardless of which geographic region you live in, with the exception of a few rural areas where team sports are difficult to organize, there are likely options to choose from for travel baseball involvement. Most medium sized cities have organizations that compete frequently in major metropolitan area tournaments. Especially in the pre-high school years, joining a competitive local organization will save you valuable time and resources to remain close to home while development improves.

Well-known organizations may offer the best resources for individual instruction and exposure, however, you should be open to finding a team where the goal is to gain experience on the field when you begin this travel ball journey. The most important consideration is to select a team where the athlete can fail, succeed, and develop with others of similar talent level.

As talent level increases and exposure becomes more important, it may be necessary to travel to a larger city to join an organization that faces better competition and is geared toward development on a national stage. If you live in a large metropolis, find a team that has players more and less talented than your athlete to maintain adequate playing time and maximize the repetitions they receive. The best players on the team will not be pushed unless there are other players of equal or greater potential, who help create a competitive environment.

Once the athlete begins to own their abilities and becomes comfortable, move toward the travel ball organizations that pursue the best tournaments, players, and programs that are managed in a professional manner. At the prospect level, these are the most important considerations because exposure and elite development is what creates opportunities for the athlete to continue their playing career.

If you decide to pursue a playing opportunity with one of the larger and more well-known travel ball organizations, be sure to do your research. Many of these organizations begin with a few elite-level teams as they provide exposure and establish a highly competitive presence with successful output and positive methods. Yet, as the organizations grow in name recognition, they may inevitably reach the threshold where they can field multiple mediocre teams for the business's bottom line, while overall quality remains reserved for the elite level teams. Be sure to understand which caliber of team your athlete is being placed on within these large, often expensive, organizations.

You may be better off with another club that can offer better playing opportunities or lower costs. Let's drive the point home once more: your athlete will not automatically be in a great situation for exposure or development simply because they are selected to play for a highly recognized organization. The third or fourth best teams in an age group will not face the highest level of competition where college recruiters and professional scouts consistently evaluate talent.

That said, before you join a team, be aware of the talent level of the other players in comparison to your ballplayer, the credibility of coaches, and the upcoming season schedule to ensure that the team will provide the expected quality of development and exposure.

Further, if your athlete is at the bottom of current ability on the team, they may not receive sufficient repetitions and playing time for development and confidence. Internal passion requires a threshold amount of success, different for each athlete, to "taste" the desire to pursue continued skill development.

Therefore, avoid teams where they will not receive ample playing time and opportunities to succeed. Sitting the bench for a brief period to observe can be beneficial during injury recovery, fill in for a talented team that needs a player, transition to a higher level of competition, or absorb high-level information from a coach with a high baseball IQ. However, this should be the exception rather than the rule in younger age groups where quality repetitions are most important. Ultimately, muscle memory and biomechanical movement patterns require consistent competitive repetitions and action on the field.

SPECIALIZATION

Similarly, specialized roles should only be permitted in unique circumstances until an appropriate age. 13-14 years old, at the earliest, is when a player might only enjoy or have the tools to play one position on the field. Learning the game by playing different positions is most advantageous for overall mental and physical development. They will always have the ability to specialize in the future and might even be required to specialize to survive. A common example of specialization is a pitcher-only ("PO") arrangement that is sometimes common with prospect age athletes. In this scenario, a player may specialize in the only position that they will likely play at the next level.

Specialization may also occur with catchers, who should not be

Learning the game by playing different positions is most advantageous for overall mental and physical development.

exempt from playing other positions, such as third base and first base and running the bases for themselves. Catchers are often substituted on the base paths for courtesy runners, which limits their ability to learn to run the bases, increase athleticism and enhance baseball IQ. Playing a position in the field will also challenge catchers' perspectives and grow field awareness from different points of view than behind the plate. We recommend that the vast majority of players experience many positions before specializing, because once a single position is chosen, it may be difficult to transition back to other positions.

In support of this view, when a player reaches the collegiate level, the ability to play multiple positions increases opportunities to earn playing time early in their career because they are able to contribute in many different areas and for multiple jobs, as opposed to only one specific position.

FINANCIAL AND TIME RESOURCE CONSIDERATIONS

As a parent, it is important to evaluate your family's desire (time priority) and financial ability to travel before committing to the travel baseball circuit. Many, if not most, travel baseball teams require a year-long commitment and are on the road multiple weekends and weeknights at prospect age during the fall, spring, and summer. Baseball is a sport that requires a large quantity of games to improve, rather than a large amount of practice time within the team, such as in football.

A typical weekend on the road consists of expenses such as: meals, hotels, laundry, vehicle and fuel, sibling and pet care arrangements, and loss of potential employment earnings. This is all in addition to the fees required to play for a specific team. Generally, team fees range from $1,500 to $6,500 per year, depending on the organization and location, with possible discounts for players who are only pitchers ("PO") due to being on the field less than position players.

The best way to budget for the many expenses is to request a tournament schedule and mandatory associated fees in advance, which will provide an estimate for your annual baseball expenditures. These fees may contribute towards: coaches' pay, practice time, uniforms, equipment, tournament entrance fees, and facility memberships. The financial strain can be overcome by alternating supervision

TRAVEL HACK

If your athlete is one of the best players on their travel ball team and you are constantly on the road, consider playing up an age bracket. This move will serve two purposes:

1. The competition level will increase immediately.
2. The need to travel regularly to expose them to better competition will decrease.

with other parents, group meals, advanced meal preparation, sharing hotel rooms, staying at campgrounds rather than hotels, or renting homes to share costs with other families. Be creative!

If you live in a region where travel is required to face elite competition or to play for an elite team, continuous travel will likely be the norm each weekend until the collegiate level. For those living within large metropolises, you may be fortunate to have several tournaments in the area annually, which does not require travel every weekend to participate in highly competitive tournaments. They may be challenged in their own backyard. Nevertheless, travel will always be part of your routine, as elite teams frequently play in other major cities to face new and improved competition.

Playing up a level will also give them the opportunity to become comfortable playing with older athletes because they will inevitably be competing with and against older players at the high school and collegiate levels in the future.

It is unavoidable that aspiring college players ages 12U-18U will spend an incredible amount of time traveling to compete for the majority of spring and summer, and that a considerable financial investment in this endeavor will be necessary. There is no other way to ensure development at the rate and level consistent with their peers. While other sports may provide a long break, continuing to pursue elite tournaments and showcases is recommended while the athlete is in the baseball prospect age and recruiting window.

Therefore, consider all of the investments of time commitment and financial resources needed to make the wisest, most practical, and most beneficial decisions when selecting a travel baseball team during your athlete's crucial stages of development and recruiting window. Equally important, ensure that your athlete understands the commitment required by your family such that they take full advantage of the development and exposure opportunities provided.

LEVELS OF YOUTH BASEBALL 6U-14U

The names for the different divisions may vary region to region, but the levels of youth baseball prior to high school competition generally are:

1 **Recreational Leagues** - This level comprises leagues that are similar to Little League, Babe Ruth, Dixie Youth, Cal Ripken, Pony, and American Legion. Participation is available through a sign up and is normally budget-friendly. These leagues provide entry-level competition with very little pressure and are a great way to gauge whether the athlete has a passion and/or ability to pursue playing at a higher level.

2 **D3/C/AA** - This level is the beginning of travel ball competition and consists of competitive tryouts and focused competition. Often, this level requires less overall travel than elite levels but will still require consistent practices, tournaments, full-season commitments, and long hours. Generally, development is more important than outcome at this level.

3 **D2/B/AAA** - This level provides mid-range to above the mid-range competition level consisting of players owning their crafts, separating from the pack, and is made up of teams of players who play at a high level. This is not the most elite travel baseball level, but many of the AAA players will see a future at the collegiate and professional levels. This level of competition may require more travel than AA to face higher caliber competition. There remains a strong development aspect, but wins and losses become a greater priority than the levels below.

4 **DI/A/Major** - This is the highest level of youth travel baseball with the most advanced teams, overall talent, and individual players in any particular age group. It is not necessary to compete at this level unless and until the athlete is physically and mentally prepared, otherwise, it could be an overwhelming experience.

WHERE DOES MY ATHLETE BELONG?

A great way to determine which level is best suited for your athlete is by attending tryouts to give a realistic comparison of the other players in their age range. Tryouts provide an opportunity to showcase abilities in front of coaches and provide accurate placement, rather than relying on parental bias. It is not in the best interest of the athlete to force them to play at a higher level than they are ready for at the present moment. A small fish in a big pond faces overwhelming pressures and frequent failures, which are the quickest paths to burnout or disinterest in the game.

Without minimal success, it is natural for a struggling player to find other activities and interests to enjoy, which could be less rewarding in the long-term. Regardless of the athlete's initial placement after tryouts, do not be discouraged. Playing time and proper fit is most important, and no situation is permanent. Even at the professional level, players continue to develop and increase their value as they adapt to new challenges and understand the game on a more advanced level. Today's disappointment could be a long-term blessing with the motivation gained from accurate assessment of their current deficiencies and exposure of areas needed to improve going forward.

Malcolm Gladwell argues in support of this concept in his book *David and Goliath*, only Gladwell uses college students as the subject, rather than young athletes. His premise is that a college student may lose confidence and motivation or be overshadowed in a particular field of study at an elite university because of the intense competition immediately surrounding the student upon enrollment. Whereas, that same student might grow and improve in a particular field of study in a less competitive but equally competent training environment, and achieve equal or greater success as a student at an elite university would in the long-term, rather than prematurely quitting the endeavor or not qualifying for future opportunities.[6]

We know that the successful professionals are not always from Ivy League schools, and the most successful athletes do not all begin in the most prestigious athletic environments. Nevertheless, it is unfortunate when athletes are forced to choose a different path before realizing their full potential or exercising grit to achieve success because the pool of competition is so strong.

While this is not a "never quit" argument, (as quitting often creates space to achieve in other areas), it does demonstrate the advantage of being a big fish in a small pond, at least for a period, to gain sufficient training, playing time, opportunity, confidence, and growth. Always seeking the biggest pond possible, whether that be in academics, athletics, or another worthy endeavor, may create a premature exit when the individual only needs more time to mature.

We recommend sitting down with your athlete to discuss current abilities, set goals, and map a plan of action for achieving those goals. Serve as a parental guide, but allow your athlete to lead. This will strengthen your relationship, prevent wasted investment, and jointly focus your efforts.

PROSPECT AGE COMPETITION 15U-18U

While younger-aged competition should be focused on team fit, travel ability, and playing time for development, prospect age decisions should be primarily focused on placement to compete at the highest level and the optimal tournament atmosphere for next level exposure and elite skills development. It only takes one good performance, or one season of consistent production, to showcase value and land an opportunity. Listed below are some of the most nationally recognized showcase tournaments that provide excellent exposure for the collegiate and professional levels.

1   World Wood Bat Classics (Hosted by Perfect Game) - Most tournaments are currently hosted in the Southeast region of the United States (Tennessee, Georgia, and Florida). Jupiter, Florida holds the premiere tournament, the World Wood Bat Association (WWBA) World Championship, which is the top annual scouting attraction in all of amateur baseball. With over 700 MLB scouts and college coaches in attendance, organizations nationwide receive invites by winning Perfect Game qualifying tournaments or by automatic bids based on program success and talent development history.

2   Perfect Game Tournaments - Perfect Game is the industry leader for prospect age athlete rankings and tournaments. Perfect Game also hosts the prospect-level Underclass All-American Games and the Super25. Any Perfect Game tournament has incredible benefits of competition, exposure, and experience among the best talent in the country. perfectgame.org

3   Top Gun Sports - Top Gun Sports is a well-run organization that hosts quality elite tournaments at excellent facilities, focusing on

talent development and exposure. Tournament winners are placed in elite national invitational tournaments versus other winners. playtopgunsports.com

④ Prep Baseball Report (PBR) - PBR has a large national following and currently runs national events at the Lakepoint Sports facility, north of Atlanta in Emerson, Georgia. PBR has an extensive prospect ranking and recruiting database, and hosts showcases nationwide. prepbaseballreport.com

Whether your team ends up in a tournament hosted by one of the above national organizations or finds other competitive options, when evaluating the tournaments, look at the list of teams attending, where they originate, and whether tournament entrance is invite-only or first-come, first-served. Next, consult GameChanger www.gc.com to research team rosters and identify the percentage of players from different high schools in the region that make up each team.

Typically, if a team has several players from the same high school, the team will not be as talented as a team consisting of quality players assembled from different regions because the players are selected from a larger talent pool. Additionally, be cautious of playing tournaments with several teams that are not affiliated with larger and widely recognized organizations. Without a history of college or professional baseball alumni, it may not be a worthwhile travel investment to play unknown or untalented teams.

PARENT ETIQUETTE DURING TRAVEL BALL

Only 20 years ago, the father of a youth hockey player beat another father to death over a dispute at a team practice. While we don't know the personal struggles of the individuals, we know that emotions run high when it comes to our kids. This extreme example certainly marks the far end of the spectrum. However, it serves as a reminder of the need to practice self-control in all situations and avoid derailing everything you have worked for and invested in to get your athlete to a competitive level.

Your athlete's opportunities will be directly impacted by the way you interact with other parents, teams, coaches, and players. Most of the seemingly important outcomes at the pre-prospect age travel levels will not dictate the final result of your athlete's baseball career.

Therefore, realize that development, passion, and respect for the game are the most important considerations, rather than results. Prepare in advance for the political climate, equip yourself and your spouse, if applicable, with patience, and appropriately discern how to respond, rather than react, to unfavorable situations. This method will pay dividends in many ways.

Your athlete's opportunities will be directly impacted by the way you interact with other parents, teams, coaches, and players.

As previously discussed, initially finding the right team for your athlete will keep many of your frustrations and potential conflicts at bay. Regardless of the situation, remain level-headed and finish the season, rather than quitting or causing long-lasting damage by acting foolish. Burning bridges and eliminating future opportunities with poor reactions will only damage your reputation, embarrass your athlete, and damage opportunities for them in the baseball community. New opportunities are presented each year as athletes develop at different rates and new teams are always looking to add fresh, new players to the roster.

TREATMENT OF UMPIRES

Learning to tolerate umpires applies to every level of competition of the athlete's career. It is no secret that umpires have the power to change the outcome of games, including no hitters and playoff championships. A study performed by Boston University researchers analyzed 4 million pitches called by umpires at the MLB level, the most experienced in the game, over the last 11 seasons. The study found that Big League umpires make incorrect calls up to 20% of the time, missing 1 out of every 5.[7] Behind the plate, MLB umpires miss up to 14 ball and strike calls per game, and up to 29% of the time when a batter has two strikes.[8] Many mistakes are made every inning, even by the best.

Umpire quality will typically be average, at best, in the lower and younger levels of competition. This is especially true when the umpire is not pursuing a professional umpiring career. Moreover, your vocalized opinion will not change the outcome of a call, and will likely embarrass your athlete and influence an umpire to show disfavor to your team.

A negative or embarrassing tone will detrimentally impact your athlete because they will not be able to ignore your voice. They should be focused on the game and proud to compete. It is your responsibility to recognize when you cross the line from a supportive to a nuisance parent whose criticism is unwanted and unwelcome. Don't be that parent! Motivate your athlete to focus on variables that they can control, and with the exception of a blown call here or there, empower the athlete to dictate their own success at the plate or on the mound.

CAMPS AND SHOWCASES

INTRODUCTION

Camps and showcases provide many benefits as your athlete seeks improvement and advancement opportunities along their development journey. The three main purposes for camps and showcases for the maturing athlete are:

1. Exposure

2. Skill Development

3. Recreation/Entertainment

A camp or showcase will most likely lean more heavily toward one or more of these purposes depending on the age, skill level, and particular event. Showcases generally focus on exposure to college coaches and professional scouts, focusing on an athlete's raw abilities and future potential. Camps, on the other hand, focus on instructing and entertaining campers, teaching proper fundamentals and skill instruction in pitching, hitting, baserunning, and defense. The exception to this rule is when a college program offers a hybrid "showcase camp," primarily for the purposes of exposure, but to gather potential prospects for observation. To remain in compliance with NCAA rules and regulations, showcase camps offer a brief instruction portion for skill instruction, in addition to the exposure aspect and tryout-style raw abilities measurements.

WHEN TO BEGIN ATTENDING CAMPS AND SHOWCASES

The NCAA defines "prospect age" when a student athlete enters their freshman year of high school. However, athletes are recruited and verbally commit earlier than their freshman year in some cases. For the typical athlete, 14-15 years old is the time to begin the process of gaining exposure, seeking insight into recruiting, and focusing on development for the next level. As stated earlier, a player reaching prospect age does not equate to reaching prospect status.

Therefore, keep in mind that showcases are only an aid to exposure and do not determine how well the athlete will perform in the future, or whether they will be considered a prospect simply from participation. Some of the best names in Major League Baseball did not receive advanced instruction until high school. World Series Champion, Gold Glove Winner, and 2-Time All-Star Lorenzo Cain, for example, did not pursue elite level baseball until well into his high school baseball career, but he is certainly the exception. His raw ability was able to compensate for the late start in development.

CAMPS (AGES 6-18)

The various camps provide opportunities for skill improvement by watching and performing drills with other players in small group settings. This environment creates competitive pressures, possibly for the first time to a camper, by practicing and performing in front of peers and coaches who evaluate each major skill. It is wise for your athlete to become familiarized with this type of skill development and evaluation atmosphere prior to prospect age. The experience will give them an advantage when the camps become more important for future opportunities and recruitment purposes.

RECREATION CAMPS VS. PROSPECT CAMPS

Understanding the purpose behind each camp is important because many are geared toward recreation and/or development, while others are for the purpose of evaluation or gaining exposure with a particular program. For example, attending a middle school-aged camp operated by the high school baseball staff, where the athlete will soon attend school, can be important for exposure.

Your athlete's attendance also demonstrates investment in the program's future with the camp fees and retail purchases. Supporting the program with your athlete's participation and financial support will create name recognition and potentially make a difference in future opportunities. We do not endorse lobbying efforts with financial support for playing time, however, this political aspect demonstrates involvement and desire to support and participate in the program.

Unlike recreational camps, attending a high school prospect camp at a specific college with the coaching staff or multiple college programs in attendance is strictly for exposure, rather than support. Recruiting decisions are often made by a coaching staff after interacting directly with the players the program has previously recruited. In a prospect camp environment, coaches are better equipped to make informed decisions on the athlete, and for the program. College coaches are not able to recruit everywhere and may have only limited information about a prospect outside of the college's region. Thus, attending specific prospect camps while in high school is a way to create exposure and form relationships.

Further, it is important to have ongoing communication with the schools that have shown interest or that you would like to show interest in your athlete. Before attending a camp, reach out to coaches who are advertised to be attending camp. This effort will separate and prioritize your athlete for exposure purposes and confirm that the coach will, in fact, be in attendance. Recruiting schedules of college coaches are ever-changing, and camps are marketed months in advance. Without confirmation in advance, the program's decision makers may not be present for evaluation and your investment for exposure purposes could be used more wisely at another school or event.

While there are many upsides, there are also downsides of camps associated with a specific scholastic program. At large universities, many of the camp instructors are only present to manage the large number of campers and may not have the baseball expertise for true development purposes. This is because most non-prospect age camps hosted by colleges are targeted toward 6U to 12U, and are operated by volunteer or graduate assistant coaches and current players in the program to supplement their incomes. These camps are focused mostly on the recreational aspect, rather than for technical skill development and instruction.

On the other hand, exposing a young athlete to the facilities, players, staff, and atmosphere of a program may be what motivates their continued growth and desire to pursue playing at that particular program or level in the future. Furthermore, the entertainment value of receiving officially licensed apparel and interacting with their favorite players from a program can be a priceless experience and create memories that will last a lifetime.

At prospect age, your athlete should only attend a college camp if invited personally or if prior contact with the coaching staff has been made, and their attendance is requested. Travel expenses to many camps can equal a semester of college tuition at the institution that the athlete ultimately attends. Therefore, it is only wise to invest if a future opportunity is realistic. Once you make the decision to send your athlete, ensure that the college coaching staff is aware that they will be attending to maximize your investment and their exposure opportunity.

QUESTIONS TO ASK WHEN EVALUATING WHICH COLLEGE CAMPS TO ATTEND:

1 Does my athlete realistically have the potential to play for the college program?

2 Does the college have the academic curriculum that my athlete desires to pursue?

3 Does the investment make financial sense for my family? If any question above is answered "no," it may be in your athlete's best interest to target schools that will give them better academic and athletic opportunities.

> 🔖 BRAMHALL: *I attended Auburn's high school prospect camp over two consecutive summers prior to my senior year in high school, and was on a first name basis with the coaching staff. My performance at camp and ongoing communication in the recruiting process led to an official Auburn athletic scholarship offer prior to my senior year in high school. Do not discount the value of prospect camp and face to face interaction with college coaches to create opportunities that otherwise would not occur. I would never have been on the program's radar without attending camp.*

PRIVATE SKILLS CAMPS

Camps are not limited to those associated with scholastic programs. Many of the most reputable and technical camps and instructors in the nation exist in the private sector and are often associated with private facilities or organizations, rather than tied to academic institutions. Quality instruction for skill development normally happens in an environment with a lower camper to instructor ratio, which is typically found at camps in the private sector where the focus is on individual athlete skills improvement, rather than the enjoyment of the recreational camp experience.

Additionally, organizations and instructors in the private sector often have individual clientele with proven success to support their credibility. Exercise due diligence by seeking instructors with a philosophy specific to your athlete's development needs such as hitting for power, throwing strikes, or improving as a defensive catcher. This may be the most important consideration of all regarding camps. By targeting a low camper to instructor ratio, proven success from organizations and instructors, and philosophies targeted to the needs of your athlete, your time and money investment in development will be more wisely spent.

SHOWCASES (AGES 14-18)

Showcases are specifically designed for exposure after years of practice and camp attendance. They are far different from skills camps geared toward repetitions and development. The format of showcases ranges from travel teams performing a pro-style workout and playing against other teams at local colleges with coaches in attendance, which is a very low-cost exposure opportunity for families and teams, to invite-only prospect showcases. Showcases are predominantly focused on evaluating physical tools such as arm strength, speed, hitting for average, fielding, and power. The methods often used to showcase talent to scouts, and are typical of a pro-style workout are:

- bullpen sessions

- live batting practice

- 60-yard dash

- home to first sprint

- exit velocity measurements off the bat

- fielding/throwing technique and velocity measurement from the outfield

- fielding/throwing technique and velocity measurement from deep shortstop

- fielding/throwing technique and velocity measurement from first to third base

- catcher "pop" time from home plate to second base

- live game simulations

When choosing a showcase early in the prospect recruitment phase, seek those with coaches in attendance from all different levels (DI, DII, DIII, NAIA, JUCO) to broaden your exposure. While development aspects will be present with peer-to-peer comparison and skill assessment workouts at showcases, the exposure to college and professional scouts will be the most beneficial aspect.

Here are a few tips to improve your athlete's showcase outcome, efficiency, and effectiveness:

1 They should wear noticeable apparel such as a bright colored shirt, hat, socks or shoes to stand out and be remembered. It is easy to get lost in the mix at a showcase with large numbers. If your athlete plays for a reputable travel organization, they should wear the team hat or jersey for the showcase.

2 Be aware that emails and letters your prospect aged player receives for costly showcases are commonly generated from large databases and sent to as many players as possible to increase the overall numbers for revenue generation. Attending a showcase for the purpose of recruiting exposure is important, but be selective in your investments in these exposure opportunities.

Showcases are predominantly focused on evaluating physical tools such as arm strength, speed, hitting for average, fielding, and power.

3 Obtain throwing, running, and swinging measurements prior to attending a showcase. The athlete will benefit twofold from having a reference for comparison with other athletes in attendance and focusing on personal growth and improvement rather than relative peer comparisons. The balance is delicate, but both are important for maximizing potential.

4 Familiarize yourself with the skills that will be measured at a showcase in advance. This preparation will help prevent excessive overwhelming and intimidating feelings from uncertainties in the competitive environment.

⑤ Research performance measurements from players in the same age group by asking around or through online databases. This will provide you with an understanding of whether the athlete is ready to attend a showcase. If they are not ready, a showcase may result in an embarrassing or miserable experience, and continuing skill development may be best for the athlete at the current time. However, every parent will testify that their child threw a 90mph fastball and gained 25 pounds of muscle last night, therefore, take the hyperboles with a grain of salt.

⑥ Attend one or more affordable showcases to become comfortable with the process and be evaluated in a pro-style workout. Understanding the layout and pressures of the experience can be psychologically overwhelming until the athlete becomes become desensitized to the "noise" and can display the same skills in any circumstance.

⑦ Understand that an athlete rarely, if ever, has a perfect showcase. Help the athlete move past mistakes and maintain positive body language. Coaches are gauging raw talent and potential, rather than perfection. A good attitude demonstrates to recruiters and scouts how an athlete handles adversity.

⑧ Interact with coaches to show confidence and personality by engaging in mature conversation and demonstrating awareness of your strengths.

HIGH ACADEMIC SHOWCASES

One of the first questions college recruiters ask coaches of travel ball organizations is to identify which athletes are academically gifted. These athletes are then marked for academic scholarship considerations, which allows the program to utilize the athletic scholarship allotment on other recruits, or are pegged by Ivy League and other academic institution recruiters who must only pursue athletes who can qualify for admission. Thus, academic showcases are specifically intended for, and very valuable to, high academic-achieving prospects.

High academic showcases have a lower total number of qualified prospects in attendance but a large number of recruiters from elite institutions who are ready to make offers quickly. Often, this is an athlete's best opportunity for exposure and admission to an Ivy League school or other high academic institution. Utilizing athletic ability paired with academic achievement is a great way to obtain a priceless education from a university in which your athlete may not otherwise gain admission.

Utilizing athletic ability paired with academic achievement is a great way to obtain a priceless education from a university in which your athlete may not otherwise gain admission.

Many of these schools are able to offer attractive scholarship packages with use of athletic, academic, and low-interest, or forgivable, family income-based financial aid. For example, Rice University, a top 15 national academic institution, implemented The Rice Investment Program in 2019, which provides full grant aid for fees, tuition, and room and board for admitted students with household incomes of less than $65,000. Students with household incomes between $65,000 - $130,000, and who are eligible to receive need-based financial aid, are awarded full tuition scholarships. Finally, students with household incomes between $130,000 - $200,000 will receive scholarships covering at least half of their tuition.

This is an incredible advancement in access to education for all who qualify. The only caveat is that the student must be admitted into school, which is not an easy feat. Although some colleges and universities offer lighter restrictions for acceptance, high academic institutions typically have higher standards and make fewer exceptions.

SHOWCASE FORMAT

The more the athlete understands the format and where they measure in comparison to their age group, the more confident they will feel attending the showcase. Most, if not all, showcases gather the following raw tool measurements from athletes in attendance:

SIXTY-YARD DASH - The sixty-yard dash is run in pairs, with a laser system and/or stopwatch to measure the athlete's running speed. Athletes have an opportunity to warm up beforehand and typically run once or twice, with the fastest time recorded for the showcase. If possible, the athlete should run with another athlete similar in speed, if not slightly faster, to ensure they run their best time. Regardless of the runners next to them on the line, the athlete should focus on their best performance.

Winning the paired race may not matter, but running the fastest time of all shortstops definitely could matter. Times vary by position, and an athlete's time is compared to prospects at the same playing position. The athlete's running speed, other raw tool measurements,

 PRO TIP

A faster time in the "Sixty" often comes from improving an athlete's explosive start rather than only by improving top end speed. To improve the sixty-yard dash time, it may be in the athlete's best interest to take a class and/or work with a speed coach prior to the showcase to give them the best chance to perform at peak performance level.[9]

Herman Demmink is the leading expert on the 60 yard dash. Watch his video, "How to Run the 60" on our website here: whosonfirstbook.com/extrainnings.

overall ability, position, and height and weight, are all factored into the overall assessment of their long-term potential as a prospect. Parents frequently ask why the measurement distance is sixty yards. Sixty yards is theoretically the furthest distance a baseball player would be required to run in a single play.

HOME TO FIRST - Similar to the sixty-yard dash, a home to first measurement provides a speed measurement out of the batter's box through first base. This measurement has been shown to have an effect on batting average and on base percentage over the course of a season. Different from a showcase, a camp conducted under NCAA regulations does not permit a 60-yard dash measurement, but permits a home to first measurement because it is considered an instructional baserunning aspect of the game.

Typically, a hitter takes a full swing, and the time clock starts with the athlete's first step out of the batter's box. Obviously, lefties have the advantage out of the box based on physical proximity to first base. At the prospect age, average right-handed hitter running times are 4.3 seconds, and 4.2 seconds for a left-handed hitter.[10]

RADAR VELOCITY FROM THE INFIELD AND THE OUTFIELD - This measurement of throwing velocity provides a gauge of the athlete's arm strength from a given defensive position. Third basemen, second basemen, and shortstops field a ground ball and throw from deep shortstop to first base. First basemen field a ground ball and throw from first base to third base, and then to home plate. Outfielders field a ground ball and throw from right field to second base, third base, and home plate at maximum effort.

While arm strength is extremely important, proper footwork and quick transitions are equally important to showcase overall ability to evaluators grading the many skills involved in fielding and throwing across the diamond efficiently. When throwing from the outfield in a showcase, velocity is the key measurement. The athlete should be as accurate as possible without losing velocity, but this is the time to showcase their arm strength and light up the radar gun. Outfield footwork can be trained at a later date.

Two-way players often shine during this evaluation because they understand how to generate maximum velocity from experience on the mound. Throwing measurements also allow coaches and scouts to determine which position players might develop as a pitcher. At the prospect age, elite middle infield and outfield recruits will throw the ball 85-95 mph, with an average velocity of 85mph.[11,12]

POP TIME FROM BEHIND HOME PLATE TO SECOND BASE - Pop time is the most common measurement for catchers at showcases in the recruiting and scouting process. The catcher receives a ball from in front of home plate, the stopwatch starts once the ball has been received, and it stops when the shortstop or 2nd baseman catches it. Footwork, rotational torque, transition time, direction efficiency, and arm strength are crucial to developing the best pop time possible. At the prospect age, average game pop time for a high school varsity catcher is 2.0-2.25 seconds.[13]

For performance as a catcher, overall arm strength is important, but footwork, transfer, and accuracy also stand out, especially when the catcher throws out runners consistently. Pop times measured in games are significantly higher than showcase pop times because at showcases, there are no hitters, the pitches are consistent for the catcher to receive before throwing to second base, and the only object of the drill is to throw to second base as fast as possible.

EXIT VELOCITY MEASUREMENTS AND LIVE BATTING PRACTICE - With the inventions of batted ball and swing measuring tools on the market, it has become much easier to measure exit velocity from a batted ball. Players in this drill usually swing the same bat and hit off of a tee to measure the velocity of the ball as it exits the bat. An old technique for measuring exit velocity that still may be used in some showcases is to hold a radar gun behind a net where the player hits a ball off a tee.

During the live batting practice portion, the player hits batting practice off of a coach or scout. They should attack good pitches to hit, focus on barreling pitches gap to gap with solid contact, and show off power during the last two to three swings in each round. In advance, verify whether the showcase will require aluminum, wood, or both for the hitting portions. If no information is provided, bring both to be prepared.

BULLPEN OR SIMULATED GAME - Pitchers throw in a bullpen session and/or a simulated game with hitters in live at bat situations. During the bullpen or simulated game sessions, recruiters and scouts evaluate the various aspects in the athlete's ability such as: pitch command, mound presence, control, deceptiveness, velocity difference between pitches, and velocity of all pitches.

If the showcase has a Rapsodo Pitching unit or similar device present, additional readings on the ball such as pitch velocity, spin rate, true spin rate, spin axis, spin efficiency, strike zone analysis, horizontal and vertical break, and release point are assessed. Pitchers should display all pitches in the bullpen and demonstrate command with each pitch. The live portion may be limited with few opportunities to throw all pitches. Many showcase formats allot 1 inning, with each at-bat beginning with a 1-1 or 2-1 count. Pitchers should take full advantage of the opportunities presented to showcase their abilities, and should never allow the count to dictate pitch sequencing decisions when attacking hitters.

LIVE AT BATS OR SIMULATED GAME - Hitters and pitchers faceoff in simulated game situations. The simulated games consist of a few innings in a scrimmage or simulated at bats in a live batting practice setting. When the count starts at 2-1, it is vital for hitters to hunt fastballs early to decrease the possibility of missing a good pitch to hit. Missing a good pitch puts the hitter in a two-strike count and approach and in a battle against a pitcher's best out pitch.

Recruiters and scouts look for a hitter's ability to drive the ball to gaps based on pitch location, presence in the batter's box (stiff and robotic vs. poised and confident), tempo (controlled movements with rhythm), and ability to generate power. Hitting home runs isn't the only way a hitter showcases raw power. Pitches that are hit high in the air also showcase power, even if they are just missed. Mechanics such as timing (leg kick, knee tuck, toe tap), swing path, barrel plane, bat control, and swing efficiency are also evaluated for repeatability, adjustability to off-speed pitches, and overall control to handle higher velocity and spin-rates.

OTHER PRE-CONTACT MEASUREMENTS - The wearable sensors from Blast Motion, Diamond Kinetics, and other state-of-the-art athletic technology companies, provide various performance measurements that are proving a correlation to success on the field. When a coach or scout directing the showcase understands which metrics translate to success, drills may be designed with these sensors to provide additional measurement statistics.

We include a chart below, courtesy of Perfect Game, that shows average, plus, and elite scores for each showcase measurement for ages 14U-17U. Visit: whosonfirstbook.com/perfectgameshowcase for more information.

HOW TO MAXIMIZE EXPOSURE AT CAMPS AND SHOWCASES

To reiterate and summarize some of the most important ways to maximize exposure from the camps and showcases the athlete attends, remember the following:

1 Send emails and letters to the coaches at the schools ahead of time before attending. Requesting your travel ball coach or instructor to reach out in advance on your behalf will help coaches identify you and ensure you are not lost in the mix of the many athletes in attendance.

LEVEL	60-YARD DASH			10-YARD DASH			FASTBALL VELOCITY		
	AVERAGE	PLUS	ELITE	AVERAGE	PLUS	ELITE	AVERAGE	PLUS	ELITE
14U	7.71	7.20	7.00	1.79	1.70	1.65	72	80	83
15U	7.52	7.10	6.95	1.75	1.61	1.63	76	81	85
16U	7.50	7.13	6.91	1.74	1.62	1.60	79	86	89
17U	7.26	6.80	6.65	1.71	1.58	1.58	82	88	92

LEVEL	CATCHER POP			CATCHER VELOCITY			FIRST BASE VELOCITY		
	AVERAGE	PLUS	ELITE	AVERAGE	PLUS	ELITE	AVERAGE	PLUS	ELITE
14U	2.20	2.03	1.98	68	73	75	71	78	80
15U	2.12	1.96	1.91	71	76	79	74	79	82
16U	2.16	1.94	1.89	73	78	80	74	80	83
17U	2.01	1.90	1.84	75	79	82	76	82	84

LEVEL	INFIELD VELOCITY			OUTFIELD VELOCITY			POCKET RADAR EXIT VELOCITY		
	AVERAGE	PLUS	ELITE	AVERAGE	PLUS	ELITE	AVERAGE	PLUS	ELITE
14U	72	80	83	75	82	85	75	82	84
15U	76	83	85	77	84	87	78	83	86
16U	77	84	86	79	87	89	81	85	90
17U	78	86	88	82	88	91	83	90	93

2 Connect with schools that are realistic to attend, athletically and academically, and a few that are seemingly out of reach because you never know which programs need certain positions filled. Don't be afraid to receive a "no."

3 Before attendance, ensure that the athlete is healthy and ready for peak performance. Their arm should be in shape, and swing and timing should be ready to showcase their talent at a high level. Otherwise, attend at a later date to make a great first impression.

4 Throw from the mound and hit in the cage and/or on the field immediately before the showcase.

5 Measure velocity, speed, and agility to set realistic goals and expectations for the upcoming evaluation. The preparation beforehand will ensure that the athlete is prepared and confident to showcase their abilities.

6 Make a personal introduction to recruiters and scouts, mention previous contact in person or through letters and email, and mention where the athlete is from.

7 Wear distinguishing apparel to separate from the group. A bright colored shirt or taped wrists are helpful for a recruiter to remember their performance.

8 Demonstrate good body language by presenting like a professional, hustling, and remaining positive.

9 Finally, follow up with thank-you notes, handwritten, preferably. Address specific content mentioned by a coach during a speech or information the player discussed specifically with the coach during their personal introduction.

When post-camp and showcase evaluations are sent to the athlete, absorb the results with a grain of salt. Many of the evaluators give higher scores to enhance the experience of the athlete and improve the chances that the athlete will give the showcase or camp high marks in return. Evaluators often have a very limited amount of time for assessments and feedback, therefore, do not be overly discouraged or excited, for that matter, when viewing constructive criticism or praise from a scoring sheet.

TOP NATIONAL PROSPECT EVENTS (AGES 16-18)

The following invite-only events feature the top ranked amateur baseball prospects in the nation. It is unlikely that your athlete will receive an invite or that it will matter to their career whether an invite is received or not. While many of the players who are invited to the top prospect events realize a bright MLB future, some do not.

BASEBALL FACTORY UNDER ARMOUR ALL-AMERICA GAME - This 4-day premier baseball experience is highlighted by formal workouts with professional scouts and a homerun derby, followed by a televised game matchup of American Team vs. National Team. It is played each summer at Wrigley Field in Chicago, Illinois. Since its inception, 365 of the 399 draft eligible players were selected in the MLB Amateur Draft, with 108 of them selected in the first round.[14]

AREA CODE GAMES - This invitation-only event showcases the Top 220 high school baseball players across the country. 8 regional teams play in a 5-day showcase in California. Scouts from all 30 MLB teams are in attendance.[15]

EAST COAST PRO - This MLB showcase event is held at the Hoover MET in Hoover, Alabama and is organized and operated by MLB scouts to educate the top prospects on what it takes to play at the professional level. Athletes are selected by professional baseball scouts to form 6 regional teams for the showcase competition. Between 80 and 110 of the invited prospects are selected in the MLB Amateur Draft each year.[16]

PERFECT GAME ALL-AMERICAN CLASSIC - This premier high school all-star baseball game is held annually at PETCO Park in San Diego, California. Since its inception, this game has featured 768 total participants from US, Canada, and Puerto Rico, and the Dominican Republic, with 680 drafted, 215 first round picks, and 182 of them playing in the MLB.[17]

RECRUITING SERVICES

We are not proponents of recruiting services as a benefit over the many different avenues to be exposed and gain opportunity at the next level. However, they do exist and it may be beneficial to be informed on what they do and how they seek to serve clients. Recruiting services generally assist an athlete with:

- Filling out questionnaires
- Athlete marketing, such as social media and contacting potential schools
- Exposure opportunity event calendars
- Identifying potential program fits

Ultimately, any athlete with potential does not need a recruiting service if they are utilizing local coaches, facilities, and attending camps and showcases. These services are often not a wise financial investment, and the majority of the readers of this book already have tools to gain exposure and opportunity without additional secondary expenses.

ADDITIONAL RESOURCES

High School Baseball Web provides resources about college baseball recruiting, scholarships, the MLB Draft, interviews with college coaches and pro scouts, "how-to's" for recruiting, information about camps and showcases, and a discussion forum to connect you with others on the same journey. Visit: www.highschoolbaseballweb. com.[18]

Go Big Recruiting has comprehensive recruiting resources to research the needs of each individual athlete. The website also provides a timeline of the stages of recruiting, information about specific defensive positions and video analysis tips, and scholarship information. Overall, Go Big Recruiting is an excellent resource to answer many questions and educate you and your athlete on the big picture from a scout or college coach's point of view. Visit: whosonfirstbook.com/gobigrecruiting.[19]

HIGH SCHOOL BASEBALL, RECRUITING, AND NAME, IMAGE, AND LIKENESS (NIL)

"Three out of every fifty high school baseball players will play baseball in college (6.4%), and 2% of high school athletes receive an NCAA sports scholarship."[20]

⚾ LYNN O'SHAUGHNESSY,

"THE ODDS OF PLAYING COLLEGE SPORTS," CBS NEWS

INTRODUCTION

Your athlete should enjoy the high school baseball years. These experiences will be the last with relatively low pressure, childhood friends on the team, and family in attendance at every game. For the final few years, you will be able to travel less than 15 minutes to watch your athlete play. At the next levels, playing becomes more of a job, with increased responsibilities, time demand, pressures of playing time, along with eligibility and performance concerns. Encourage your athlete to cherish the privilege of representing their school and local community, and competing with classmates.

PROGRAM STRUCTURE AND SEASON LAYOUT

Generally, high school baseball is organized by levels that separate the highest level, the varsity, from the teams that are working toward the varsity. The varsity is the only team that is able to compete for a spot in the playoffs and a chance to win a championship, whether that be as a member of a private school athletic association or public school state championship. Different states and regions have varying competition formats based on school enrollment. Private schools may also be separated into conferences based on the ability to recruit and provide scholarships to athletes.

At the entry levels of high school baseball, programs may fill a freshman and/or junior varsity team ("JV"), based on participation numbers. The varsity team consists of the most experienced and talented players in the program. Players move up and down throughout the season between the JV and varsity squads due to player performance and roster needs. Depending on the number of teams, the varsity likely travels independently of the freshman or JV teams. This allows the high school ballparks to be utilized for the freshman or JV games when the varsity is away. If a program has enough participants to field all three levels, the JV and varsity teams generally travel together, and the JV plays either before or after the varsity.

The season typically begins with up to four weeks of practice and intra-squad practice games before playing inter-squad scrimmages versus other schools that are not on the regular season schedule. In many cases, the scrimmages are followed by tournaments consisting of several schools in either round-robin format, or classic tournament brackets to determine a tournament champion. In certain regions, the tournament portion is a spring break trip where a team uses the opportunity for bonding, and as a measuring opportunity to set improvement goals going forward.

Following tournaments, district or conference play completes the remaining games on the schedule prior to playoffs. Depending on the number of teams in the district or conference and the length of the season, there may be one or two games played against each district or conference opponent. The number of playoff spots awarded and rounds of playoff competition vary state to state and by classification. The playoffs are undoubtedly the most exciting and heartbreaking part of the season as community involvement increases with each round, the end of the school year approaches, and many athletes compete in their last organized baseball games of their careers.

THE POLITICAL LANDSCAPE AND PARENT ETIQUETTE

It is in a parent's nature to care for, protect, and provide for their kid. However, you must recognize your inherent bias and desire for your athlete to receive the most opportunities. Otherwise, you may detrimentally influence their career by voicing your opinions about playing time or treatment in a negative manner and lose important relationships with coaches, other parents, and other players. When these situations arise, identify your bias, and then abstain or respond appropriately. Likeable parents create opportunities for their athletes, make no mistake about it. Allow the player to find their way without adding needless drama or negative energy from coaches or teammates caused by your actions.

A baseball season spans from early workouts at the end of winter through the end of spring, which provides several windows of opportunity for the athlete to make positive strides. If you behave poorly and come across as a problem parent, the athlete's opportunities will not be maximized when college coaches and professional scouts inquire about your athlete. Your actions follow your athlete's reputation and the overall package they will bring to the next level, both on and off the field. Awareness of your actions should be of utmost importance as your athlete is working on the field for their future.

Positive actions to form relationships with other parents and coaches include: volunteering for field maintenance, taking concession shifts, preparing team meals and snacks, collecting tickets, purchasing team apparel, and other booster club responsibilities.

Participating positively forms relationships and sparks conversations beyond baseball specific discussions about the athlete. While there can be a fine line between supporting the program and seeking political influence or favor, be aware when you may be taking away opportunities by not doing your part as a supportive parent.

INSIDE THE MIND OF A HIGH SCHOOL BASEBALL COACH

Coaches affiliated with high school programs are most often teachers or employed by the school district in another full-time role. Coaching may be their passion, but the vast majority of their income is often earned from the responsibilities associated with academic or administrative duties. That said, coaches do not need advice or input from parents to maintain their jobs within the school district.

Sure, a high school baseball coach has goals of winning to advance their career, to keep their current job, or simply because they love the game. However, they do not spend afternoons and evenings on the high school baseball diamond for the money. Coaches are involved for impact, purpose, and passion for the game. The median high school baseball head coach's salary is $30,830 for their teaching or administrative duties, earning only an additional $800-$3,000 for baseball coaching duties and sacrificing precious time away from family or personal life to coach young athletes.[21]

Awareness of your actions should be of utmost importance as your athlete is working on the field for their future.

A high school baseball program has time constraints that prevent coaches from focusing on individual development. In order to most efficiently use the practice time available, situational aspects of the game such as bunt coverages, run downs, and cuts and relays are more often the focus of baseball practice. As a result, your athlete's individual technical skill development and baseball IQ will likely come from sources outside high school baseball practice or instruction. When team practice is over, coaches return home to their families from long days at school and on the practice field.

A high school baseball coach is looking for players who can play in their system and who demonstrate potential to improve the team, represent the program, and if fortunate, have parents who support them in management decisions. You will not agree with every decision made by a high school coach, and each situation may bring unique challenges and calls for action, but the coach has many concerns and considerations influencing their decision-making process.

Coaches do not seek opinions about playing time from biased parents and approaching a coach can be detrimental to the athlete. On rare occasions, coaches may hinder the development opportunities for the athlete, which may warrant a scheduled discussion. More often than not, though, throughout the course of the season, the athlete will have several opportunities to prove their value without your involvement.

A high school coach may be a bridge of communication with professional scouts or college recruiters. Coaches have direct access to share opinions that could influence future opportunities necessary for the athlete to reach the next level. As a parent, it is best to allow the athlete's skill set and on-field production to dictate their opportunities at the next level without hindrances from you. High school baseball coaches often have years of baseball knowledge, resources, and are likely proud of their positions as both coaches and baseball evaluators. Be mindful of a coach's ego, support their mission, and adapt to their system as necessary, while preserving your player's individuality, unique talent, and uncapped potential. Let not your high school baseball coach prevent your athlete from playing time or a bright future because of your actions as a parent.

EARN YOUR KEEP

It is important to realize that many of the varsity players likely have been in the system for at least two years, earning performance credentials and playing familiarity with coaching staff. Depending on coaching philosophy, some coaches will play the best athletes available, while others allow seniority to weigh significantly in lineup decisions. We support the philosophy of playing the best athletes, regardless of age or time in the program. If younger athletes in the program are more talented and receive the playing time, that immediately helps a program's current strength and future success in the coming years, politics aside.

Each year in programs nationwide, a young, talented athlete rises to the varsity and replaces an upper-classman. Grab some popcorn for those parents to coach conversations! The younger athletes should respect the upper-classmen for reasons on and off the field, but should not hesitate to take their positions and never look back. Seniority as a means of playing time security is old news, winning is about having the best players on the field.

A high school head coach's career success depends on coaching with integrity, wins, depending on the talent they have available, playoff appearances, and championships to continue to earn the favor of the athletics director and community. Therefore, a player who proves their value should ultimately be awarded playing time because wins matter in competitive baseball. Winning is the central concept that pervades amateur sports, and the reason that the game is played.

Regardless of your athlete's opportunities, give your ballplayer the best chance to earn their keep by seeking the best independent coaching and training within your financial means, and by instilling mental fortitude to positively contribute to their program. Players who play among the best, and are trained by the best, stand out. This is also true for parents who carry themselves diplomatically.

It may take time for an athlete to showcase talent and gain favor with the baseball coaching staff due to competition or many on and off the field political factors. These forces may work in favor of or against your athlete from time to time. Yet, how you respond, and have behaved in the past, is vitally important for your athlete's current and future opportunities. Much like surviving in the wild, how you have prepared, the paths you have previously cleared, and respecting variables out of your control will determine whether you make it through unscathed and move on to the next challenge.

HOW TO BE A GOOD TEAMMATE

Human behavioral research reveals that struggle and joint pursuit are the greatest predictors of bonding and friendships. Working together toward a common goal, whether that be in family relationships, business partnerships, military assignments, or with teammates in athletics, produces lifelong bonds and connections. It is no secret why teammates refer to one another as "brothers" and "family" after high-pressure demands that require substantial investment of time, effort, sweat, emotion, and overcoming challenges. Becoming a great teammate begins with self-accountability and a commitment to the journey.

An athlete must understand and embrace their role and contribute to the overall purpose in whatever capacity necessary. This is what separates great teammates from individuals. Holding a teammate accountable is equally as important as supporting a teammate during challenges and failures. A teammate should strive to be even-keeled in attitude and body language so that no coach, player, or evaluator can distinguish whether the athlete is in a period of success or failure.

Players who play among the best, and are trained by the best, stand out.

The ability to compartmentalize outside distractions is necessary to stay focused on a common team goal and positively contribute to the team dynamic. All players and coaches have outside distractions on occasion, however, remaining focused on baseball while at the stadium is just as important as leaving baseball at the stadium when returning to family and friends. Learning to become a good teammate at the high school level will pay dividends at the next levels and in life after baseball.

RECRUITING

A majority of recruiting exposure comes from the travel ball circuit and showcases as a high school athlete. High school programs are also important during the recruiting process because college programs often utilize high school coaches as resources for recruiting, character evaluation, and analyzing an athlete's overall makeup. However, as a parent, do not entirely depend on a high school coach's influence with college programs or scouts to get your athlete to the next level. You may or may not have a high school coach with time and/or resources to network and advocate for your ballplayer's career opportunities. Some high school coaches devote time and effort, while others do not make it a priority.

Regardless of the exposure the athlete receives from their high school program, successful performance will always help pave the way to the next level. Success against other college prospects will often lead to open doors when scouts are present. Often, a scout or coach attends a game to evaluate a specific pitching prospect but leaves the game with a list of potential prospects who performed well against the talented arm. Do not discount the exposure value of a successful hitting performance versus a college or professional prospect. Performance is the ultimate eye-opener, and it only takes one scout or evaluator's positive report to become a prospect.

Professional scouts initially watch players on the immediate national or regional radar to generate early reports of draftability, future projections, and performance evaluations. After the excitement of the season's beginning fades, the scouts evaluate other talented players and send letters to those athletes to gather information for MLB organizational databases. Do not expect many college coaches to attend high school regular season games due

> **Excellent communication could be the difference in receiving a college offer or professional contract, rather than the evaluator moving on to other prospects.**

to conflicting game schedules. This is what makes the previously discussed travel ball circuit so important. Nevertheless, college coaches will receive reports about high school games and have various contacts to relay information about prospects to watch in the upcoming summer travel ball seasons.

Contact by a college coach or recruiter to a prospect will likely be made to a prospect in the form of text, phone call, or email. Distinguish between a camp invite email or letter that has been sent to a mass list of players to generate attendance and revenue, and a personal invite or communication from a college coach specifically recruiting your athlete.

Similarly, a scouting letter will come from an MLB organization requesting general information such as: graduation year, contact information, HS team, summer baseball team, and desire to be drafted. If your athlete is contacted by a coach or scout, be sure to respond, regardless of their intention. Rejecting exposure opportunities before the athlete has made a definitive career choice can be detrimental because word travels quickly and the baseball community is tight-knit.

The coaches and scouts who have shown interest deserve a response and frequently move to other programs and organizations throughout the course of their careers. Your athlete should keep options open, provide schools and organizations the requested information, and remain approachable. Coaches frequently discuss recruiting with other coaches, therefore, an athlete's reputation for approachability and communication is important.

This is especially true if the athlete is a borderline Division I player, or a borderline MLB Draft prospect. Excellent communication could be the difference in receiving a college offer or professional contract, rather than the evaluator moving on to other prospects. Use the interest from multiple schools and professional baseball organizations as leverage, even if the athlete is heavily leaning one particular direction.

WHAT IS SIGNING DAY?

Signing Day is designated for athletes to finalize commitments in writing with the programs they will join at the next level. This memorable day is often celebrated with family, media, coaches, and teammates in attendance. Formerly, there was an early signing period in November, which accounted for about 20% of players aspiring to play college baseball. The standard signing period took place in April of the athletes' senior year in high school.[22]

However, in all sports besides football and basketball, beginning with the 2019-2020 school year, players now may begin signing scholarships on November 13th, and may continue signing scholarships through August 1st of their senior years. This will likely result in Division I schools completing the recruiting process earlier than in years past, which will allow DII and DIII schools to accelerate their signing dates.[23]

Different from a verbal commitment, which has no legal ramifications, scholarship athletes typically sign a legally binding contract called a National Letter of Intent ("NLI") to formalize the commitment and allow the school to begin academic and athletic preparations for their arrival in the upcoming semester. Signing an NLI means three things for a future collegiate student athlete:

1   Your student athlete is committed to one year at the university. The school is required to inform student athletes that their scholarship is or is not being renewed after the first year.

2   The university is promising to provide an athletic scholarship for that year. Note: the athletic scholarship and financial aid forms are two separate documents, the athlete will need to sign both.

3 Your student athlete may not be recruited by another school.

While verbal decommitments are common among college football recruits, who frequently change their decisions prior to Signing Day, it is rare to see baseball student athletes decommit for purposes outside of coaching changes or family emergencies. This is because college baseball programs have fewer scholarships and roster availability to make frequent changes in offers to players, and college baseball prospects do not receive the same level of media and social media attention.

Final certification with the NCAA Eligibility Center is not required to sign an NLI, but if certification is not achieved by June of an athlete's senior academic year, the NLI becomes null and void. An NLI is not used by all schools, and junior college and NAIA schools have their own versions of an NLI. Further, signing an NLI does not guarantee admission to the school, as all athletes are required to apply and gain admission with other students.

Walk-ons and preferred walk-ons are not required to sign an NLI. A walk-on is an athlete on a college team who undergoes a tryout and secures a spot on the team, but does not receive athletic scholarship aid. At the Division I level, it is extremely rare and highly unlikely that a previously unrecruited student walk-on will earn a spot on the team and make a meaningful impact, though there are exceptions. A preferred walk-on, on the other hand, is different because the athlete is previously recruited by the program and guaranteed a spot on the team. Preferred walk-ons are not required to try out and may later earn athletic scholarship funds through performance accomplishment.

PERSONAL BRANDING AND THE RIGHT OF PUBLICITY (NIL)

Social media has a major impact on recruiting and character evaluation in the baseball industry and beyond. Not only does it provide a platform for an athlete to showcase their talents, similar to entertainers, through photos and videos, statistics, and other performance content, it also displays a reflection of the athlete's internal makeup, character, and personality, which may be a deciding factor for potential fit for a college program or professional organization.

While it is crucial for an athlete to exercise wise judgment in their actions and social media postings, an athlete should be able to maintain individuality and monetize their name, image, and likeness ("NIL") for personal gain. In this new "Wild West" opportunity, athletes should uphold a certain amount of professionalism and be a positive influence and asset to a future program or organization while utilizing the public platform that they have earned to generate revenue.

College sports leagues, schools, booster clubs, sponsors, agencies, athletes, and parents are currently navigating uncharted waters with the first opportunity for NCAA student athletes to monetize NIL as other public figures have been doing for years.

> **In this new "Wild West" opportunity, athletes should uphold a certain amount of professionalism and be a positive influence and asset to a future program or organization while utilizing the public platform that they have earned to generate revenue.**

 PRO TIP ——————————————————

Ask coaches and recruiters of prospective institutions whether they plan to, or have a history of, accessing NIL income opportunities for their athletes.

Rules and regulations are rapidly changing and forming around the third-party relationships with student athletes, but the NCAA relinquished its efforts to control the student athlete's NIL when the Supreme Court stated in late June of 2021 that "The NCAA is not above the law." This opened the floodgates of opportunity for athletes to pursue and monetize their NIL, which for many athletes, is already generating revenues in excess of $500,000.

In late 2020, several other states initiated legislative action, and a Senate bill underwent consideration to put the legislation under federal control.

BRAMHALL: *In response to this new age in college athletics, I started Athlete Licensing Company ("ALC") www.athlete-licensing.com with two partners who are former college athletes. ALC is the leading market resource for NIL opportunities, placing the athlete at the center of the NIL ecosystem. We recognized the need to assist athletes in realizing their commercial NIL potential and the importance of keeping their interests as the number one priority. ALC provides a tech-enabled platform for:*

- monetization
- IP protection
- facilitation of deals
- transparent accounting
- royalty statements
- tax withholding
- NCAA, state, and federal compliance, and
- required reporting

ALC partners with universities, collectives, agencies, and athletes. In addition to ALC's back-office NIL management benefits, our monetization platform creates custom merchandise, NFTs (non-fungible tokens), and ticketed event opportunities for the athletes we represent.

Follow ALC www.athlete-licensing.com. Athletes will continue to benefit from their personal platforms for potential public influence and financial gain in many ways, and it is in your best interest to stay informed on how your athlete can use these tools to further their brand while maintaining eligibility.

JUNIOR COLLEGE BASEBALL

INTRODUCTION

This chapter will provide you with the most detailed information available about junior college baseball. In fact, there is very little written anywhere about this level, which has many benefits for ballplayers nationwide. After reading, you will know about the pros and cons, competition schedules, academic requirements, and professional scouting that occurs in this competitive environment.

WHY ATTEND A JUNIOR COLLEGE?

An outstanding opportunity awaits your athlete if they are fortunate to play junior college or community college baseball ("JUCO"). Junior colleges are two-year academic institutions that provide an associate's degree upon graduation, and offer many credits that transfer into 4-year institutions. Regardless of your athlete's career aspirations outside of baseball, attending a junior college will not hinder admission into a 4-year academic institution as a transfer at a later date. In fact, it may help.

Many parents have academic curriculum quality concerns that may or may not be justified. In addition to decreased class sizes and better access to professors based on student to teacher ratio, fully funded JUCO baseball programs may provide up to 24 athletic scholarships for the players on the roster, which means a free or low-cost education for the athlete. A JUCO athletic scholarship is not only an educational stepping stone but also an opportunity to continue to develop baseball skills, baseball IQ, and physical attributes.[24]

Further, if the athlete is unprepared for a 4-year university academically, junior colleges typically have more lenient admissions criteria and less stringent curriculum than 4-year universities. This allows student athletes to gradually develop study habits and improve self-discipline. Athletes can earn manageable credits for future transfer, while focusing on baseball and adapting to college routines.

Transferring into a 4-year institution can be an easier admission process than applying as a freshman candidate because qualifying test scores are not required or calculated in the overall class averages and university admissions statistics. Thus, JUCO attendance is also a way to sidestep the impact of SATs and ACTs on admission statistics if the athlete did not receive adequate scores on these exams in high school.

Another reason to attend JUCO is if the athlete is on the fringe of playing time at a 4-year university but likely will not receive a starting opportunity during their first season. These athletes often benefit from playing every day, rather than spending a season as a "redshirt" or receiving limited playing time in high pressure situations as a pinch hitter or relief pitcher. "A 'redshirt' season refers to a year in which a student-athlete does not compete at all against outside competition. During the redshirt season, a student can practice with his or her team and receive financial aid."[25]

The COVID-19 pandemic shut down college baseball mid-season in 2020. The NCAA and NJCAA created an eligibility extension of one year for each athlete, which resulted in a log jam across all levels of college baseball. High school graduates had already committed or signed for the upcoming 2021 season, and the NCAA and NJCAA member schools honored the scholarships of existing players. Many programs reported fielding 50-plus eligible players for the 2020-2021 academic year, when rosters normally max out at 35-40 players. One DI coach referred to 2020 Fall Ball practice as "a sea of players on the field, like spring football practice."

This unique situation will take 3-4 years to normalize into pre-COVID roster numbers. It also means that JUCO leagues will be more competitive due to the number of quality players seeking playing time, who otherwise would fill a roster at a 4-year institution. Professional scouts will have the opportunity to snag a would-be 3- or 4-year college player after their first or second year of JUCO ball. Unfortunately, it will also prevent many openings at the higher levels of competition for talented high school and JUCO players looking to get to the next level.

> **4-year institutions recruit athletes from junior colleges to fill major roster gaps each year.**

Ultimately, the expectations of the athlete and how their playing opportunities may be impacted will be crucial when deciding whether attending a JUCO or 4-year institution will be more beneficial, especially given the roster saturation as of 2021-2022. Athletes mature exponentially in the transition from high school to college, and 4-year institutions recruit athletes from junior colleges to fill major roster gaps each year.

Finally, MLB Draft and transfer considerations play a major factor in determining whether attending a JUCO is a beneficial choice. JUCOs are not under the same draft or transfer rules as 4-year institutions. JUCO baseball players are draft eligible after one year and may sign a professional baseball contract rather than returning for a second season. Likewise, a junior college player may transfer to another JUCO or 4-year institution at the semester break, after 1 year, or after 2 years. This boosts the competition level at the JUCO level because draft prospects may prefer to maintain draft eligibility and contract opportunity throughout the first two years of their collegiate careers.

JUCO REALITIES

With all of the benefits that JUCO attendance provides, there are unpleasant realities and challenging aspects that require mental fortitude to be successful. The first challenge is that the funding is limited and athletes are responsible for themselves in many ways. As a whole, JUCO baseball is not funded anywhere near 4-year DI institutions in nutrition, travel, sports medicine, facilities, equipment, or development.

In fact, the athlete may have experienced better while playing at lower levels. There are certainly perennial powerhouse JUCOs that may provide an experience more similar to DI, but these exceptions are few and far between. Success is reserved for the hungry who desire to push through challenges and remain focused on becoming a better player throughout the experience.

Secondly, this may be an athlete's first experience playing with individuals from different socio-economic backgrounds, with potentially different ethical and moral considerations. The athlete's decision-making processes may be challenged by this immersion into a new group of teammates who hold different values and may make questionable decisions. To expand, many of these JUCOs are located in rural areas with low enrollment and many opportunities to make poor choices due to limited entertainment, and lack of foresight and supervision.

🔻 HEADLEY: *As a perfect example, my first two weeks of JUCO were almost my last because of my roommates. I reported to my JUCO 2 weeks before classes started for fall baseball workouts. A few days after moving into the dorm, one of my new roommates purchased a used BBQ grill and brought it to the dorm building. Grills were prohibited on campus, so we took it to a friend's house on the last weekend before school began to grill burgers before the start of school and fall baseball.*

The following Monday, the first day of classes, the police knocked on the main dorm door at 5 A.M. yelling, "Cops, open up!" When I opened my personal door to enter the common living room, it was redecorated with lawn furniture that was not there when I went to sleep the night before. Apparently, some of the guys went on a shopping spree around town stealing local lawn furniture. 3 out of 8 were arrested and taken to the police station.

A few hours later, sitting in my first college class (pre-law, political science), a policeman I recognized from our dorm entered my class, spoke with the professor, and told me to pack my stuff because I would not be coming back. He arrested me based on my connection with the others, and took me to the station for questioning. After explaining that I was not involved in the lawn furniture theft, and that I suspected a BBQ grill theft was also connected to these individuals, the police allowed me one hour to prove my case by picking up the grill and bringing it to the station. Thankfully, after doing so, all charges against me were dropped. The other 3 three guys were charged with felony theft and dismissed from the baseball team and the school.

Needless to say, my welcome to JUCO was not how I envisioned it. Similar to my experience, your athlete may be thrust into challenging and unavoidable situations with roommates or teammates, especially those with different values. It is extremely important that the athlete stay focused on school and baseball, and practice self-control. This will elevate them above the many distractions that could limit their future opportunities. Counsel your athlete to stay the course, avoid those who bring them down, and make a positive impact with what they can control.

SCHEDULE

JUCO schedules consist of a fall and spring season. The spring season is considered to be the championship season with playoff implications. The fall schedule includes practice, intrasquads, and a number of games against other institutions or organizations at multiple levels. The fall games are important for development and depth chart evaluation. Many jobs are won or lost in the fall. Similar to other collegiate baseball season models, the fall games do not count toward a program's regular season schedule and may consist of extended games, cancellations without consequence, and rolled innings. Rolled innings are innings that are terminated prior to the defensive team getting 3 outs. Often, an inning is rolled based on a pitcher's pitch count, number of batters faced, or runs scored in a single half inning.

The NJCAA Division I JUCO World Series is the premiere tournament featuring the top JUCO programs in the country.

The regular season spring schedule is a hard reset with new goals and opportunities. It begins with team practice in early January close to the start of classes, and consists of roughly 50-55 games. JUCO is known for double-headers on any day of the week. Depending on travel arrangements, weather delays could push a weekend series or game to Sunday, but most games are played on Fridays and Saturdays.

The regular season is followed by playoffs for qualifying teams, with the end goal of reaching and winning the JUCO (NJCAA) World Series in Grand Junction, Colorado. The NJCAA Division I JUCO World Series is the premiere tournament featuring the top JUCO programs in the country. Many 4-year universities and professional scouts attend. This is a great opportunity for players to advance to the next level because NCAA programs are recruiting for their rosters for the upcoming season.

RECRUITMENT, TRANSFERS, AND ACADEMICS

The JUCO experience can last 1-3 years. An athlete only needs one season to be exposed to the recruitment and transfers that frequently occur, which cause changes in team dynamics each season. Although the end result appears the same, there is a difference in perception between recruitment and transfer.

Recruitment generally occurs when a player fulfills their playing commitment to the JUCO and coaching staff, and is recruited away by specific college programs to finish the remaining years of collegiate eligibility. Coaches assist in the process and their programs benefit by having players advance to successful careers at 4-year institutions or sign professional contracts. A transfer, on the other hand, is often when an athlete unilaterally seeks to exit a program for other opportunities and better fit. Transfers may also come into the program from a 4-year institution or another JUCO at the semester break due to roster cuts and/or changes.

Coaches are more likely to be proactive in the recruitment process and placement of graduating or high performing players when the player has fulfilled their commitment to the program. Whether a player intends to stay another year or transfer, they should communicate with coaches about their intentions to ensure that coaches are not blindsided by the decision. These coaches have provided a development and playing opportunity, and deserve a certain amount of respect and honest communication in return.

During the recruitment and/or transfer process, a common issue faced by athletes is determining which class credits will transfer to the next institution. When the opportunity arises to further a baseball and/or academic career, credits that do not transfer can cause unforeseen eligibility and financial issues. Insufficient transferable credits may require additional classes or semesters to obtain a degree and might result in insufficient prerequisites to pursue a chosen degree path. It is important to avoid any potential future issues during course registration.

The wisest route is to enroll in transferable 4-year institution prerequisites or core subject matter classes, regardless of the perceived difficulty of schedule. The athlete should be challenged and take pride in their education. Proper depth of course selection will provide the athlete with the best opportunity to transfer the credits earned and avoid wasted hours and effort that do not benefit their future. Many academic advisors may suggest a lighter introductory course load for the first semester to acclimate, but we do not recommend this for spring sport JUCO athletes. As a consequence, the athlete endures a heavier load during the season to remain on track and eligible for the following year. This can be burdensome with schedules of multiple games and overnight bus trips each week.

If your athlete requires academic assistance or struggles to keep up with athletics and academics concurrently in the first semester, they should discuss the challenges in advance with their head coach or academic counselor and they will arrange tutors and schedule modifications. The athlete and counselor can develop proactive strategies together before problems arise. Demonstrating the ability to perform in the classroom is important as the athlete seeks to further their education, transfer JUCO credits earned after graduation, and aspire to further their playing career at a 4-year institution.

SCOUTING

We will discuss the many facets of scouting in the upcoming Amateur and Pro Scouting chapter, but a brief understanding of the JUCO scouting scene will be helpful as your athlete's career progresses.

Professional scouting is consistent throughout the JUCO season because all players are draft-eligible. Fall scouting is essential for MLB organizations because scouts spend an incredible amount of time on the road in the regular season. Evaluating talent in preparation for the upcoming regular season and MLB Draft projections is crucial. In fall games, scouts often make requests to JUCO coaches to evaluate specific athletes to maximize the efficiency of the time.

Area scouts are visible throughout the fall and regular spring seasons to evaluate talent and provide reports on potential draft picks to their organizations. Cross-checkers and scouting directors also make appearances to verify evaluations and make final decisions. Scouting, which relies heavily on potential and projectability, focuses on evaluating the physical upsides of athletes to fill professional rosters and stockpile talent in the minor league systems. While statistics and overall performance success help a player's draft stock or to gain initial recognition, scouts generally evaluate an athlete's tools for potential impact in professional baseball.

Many pro scouts converse regularly with 4-year school coaches. This could lead to an opportunity for your JUCO athlete if the best next step in their career is at a 4-year institution, rather than the pros. As previously discussed, the flexibility offered by JUCOs to be recruited by a 4-year institution, transfer, or maintain MLB Draft eligibility, are some of the benefits to deferring a 4-year university commitment or waiting for a more opportune time to sign a professional contract. The JUCO experience can be a valuable but unglamorous opportunity to develop grit and passion for the game, increase baseball IQ, develop physically, and gain experience necessary to advance to the next level.

FOUR-YEAR COLLEGE BASEBALL

INTRODUCTION

There are four distinct levels associated with four-year academic institutions that field college baseball programs[26]:

NCAA DIVISION I

- The highest-level programs with national or regional audiences

- Able to offer athletic scholarships

- 350 participating schools (32% of overall)

- Median undergraduate enrollment of 8,960 students

- 4.3% of students are student athletes

- 57% of athletes receive financial aid

- World Series: Omaha, NE

NCAA DIVISION II

- Regional schools with less athletic funding than Division I

- Able to offer athletic scholarships

- 310 participating schools (28% of overall)

- Median undergraduate enrollment of 2,428 students

- 10% of students are student athletes

- 25% of athletes receive financial aid
- World Series: hosting rights vary year to year

NCAA DIVISION III

- Unable to offer athletic scholarships
- 438 participating schools (40% of overall)
- Median undergraduate enrollment of 1,740 students
- 16.7% of students are student athletes
- World Series: hosting rights vary year to year

NAIA

- Subject to different rules and regulations than NCAA members
- Able to offer athletic scholarships
- Athletic budgets similar to NCAA DIII schools
- 212 NAIA baseball programs
- No recruiting restrictions for coach and student athlete communication
- 12 scholarships vs. NCAA Division I 11.7 scholarships
- World Series: Lewiston, ID

Despite the differences between the divisions, you will gain a better understanding of each during the recruiting process. During this time, the athlete will benefit from parental wisdom and guidance to weigh various options and understand the bigger picture. Once they make a decision, your involvement must shift to support and encouragement, while the coaching staff assumes responsibility for the development of your athlete and winning games for the program.

This chapter will focus on the Division I level because it is the highest level of college baseball. However, many athletes fall into the trap of considering only DI schools due to the attention these schools receive. In reality, each level presents competitive opportunities to continue playing at a high level. Although the talent level and roster depth are generally the highest and deepest at the DI level, the cream rises regardless of where and when the athlete lands, and elite level talent is found at every level each year by professional scouts.

DI BASEBALL

DI Baseball receives the most attention because of the funding provided, level of competition, and public awareness. It is likely the most celebrated and rewarding of all levels of baseball, aside from Major League Baseball. Here, amateur level competition peaks with mentally and physically developed talent on the field, recognition, funding for recruiting, development, excellent facilities for the student athletes and fans, and a higher percentage of athletes who sign professional contracts compared to other levels of baseball.

Further, DI universities whose athletic programs are generally funded through football revenue and donor investments, are able to offer added benefits of nutrition, strength and conditioning programs, experienced coaching, tools and technology to improve results, impressive hotel accommodations, and academic career networking and education for student athletes. These benefits improve the student athlete experience and make attendance at a DI over other divisions more attractive to prospects during the recruiting process.

The fan engagement at this level is tribal in nature and drives the recruiting and prestige. Power 5 DI baseball schools

Power 5 DI baseball schools average between 1,000–5,000 fans per game, and some schools reach as high as 11,000 fans in a single regular season game.

average between 1,000-5,000 fans per game, and some schools reach as many as 11,000 fans in a single regular season game. All factors contribute to a higher quality of life, more notoriety (including name, image, and likeness benefits), prospect visibility, and ultimately, a better probability of a professional baseball opportunity for the student athletes.

A DAY IN THE LIFE OF A DI BASEBALL STUDENT ATHLETE

The transition from high school baseball as a hobby to the full-time job of college baseball and academics presents challenges that are consistent among all levels of college baseball. These include: athletic commitments, full-time school responsibilities, family and social time demands, and personal discretionary time during their collegiate career.

Most athletes follow a general pattern. They attend class in the morning and have strength and conditioning workouts before or after class, in addition to team practice, study hall, and "individuals." "Individuals" are workouts typically consisting of 4-6 players, commonly held before team practice time. These workouts consist of specific drills and instruction according to defensive position, and offensive drill work with a coach. The competition is intense with workouts grouped according to position, and the motivation to be your best is at an all-time high.

From the moment an athlete wakes up for class or morning workouts, the schedule is full. Mealtimes may be the only designated opportunities to regroup before the next commitment.

HERE IS A TYPICAL STUDENT ATHLETE'S DAILY SCHEDULE:

5:30am - Alarm

6:00am - Strength and conditioning

8:00am - Shower and breakfast

9:00am -12:00pm - Class attendance

12:00pm - Lunch

1:30pm - Individuals

2:30pm - Team meeting

3:00pm - Team practice

6:30pm - Dinner

7:30pm - Library or study hall

9:30pm - Social

10:30pm - Lights out

Gamedays, which require 8-10 hours of commitment after classes, present additional challenges with exams and academic deadlines, regardless of team travel or extracurricular activities. This drastically reduces the time available for academic studies and recovery. Time management, compartmentalization, and self-accountability are crucial for an athlete's success, in addition to their athletic duties.

To whom much is given, much is expected. The opportunities afforded to DI athletes bring responsibilities that other non-athlete students do not experience. Increased expectations to perform, social distractions and pressures, and academic commitments in preparation for life after athletics are all possible to manage with proper time management and prioritization.

AMATEURISM, ACADEMIC, AND ADMISSION REQUIREMENTS

The National Collegiate Athletic Association (NCAA), the governing body of collegiate sports, requires achievement of certain qualifications and preservation of amateur status for an athlete to play sports at an institution. An individual loses amateur status and will not be eligible for intercollegiate competition in a particular sport if the individual:

A Uses his or her athletics skill (directly or indirectly) for pay in any form in that sport;

B Accepts a promise of pay even if such pay is to be received following completion of athletics participation;

C Signs a contract or commitment of any kind to play professional athletics, regardless of its legal enforceability or any consideration received, except as permitted in Bylaw 12.2.5.1;

D Receives, directly or indirectly, a salary, reimbursement of expenses or any other form of financial assistance from a professional sports organization based on athletics skill or participation, except as permitted by NCAA rules and regulations;[27]

E Competes on any professional athletics team per Bylaw 12.02.12, even if no pay or remuneration for expenses was received, except as permitted in Bylaw 12.2.3.2.1;

F After initial full-time collegiate enrollment, enters into a professional draft (see Bylaw 12.2.4); or

G Enters into an agreement with an agent. 12.1.2.1 Prohibited Forms of Pay. "Pay," as used in Bylaw 12.1.2 above, includes, but is not limited to, the following: 12.1.2.1.1 Salary.[28] These include athlete and agent relationships pertaining to professional sports playing contracts.

Further, the amateur student athletes must register with the NCAA Initial-Eligibility Clearinghouse to be eligible to play NCAA Division I or Division II sports. Athletes playing in NCAA Division III do not have to register, but athletes planning on attending an NAIA institution must register with the NAIA Eligibility Center. The NCAA recommends that the student athlete register with the clearinghouse at the beginning of their junior year in high school, but a student athlete may register after their junior year. There is no registration deadline. However, a student must be cleared by the Clearinghouse for amateur status determination and before they receive athletic scholarships, or compete at a Division I or Division II institution.

Students may register online at the NCAA Eligibility Center[29] to ensure all required criteria have been met. The prospective student athlete will enter personal information, answer questions about athletic participation, and pay a registration fee. They must also send their high school transcript and ACT or SAT scores to the Clearinghouse.[30] Please refer to the chart available here: whosonfirstbook.com/academics, which establishes the sliding scale that is required to be admitted and remain eligible during the athlete's collegiate career, with respect to GPA, SAT, and ACT scores.[31]

SUCCESS IN THE CLASSROOM

Regardless of talent, if certain academic standards are not met, eligibility and playing opportunity can be withdrawn from the athlete before or during their collegiate years. As mentioned in the JUCO chapter, a route for the less academically inclined player is to attend JUCO for a year or two, which has more lenient admissions and academic eligibility requirements. At these less academically demanding schools, whether they be two- or four-year institutions, the athlete has the opportunity to develop study habits with less academic pressures as their game develops on the field.

Do not discount the value of the opportunity to gain an education and pursue a degree that will carry your athlete after baseball is over. Many players, even former Major Leaguers, struggle after baseball without a degree or formal training. Each institution offers tutoring for student athletes, and depending on the academic success of the athlete, may require study hall hours. The amount of study hall hours required is typically based on their progress reports, classroom attendance, and academic year in school. Division I institutions often have academic counselors and members of the coaching staff available for one-on-one tutoring, classroom checks, progress reports, and mentoring. For example, Texas A&M University employs 26 full-time athletics academic staff members to support the student athletes.

Tutoring aside, sometimes the relationship an athlete establishes with a professor can be the difference in achieving a desired outcome in a particular course, especially when the demands of travel and outside responsibilities conflict with that course. Constant communication will improve the relationship and ability of the professor to accommodate for absences, allow alternative assignments, and adjust exam schedules. When attending class, athletes should sit toward the front, be attentive, and participate as a member of the student body, without expectation of privilege. This will bode well with the professors. Once the athlete realizes they are responsible for the outcome of their academic and athletic career by maintaining a proactive mentality with proper time management, academics will likely not be a problem. Especially with the numerous resources available to succeed.

COMPETITION FOR PLAYING TIME

A college coach must engage the donor fanbase, establish a cohesive team culture, and generate success on the field to maintain their job. At the collegiate level, the lineup decisions are based on winning, the likelihood of future success, and ultimately, putting food on the table for coaches' families. "Daddy Ball" is over. This means that playing time is not guaranteed, regardless of your involvement or influence during the recruiting process. In this meritocracy, coaches will indirectly, and frequently, ask players – "What have you done for me lately?" Consistent production and measurable results are the greatest insurance policies for playing time, scholarship money, and opportunities going forward.

SCHOLARSHIP INFORMATION

You may have assumed that baseball scholarships are "full rides," as is common in college football and basketball. Unfortunately, a full baseball scholarship is rare because of the scholarship allotment per team and the number of players on a baseball roster. Currently, the NCAA permits each school to provide only 11.7 athletic baseball scholarships for DI, 9 for DII, and none for DIII. The NAIA permits 12 athletic baseball scholarships per school. Excluding special exceptions and changes in the rules for 2021, at the DI level, the scholarships may be divided between a maximum of 27 players, with each scholarship athlete receiving a minimum 25% scholarship. At the DII level, the athletic scholarships may be divided among the athletes, in any manner. Remember this during your investments of time and money in travel baseball throughout your athlete's early career.

Ensure the pursuit is for the love of the game, involvement for the family, and challenge and enjoyment of the experience, rather than for a chance at a partial scholarship that may never produce the return on investment that you expected. Additionally, athletic scholarships are generally only guaranteed year to year, rather than for the entire duration of a player's academic career at the institution. High academic institutions, such as Rice University, are the exception to this rule. Rice requires that scholarships awarded to athletes be honored for the entirety of their tenures at the University. Honoring the scholarship encourages the athlete to pursue their academic future with the promise that the educational benefits will be guaranteed, regardless of athletic performance or roster decisions.

However, these institutions are the rare exception, and each year programs are forced to renege on promises made and scholarships originally offered. This often creates challenging circumstances for the student athletes, and their parents, who depend on the scholarship financially. When an athlete's scholarship support is removed, they are forced to transfer schools to another scholarship playing opportunity or obtain financial assistance through other means to stay enrolled at their current school.

Coaches must use creative tactics when dividing scholarships to recruit quality talent and fulfill offers. This can result in promising more scholarship money than is ultimately available. A common situation occurs where multiple committed recruits, who were expected to sign in the MLB Draft out of high school, end up enrolling in school. Scholarship money must be removed from players currently on the roster to honor the offers previously extended to those prospects.

For programs in these situations, having talented committed recruits that do not sign professional contracts can be a fantastic bonus. Yet, it may create scholarship allotment issues to remain in compliance with the NCAA. Further, when a top recruit signs in the draft, many of the other prospects have already accepted offers at other programs. Thus, college coaches must balance the desire to have a high-ranking recruiting class and risk losing players to the draft, with a more dependable recruiting class consisting of recruits who are sure to become student athletes, but who may initially show less future potential.

This is a great opportunity to discuss some of the recruiting advantages some college DI baseball programs have over others. LSU, for example, considered to be one of the top programs in the country, has an in-state tuition waiver for students and athletes from the state of Louisiana. This advantage allows the allotted 11.7 athletic scholarships to be used on players from out of state. In effect, this results in a higher percentage of athletes to be on scholarship than at other DI programs.

Other similar examples include many private and some public institutions with a high cost of attendance or a difficult admissions process based on high academic requirements such as Tulane, Vanderbilt, Rice, and Stanford, among others. These institutions frequently extend need-based financial grants and aid to families that qualify based on annual income, rather than requiring those athletes to be factored into the NCAA athletic scholarship allotment. As a result, this creates a steep advantage to increase roster depth and promise scholarship funding to many more prospects than institutions under normal restrictions.

THE SECRETS TO SUCCESS

At this level, there are a few key suggestions that, if followed, will greatly improve your athlete's chances of reaching the goals of their college playing career. The first recommendation is that the athlete should prioritize commitments that make them better individuals, athletes, teammates, and academic students. Nothing should impede a relentless pursuit of these priorities during the finite years of college. The athlete will have the opportunity to participate in leisure and entertainment in the years after college, but optimizing performance in school and baseball should be the top priority during this period in their career. Maintaining a keen awareness of the necessary mental and physical preparation required, including balanced nutrition and sleep habits, will pay dividends in daily output throughout the longevity of the season.

Second, understanding what creates value in the coaches' eyes is critical. Some programs enforce strict conditioning and discipline regimens to be the "toughest" and most physically prepared, while others enforce mental fortitude and tests of character as a means of encouraging teamwork and fireproofing the emotional strength of its athletes. It is vital to the success of the player to understand the way in which their program chooses and respects players and leaders, and to develop fortitude and a winner's

> Maintaining a keen awareness of the necessary mental and physical preparation required, including balanced nutrition and sleep habits, will pay dividends in daily output throughout the longevity of the season.

mentality. It may be difficult to prepare for these challenges or to pick up on these psychological insights entering as a freshman. With time, however, your athlete can cultivate the mindset of adapting to any style of coaching by becoming aware of the underlying motivations of a coach.

One of the best examples of this emotional strength and determination paired with talent was by a player named Parker Dalton, who was caught in the middle of a coaching change. The previous staff, who recruited him and who he earned his stripes with, was terminated. Staff changes at any level can present difficult changes, but how you respond as an athlete greatly influences the outcome. Parker had previously survived cancer and knew this challenge was simply another test of his willpower.

After fall evaluations and meetings entering his senior season, he was told by the staff he would be a bench coach and veteran presence, but that he would not be a player because there were 2-3 players ahead of him on the depth chart. In the meeting, Parker calmly absorbed the news and season's projection by his head coach and replied, "Coach, you don't know it yet, but I am going to start at second base for you." That season, Parker went on to achieve Second-Team All-Big 12 honors, finishing 3rd in conference batting average, and was drafted by the Los Angeles Dodgers in the 2007 MLB Draft. Be that guy.

Finally, as difficult as it may seem to remain focused and practice fortitude with increased social pressures, responsibilities, relationships, or academic demands, success at this level is born from time management. Succeeding here contributes to maximizing potential and output as a baseball player and student athlete. This is accomplished with a marathoner's mentality of consistent progress, and making everything they do about the end goal.

The collegiate level is where the athlete will make lifelong friends, earn respect, enhance their future on and off the field, and develop character through the trials that will certainly grow in significance over time. They do not get this time back, and there are no redos. A business professional may have multiple opportunities to be successful or move to another job in their career. But in college sports, athletes get one 5-year period to establish a legacy and prepare for the grind of professional baseball, or life in the real world.

PARENT ETIQUETTE IN COLLEGE BASEBALL

At this level of collegiate baseball, your number one priority should be to support your athlete and cultivate a positive personal relationship with them. Your involvement beyond that is no longer necessary or desired, even if you were able to impact the athlete's career at previous stages of development. Any involvement here most likely hinders their opportunities because a college program is much bigger than any single athlete, and any helicopter parents. Therefore, be invisible and supportive at the same time.

> **Awareness of your actions should be of utmost importance as your athlete is working on the field for their future.**

The more positive and supportive you can be, with a poker face on tough days, the better chance your athlete's abilities will dictate the future. Despite what you think you may know, you do not have all of the information about internal team dynamics. Coaches at this level are making decisions to feed their families. Support the program and your athlete regardless of the situation. Awareness of your actions should be of utmost importance as your athlete is working on the field for their future.

PRO TIP

The best website to stay informed on Division I Baseball is d1baseball.com.

FALL BALL

"Fall Ball" is the non-championship practice season. It is comparable to spring football practice, where positions are earned, incoming athletes are introduced to the increased level of competition, and the clubhouse dynamic is formed for the upcoming season. Academic work, strength and conditioning, individuals, and team practice must be properly managed and balanced within the athlete's new routine as a student athlete during this period.

Fall Ball generates a unique intensity of competition and "weeding out" period, which results in some players transferring at semester's end or getting cut from the team. In the military, boot camp is the first phase of becoming a trained soldier and member of a team. In this period, the weakest links are exposed, trials and failures become the norm, and self-discovery leads to personal growth to benefit the whole.

Similarly, Fall Ball is a necessary time of integrating athletes into the team, with up to 20 permitted hours of training each week. 20 *documented* hours, anyway. This period is designed to prepare the ballplayers for a multitude of challenges they will face in the upcoming season.[32] An athlete should focus on individual development during this period and persevere as an initiated member of the team for the upcoming season. There is a light at the end of the tunnel knowing the end of Fall Ball is followed by a holiday break, and the excitement of the upcoming regular season is just around the corner.

Fall Ball begins with "individuals" consisting of up to 4 players and a coach, practicing specific defensive drills for a position, bullpens and pitching development, or hitting instruction. The Fall Ball practice season is roughly 6 weeks in duration and includes team practices, intrasquads, and intersquad games versus other JUCO or 4-year programs. The intersquad games are generally regional, few in number, and often on the weekend. This helps to minimize travel demands for budget conservation and academic focus for the student athletes. Programs typically conclude the fall season with a 7-game World Series within the program to heighten competition, simulate the elite-level atmosphere, and include the fan base to generate support.

If your athlete desires to make an impact early, which they should, performing well in fall practices and games is the best avenue. Although the first opportunity an athlete has to demonstrate their abilities is during individuals, the coaches are most likely evaluating impact players to fill travel rosters and starting lineups for the upcoming season based on success in *game* situations.

Remember, prior to this first impression opportunity, the coaches may have only recruited the athlete through word of mouth or limited evaluation at a showcase or travel ball tournament. Coaches must be reminded that their decision to bring the athlete into the program was and remains beneficial for the program's future. Fall practice is a crucial first step in evaluating each player and the team's overall potential.

It is not uncommon for coaches to ask a player to transfer at the end of the semester after realizing that the player will not be a good fit or will not be talented enough to succeed at the D1 level. This allows the player to seek a more beneficial situation for their playing career, which will provide more playing time and repetitions. When an athlete decides or is asked to transfer, it is only the end of the playing opportunity at that school and could lead to a better situation going forward at a JUCO or another 4-year program.

The athlete should take advantage of the challenges and growth opportunities presented by Fall Ball to be an established member of the team and prepare for the upcoming regular season. While the pressures of school will accompany baseball, possibly for the first time, this necessary growth period will prepare them for the unique demands as a student athlete in a competitive athletic environment.

REGULAR SEASON

The opening of the college baseball regular season generates unmatched excitement across the country because it is a fresh start on the road to Omaha for players, fans, and staff. It is also the first opportunity of the year for fans and scouts to get outside and watch the future stars of the game. Practice begins in January near the start of the academic semester, which is 4-6 weeks before MLB Spring Training. Practice routines and itineraries are already well-established by the coaching staff and understood by the players. However, the new season presents new degree coursework for student athletes and increased focus on the championship season.

Team practice gradually establishes a depth chart, pitching rotation, bullpen roles, and starting lineups for the opening series or tournament. Yet, there always remain opportunities for roles to be earned, as many decisions are not solidified until several games into the season. Windows of opportunity open and close, and it is up to the athlete to be prepared to take advantage, however small those windows may be. Most freshmen are further down the depth chart to begin the season. Consistent success in practice and engagement during games by supporting the team in various aspects improves their chances at playing opportunities.

Many of these early opportunities may be as a defensive replacement, pinch-hitting roles, or relief pitching appearances. Regardless of the potential impact, the young athlete should approach each situation fully committed to earn a future opportunity in the field, at the plate, or on the mound. Regardless of the outcomes, the athlete should put forth their best effort, embrace and learn from failure, and exhibit poise and maturity. Always expect another opportunity to make an impact.

Most programs play an early-season schedule consisting of 3-game series and mid-week games versus non-conference opponents and/or weekend tournaments. This portion of the season is important for Rating Percentage Index ("RPI") and at-large bids during playoff seeding and selection. RPI is a metric used to rank NCAA Division I college teams. Since college sports are divided into conferences with varying levels of caliber, RPI provides a team comparison by using strength of schedule and strength of opponents' schedules.[33] Although the non-conference games do not affect the team's conference standings, RPI impacts the regional playoff selection and seed placement in the postseason tournament. It is also important to establish a winning mentality heading into conference play.

Conference schedules vary based on the number of schools in the conference. Generally, conference games are played in a 3-game series played on Friday evening, Saturday afternoon or evening, and Sunday afternoon, with the possibility of a doubleheader the following day to compensate for weather cancellations. The conference regular-season standings determine the placement in the conference tournament, which is the reason a team's focus entering a weekend series should be to win the series, improve conference standing, and improve overall record.

The remainder of the schedule consists of mid-week games versus regional non-conference opponents, generally on Tuesdays and/or Wednesdays. While seemingly less important than conference games, the mid-week schedule can be intense and have a major impact on in- or out-of-state rivalries and RPI standings. It allows playing time for athletes who will have important roles in the upcoming conference tournament and postseason.

Games against seemingly lesser opponents can be dangerous when the other team uses its best pitchers in hopes of a shocking win to bolster RPI, reputation for recruiting purposes, and momentum for the program. These games can also be beneficial for the smaller programs to gain exposure to professional scouts when players have success against competition that they may not see on a consistent basis in their respective conference matchups.

> **Regardless of the mode of travel, maintaining a disciplined "business trip" mentality during the demands of a road trip, provides the athlete and program the best chance of accomplishing the end goal of winning games, maintaining momentum, and remaining academically productive for the athlete's future.**

The program's location, conference, and budget dictate the travel itineraries and transportation experience. These result in new challenges to overcome, such as sleep deprivation, time management, and mental preparedness in the rigors of a long season. For most schools, a charter bus or a sleeper bus is used for transportation to regional opponents. However, there are some schools with budgets to provide commercial airline or charter airline arrangements.

Regardless of the mode of travel, maintaining a disciplined "business trip" mentality during the demands of a road trip, provides the athlete and program the best chance of accomplishing the end goal of winning games, maintaining momentum, and remaining academically productive for the athlete's future.

Distractions are numerous during the season without the consistency of regular class attendance and a constantly changing environment with travel to numerous cities for competition. Without clearly established deadlines and structure, it is easy for an athlete to forget to focus on individual responsibilities with the temptations to engage with yahoos on social media, participate in tomfoolery, or procrastinate with other modes of entertainment. An athlete should take care to establish regimented practices of self-discipline in advance and seek to succeed in every aspect.

CONFERENCE TOURNAMENT

One of the unique experiences of playing in the baseball postseason, unlike most collegiate sports, is that the postseason occurs after the school semester. Focus is on baseball alone, rather than including the stresses of academics during the quest for a championship. A conference tournament championship results in an automatic bid into the NCAA postseason, regardless of the team's regular season RPI or conference ranking.

Most conference tournament formats match the team with the best regular season conference record against the team with the worst qualifying record to begin the tournament in a double-elimination format. This is similar to a college basketball conference tournament layout. In large conferences, the regular season record determines which schools qualify to compete at the conference tournament. In addition to the incredible privilege of representing their schools, players are provided gift packages and treated as royalty in this unforgettable experience.

Fanfare is filled with energy and excitement at the week-long conference tournaments, as each program's fanbase flocks to support their favorite teams and players for bragging rights. This is also a preview of the contenders in the upcoming NCAA postseason tournament. If your athlete has never attended a Power 5 conference tournament, prioritize a trip for family entertainment at least once during middle school or high school. In addition to the enjoyable experience, it will motivate your athlete and provide a glimpse of this level of baseball.

As the tournament progresses and teams are eliminated, the crowds diminish, which increases the intensity for the teams still standing. Winning the conference tournament not only provides automatic postseason selection into the NCAA Tournament, but can also cement a national seed or regional host site for teams in the top 16.[34]

THE NCAA PLAYOFFS AND THE COLLEGE WORLD SERIES

The NCAA Division I playoffs, hosted at sites nationwide, and the

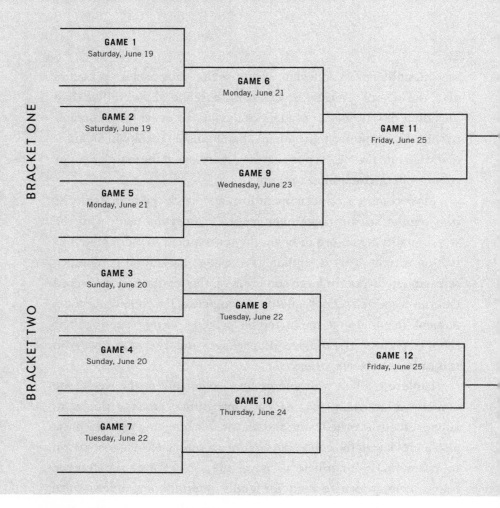

BRACKET ONE

GAME 1
Saturday, June 19

GAME 6
Monday, June 21

GAME 2
Saturday, June 19

GAME 11
Friday, June 25

GAME 9
Wednesday, June 23

GAME 5
Monday, June 21

BRACKET TWO

GAME 3
Sunday, June 20

GAME 8
Tuesday, June 22

GAME 4
Sunday, June 20

GAME 12
Friday, June 25

GAME 10
Thursday, June 24

GAME 7
Tuesday, June 22

College World Series ("CWS"), hosted annually in Omaha, NE, are two of the most memorable aspects of the college baseball player's career, fulfilling lifelong goals and dreams in one special tournament. NCAA Divisions II and III, and the NAIA also hold annual playoff tournaments that follow a similar format and fanfare, but we will focus primarily on the largest stage at the collegiate level.

The playoff field consists of 64 qualifying teams, separated in 16 regional sites nationwide. The hosts of the regional sites have earned a top seed in most cases, with a rare exception when a two seed is chosen to host. As previously mentioned, the 8 national seeds host regional and super regional tournaments, assuming

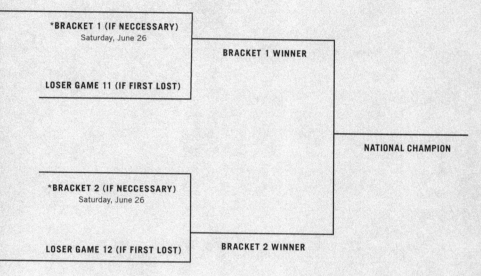

2021 NCAA MEN'S COLLEGE WORLD SERIES
TD AMERITRADE PARK OMAHA
JUNE 19-29/30 • OMAHA, NE

*BRACKET 1 (IF NECCESSARY)
Saturday, June 26

BRACKET 1 WINNER

LOSER GAME 11 (IF FIRST LOST)

NATIONAL CHAMPION

*BRACKET 2 (IF NECCESSARY)
Saturday, June 26

LOSER GAME 12 (IF FIRST LOST)

BRACKET 2 WINNER

CWS FINALS
Game One - Monday, June 28 - Time
Game Two - Tuesday, June 29 - Time
#Game Three - Wednesday, June 30 - Time

these national seeds win their respective regionals. The 16 regional tournaments consist of a 4-team, double elimination bracket. The winner advances to the super regional versus the winner of another regional's pre-determined pairing. The super regional is a 3-game series, with the winner receiving a bid to the 8-team College World Series, and a chance to compete for the National Championship.

The CWS is among the most exciting events in all of sports, consisting of the top 8 programs in the nation competing for the ultimate prize in college baseball. Teams arrive for opening ceremonies and practice for two days prior to the first round of play. Players engage in fan autograph sessions, media appearances, concerts, and other

◆ **BRAMHALL:** *In the 2006 Super Regionals, my team, Rice University, hosted the University of Oklahoma in a best-of-3 series to determine which team would advance to the College World Series.*

Before game 3, Wayne Graham, one of the greatest college baseball coaches of all-time, began reading the comments about the upcoming game from the online fan forums during our team meeting in the locker room. As he read comments out loud questioning player performance or coaching decisions from the previous games, his tongue stuck to his cheek, his bottom lip curled, and his eyes watered. "Fuck 'em," he said. He said it twice, boldly, and walked out of the meeting into the dugout.

That afternoon, we dogpiled on the pitcher's mound and made plans for our next stop, Omaha, NE. Below is an emotional photo of my dad and me meeting at the backstop behind home plate after the dogpile, realizing a lifelong dream we both shared for years.

entertainment. The format consists of two 4-team double elimination brackets, with the winners advancing to a final 3-game series to determine the National Champion.[35]

In the first two rounds of bracket play, teams receive one day off if they win their first game and two days off if they win the second, which places them in the bracket championship. This period allows for pitching staff recovery and scouting of the remaining teams in the tournament. But it can also result in a loss of momentum from waiting multiple days for the next game.

An athlete frequently plays in double-elimination tournaments in their career, yet the intensity and focus required to perform in Omaha is incomparable. Remaining physically and mentally prepared during this 10-day event requires intense focus and can be the difference in winning or losing the National Championship.

We recommend a trip to Omaha to watch the CWS, an event with many entertaining aspects available for athletes and their families. It is an opportunity to witness some of the most talented players and cohesive team dynamics in the country. There is truly nothing like it, and only a firsthand experience will do justice to its significance and allure.

COLLEGE SUMMER BASEBALL LEAGUES

OVERVIEW

Collegiate wood-bat summer leagues are a cherished experience for those who get to be involved. Summers are filled with stories of host families and teammates forming lifelong friendships, players working various jobs each morning before games, community involvement during the summer season, and players rising up in their development as ballplayers.

It is important for a college athlete to prioritize placement on a summer ball team at the start of the fall semester before Fall Ball. Team rosters are decided and contracts are signed no later than the end of the fall school semester. If the athlete waits until the end of the regular season to reach out to a summer ball program, it may be difficult to find a spot in a competitive league or receive adequate playing time for development.

Not every college coach reaches out on behalf of their players, which leaves the player responsible to network and find a spot for the upcoming summer season. Incoming freshmen who have yet to compile statistics at the collegiate level may have difficulty finding a place to play in the premiere summer leagues after their first season. Those with contracts or commitments in advance have the advantage of guaranteed playing time that is not dictated by the previous college season's successes, failures, or lack of repetitions.

Some of the unique advantages of Summer Ball are that the new team provides a clean slate for players to earn playing time, gain experience at different positions, and perform in a new environment unconnected to their current college program. Additionally, rosters in the most competitive leagues typically have players who are still in the NCAA postseason when the summer league begins. This provides an opportunity for temporary players ("temps") from schools that have completed their seasons to gain experience. In fact, many of these temp players end up with permanent positions on the team based on performance over the course of their temporary contracts.

Another unique advantage of playing for a summer team unconnected to the athlete's college team is that players who wish to transfer form bonds with other players on the summer collegiate rosters. This provides a network to relay information to coaches through these players who can assist in a possible opportunity. One of the best examples of this transfer opportunity happened on my Cape Cod League summer team when two San Diego State standouts became close friends with former MLB All-Star Justin Masterson. Masterson was attending Bethel College, an NAIA institution, at the time. By summer's end, Masterson transferred from Bethel to join the players at San Diego State under coach Tony Gwynn.

If the athlete waits until the end of the regular season to reach out to a summer ball program, it may be difficult to find a spot in a competitive league or receive adequate playing time for development.

Overall, without the added academic responsibilities of the regular season and experiences of a new environment, Summer Ball is a refreshing opportunity to return a player's passion and focus back to playing the game. This is as long as they avoid the temptations to break team rules, which is known to earn a plane ticket back home!

To realistically discuss each collegiate summer baseball league in sufficient detail would require another book, however, we will touch on each of the most respected leagues to illustrate the incredible experiences offered by the leagues and the communities that support their existence year after year. For a complete list to research and find a fit for your player during their summer break, visit: baseballnews.com/summer-collegiate-leagues/.[36]

THE CAPE COD BASEBALL LEAGUE

"You talk about baseball players being a brotherhood, there's a brotherhood within a brotherhood and that is those who played in the Cape League. When you meet, there are always two questions: Who was your host family, and what was your job?"

🔻 NOMAR GARCIAPARRA, TWO-TIME MLB BATTING CHAMPION, SIX-TIME MLB ALL-STAR

Otherwise known as "The Cape," this premiere collegiate baseball summer league is the most competitive and highly scouted summer league in the country. As of 2018, there were 303 Cape Cod Baseball alumni who were active players on 40-man MLB rosters. This makes up more than 25% of all big leaguers. The 44-game season showcases the top talent, which can turn an unknown player into a professional prospect in one summer, or can quickly humble a highly touted prospect by exposing weaknesses in their skill set.

Unlike regular season college schedules, each game consists of the top starting and relief pitchers from various colleges nationwide. As a result, hitters must adapt to the higher level of competition with a wood bat to have a productive summer. Many struggle to succeed. The Cape is the best place for professional scouts to evaluate and project talent because this league is as close to professional baseball as can be simulated at the amateur level. Like pro ball, hitters and pitchers square off with wood bats on a daily basis.

Host families have a memorable impact in the summer experience for the athletes and frequently maintain lifelong friendships with the Cape League alumni. These volunteer families provide a "home away from home," providing transportation, neighborhood cookouts, fishing expeditions, golf outings, and countless other enjoyable memories that an athlete would not experience back at school. The movie *Summer Catch* is Hollywood's spin on this league and these player-host family relationships.

OTHER REPUTABLE SUMMER BASEBALL LEAGUES

Although the Cape is known as the most elite college summer league and has the most hands-on community participation, there are many other leagues that are highly competitive and nationally recognized:

TEXAS COLLEGIATE LEAGUE - Founded in 2004, the "TCL" is a 5-team summer collegiate league located in Texas and Louisiana. Competition is held from May to August.

NORTHWOODS COLLEGIATE LEAGUE - Founded in 1994, this league is famous for its record-breaking fan attendance with some teams averaging over 6,000 fans per game. The Northwoods League consists of 22 teams located in North Dakota, Wisconsin, Minnesota, Ontario, Canada, Iowa, Michigan, Indiana, and Illinois.

JAYHAWK LEAGUE - Formed in 1976 and recognized as a Premier League with National Baseball Congress (NBC), this 8-team league is located in Kansas and Oklahoma.

FLORIDA COLLEGIATE LEAGUE - Founded in 2004, this 6-team league is located in Central Florida.

GREAT LAKES LEAGUE - Founded in 1986, this 12-team league is located in the Great Lakes region of the United States.

COASTAL PLAINS LEAGUE - Founded in 1997, and deriving its name from the class D minor league baseball league that operated in the area from 1937 to 1952, this 16-team league in the coastal plains region spans Virginia, North Carolina, South Carolina, and Georgia.

NEW ENGLAND COLLEGIATE LEAGUE - Founded in 1993, The "NECBL" features 13 teams that play a 44-game schedule through June and July, with playoffs in early August.

ALASKA BASEBALL LEAGUE - Founded in 1969, the ABL features 5 teams located in the state of Alaska. The unique experience of a summer in Alaska features highlights for players such as fishing expeditions, playing in the "Midnight Sun Game" which begins at 10:30pm, and experiencing 24 hours of daylight.

Leagues that are associated with the National Baseball Congress (NBC) compete in the annual NBC World Series featuring the top teams from 17 of the collegiate summer leagues, while other leagues host their own playoffs and championships. The playoffs are a memorable experience in any league, but to be truthful, by summer's end, players are looking forward to returning home for a short break before the school semester. Fall Ball is just around the corner after a long summer on the job.

AGENTS AND ADVISORS

"I can't hear you, Jerry. Show. Me. The Money!"

♥ JERRY MAGUIRE

INTRODUCTION

In this chapter, we provide you with a 360-degree overview of the often obscure yet essential aspects of athlete representation, agents and advisors. An advisor is a representative who has no legally binding contractual obligations with an athlete, but provides guidance and advice with the hope of earning the right to represent an athlete in the MLB Draft and throughout their career. An agent, on the other hand, is a representative who generally has a financial interest and investment in a professional athlete, including a legally binding contract.

Advisors are common in the pre-professional phases of high school and college baseball. You may not be aware of advisors and agents until your athlete or their teammates reach a level where representation is needed. Nevertheless, understanding the purpose of agents and advisors will allow you to quickly recognize their presence and value in the journey towards professional baseball. Until now, the only way to become aware of agents and advisors was through direct experience by the fortunate few who achieved prospect status. This section will surely increase your awareness, answer the many questions you may have, and prime you to identify and select the best representation for your athlete.

Always remember with each public appearance or athletic performance, an athlete's brand, reputation, self-image, and income are their responsibility. A player may play for a team and have contractual requirements, restrictions, and organizational responsibilities for a period of time, but it is ultimately performance and notoriety that dictate their career and financial success.

Therefore, it's important to understand that athletes are the CEOs of their own companies and should be surrounded by those who are looking out for their best interests. Agents are incredibly valuable to the baseball industry because they are the counsel for the athletes in many career aspects and act as a bridge between front offices and the players. This chapter validates the value of an advisor or agent, and may cause you to re-evaluate many of your preconceived ideas that baseball career success only revolves around on-the-field success.

OVERVIEW

Agents act as the intermediaries, legal advisors, communicators, negotiators, and protectors of the athletes' careers. These individuals represent the interests of the athlete, not only financially but as negotiators and promoters. They leverage an athlete's talent and value in the market to maximize advancement and manage career success efficiently. The agent mediates the relationships and opportunities an athlete generates through their on-the-field product, NIL, political standing, and community involvement through commercial sponsorships and playing contracts. Agent involvement often extends beyond career negotiations and representation to travel arrangements for family, outside investments, emotional support, and apparel deals.

Without a representative who understands the market, has resources, and is able to influence outcomes, the potential organizations and commercial sponsors may hold unequal bargaining power during pivotal negotiations in the player's career. It can be difficult for a player to detach emotionally when negotiating rights, responsibilities, and preferences with an organization or sponsor because each side represents different interests. The organization or sponsor looks out for their best interests, and so should the player. That said, the player and their family will likely have a different perspective than the organization or sponsor at some point in time regarding various key aspects.

This is why an advocate to mediate and communicate effectively between the two parties ultimately leads to better results than if the player negotiates without assistance. A skilled representative with an understanding of the business and a pre-existing relationship with the organization can mediate a mutually beneficial outcome for both parties. As an attorney meets with opposing counsel on behalf of an individual, similarly, an agent represents a player in essential matters with the baseball organization in order to work toward the best outcome for all parties involved.

Often, an agent's power and prestige within baseball, which athletes they represent, and which agency they work for, determine whether a player receives certain sums of money, additional benefits with the organization or commercial sponsors, or a playing contract. A few examples of potential benefits negotiated in an MLB contract include: trade bonus or constraint clauses, performance incentives, or options to extend or terminate a contract. A player's agent can determine the outcome of an opportunity simply based on the relationships previously established and trust or leverage between the parties.

MLB organizations are businesses tasked to build a brand and put a product on the field that generates revenue at all levels. This is true whether those decisions are based on winning, managing talented athletes, culture, or image. Sometimes this leads to promotions for the most marketable athletes, rather than the most productive. Contrary to popular belief, many players fall within a similar talent range and are indistinguishable from the next talented ballplayer.

Michael Lewis, author of Moneyball, was the first journalist to dig into this phenomenon. After interviewing Billy Bean, GM of the Oakland Athletics (A's), he discovered that the A's were looking for underappreciated baseball players as a business model for success just as an investor looks for underappreciated stocks. Lewis, and the A's, have found that between two players with similar stats, the player appearing more physically fit is usually paid more, which creates the opportunity to sign an equally productive but undervalued player. "It became a very universal story about the mistakes we make when we look at another person [and determine their value]."[37]

Thus, the unknown athletes beginning their careers are largely replaceable and provide far less economic value than seasoned Major League players with social status and proof of career success.

In the grand scheme, there are between 7,500 and 8,000 professional baseball players across all MLB organizations, with only 1,200 of those competing at the MLB level, or approximately 15%.[38] As you can see, until the young professional athlete earns MLB prospect status based on their draft slot, projectibility, or produces consistent dominant statistics to create a market early in their minor league career, they essentially have no market or bargaining power. Players can easily get lost in a minor league system composed of many players competing for the few available Major League spots.

Additionally, a good organizational fit is crucial to either the realization, or collapse, of the 20+ year marathon and lifelong dream. The subjective evaluations of coaches and administration will often dictate opportunities based on this fit. That is why agent involvement is extremely important to highlight successes, remain in contact with the front office, and keep the athlete "top of mind." Otherwise, the athlete is at the mercy of the organization for playing time and exposure.

Without representation, a player who did not receive a large signing bonus in the draft may fall into the mix of roster-fillers who will never receive a chance to rise to the top. In fact, a study performed from 1996-2011 tracked the odds of a drafted player reaching the Major Leagues and obtaining MLB service time, according to the drafted round (often correlated with projectibility) and the amount of service time gained.[39]

ROUND	1	2	3	4	5	6	7	8	9	10	11 -15	12 -20
MLB%	66.7	49.4	39.7	35	33.3	24.4	20.4	24.4	17.8	17.5	12.7	9.9
3+ YRS IN MLB%	46.8	31.5	21.6	18.6	18.6	10.6	9.0	10.6	7.8	8.3	5.2	4.4

AGENT INVOLVEMENT

For MLB players, agent involvement is critical as they navigate their careers, reach arbitration, sign guaranteed contracts, communicate with the player's union, and negotiate terms that can have a major impact on the player's life. As an example of how valuable an agent's involvement is, let's take a look at arbitration, which provides an opportunity for a player's pay to level-up relative to their contributions and performance at the MLB level, even though they are still under their original 7-year contract.

Arbitration is the process by which eligible players, those with 3 or more years of service time but not yet six years of MLB service time, bring a salary dispute case against the baseball club in front of a panel of independent arbitrators. This panel decides in favor of either the player or the club on the proposed salary.

In certain cases, a player may be eligible for arbitration prior to serving a full three-years of service time. This player is known as a "Super Two" – a player who has more than two and fewer than three years of MLB service time,[40] but ranks in the top 22% of peer players who have between 2-3 years of MLB service time. In effect, this accelerates the player's arbitration clock, giving him an additional year of arbitration eligibility.

The cutoff date for Super Two eligibility varies from year to year, depending on when that top 22 percent of players were placed on a 25-man roster. In 2019, the Super Two cutoff date was placed at two years and 115 days of service time, which was the earliest cutoff in years."[41] Interestingly, teams will often forgo calling up a deserving player to avoid starting the player's MLB service time clock, despite his potential positive impact on the big league team.

The bottom line is that an agent is an extremely valuable asset for pivotal moments like this in a player's career. An agent helps with education on the rules, understanding the market, gauging player value, navigating negotiations, and developing relationships with the organizational leaders to ultimately get deals done. A baseball player knows the game and about performance, but they are not a match against an organization on business matters. The bigger the stakes, the more management and preparation required, which makes an agent's advocacy and expertise necessary for career longevity.

SELECTION PROCESS AND VALUATION OF AN AGENT

Understanding how to wisely select and maintain an agent is crucial to making the most informed decisions on who your athlete ultimately pays and chooses to represent them throughout the course of their career. After all, agents have incentives and defined measures to determine your athlete's value for their purposes, so should you.

Scott Boras, the most successful baseball agent in history, once said that 70% of his job was not negotiating contracts or interpreting contract clauses. Instead, his job was to understand the game and its psychology; to aid and grow a player through high school, college, or a professional season; and to advise during the draft to create an environment centered on the player's needs to succeed and persevere through a successful Major League Baseball career. Consider Boras' summary of his duties often to ensure your athlete's agent has a well-rounded approach and can offer them a multitude of benefits throughout their career.

When evaluating the potential impact an agent may have, it is important to research the following:

- their former and current clients

- results of arbitration case settlements

- contracts they have negotiated for clients

- their reputation among the 30 MLB teams

- relationships with commercial entities who offer marketing deals and sponsorships

- retention and turnover of clientele, and

- opinions of current players

Connecting with both a current client of the agent and a client who has parted ways with them will provide a better understanding of the agent's strengths and weaknesses, along with a balanced assessment from multiple sources.

The difficulty lies in understanding whether the agent's particular network or negotiation ability will benefit your specific athlete's playing career. Will they be proactive or back down when an organization refuses to promote a player, despite statistical evidence and indisputable production? Is the agent a skillful negotiator while building trustworthy relationships? Are they respected by colleagues and the organizations in which they are in communication?

The answers to these questions are vital because the athlete's career opportunities could hinge on timely advocacy and influence by their agent. When a player is deserving of recognition through promotion or opportunity, they need a representative in their corner. If your athlete is simply another client on a long list of obligations, it is doubtful that the agent will be incentivized to go to bat on their behalf.

While it is true that a team will ultimately act in their own perceived best interests, it is important to have an agent who believes in the athlete and has the skills and resources to enhance and accelerate an athlete's career path or a particular opportunity. The agent, playing the role of intermediary between the organization and the player, maintains the balance between the parties to mediate communication. Tensions will inevitably arise between the player and the organization during negotiations, and the agent-mediator prioritizes the focus on a final mutual agreement, while representing the player's best interests.

One example of an agent's value is when the player has a conflict during the season with a coach or the organization. Having representation here is priceless. An issue is more often calmly and effectively resolved with a mediator or liaison standing in the middle to discuss the matter and work toward a solution for both sides. This could be the difference in the outcome during a conflict, and ultimately, a player's career longevity.

The drafting organization invests in the player, and the player builds equity over their years in the system. Once a relationship is severed, or the athlete has to seek other opportunities as a free agent, it is exponentially more difficult to build comparable equity in a new system. Due to this reality, prior to an MLB contract, differences of opinion without an agent as an advocate can effectively wipe away future MLB opportunities, despite performance.

In most cases, a player must achieve MLB service time before their voice will be heard without career destroying consequences. At this place, on the brink of reaching the summit and in the most difficult portion of the climb, when 90% of all players have fallen away, the player is ironically most vulnerable to losing it all due to an imbalance of negotiating power.

Forty-man roster players receive union protection (MLBPA),

fair pay and treatment, and influence for future longevity. This status alone takes care of many everyday conflicts and issues. However, before that moment of protection and respect, the window is narrow, and the organizations hold the power to make or break a career. Without representation to work through an issue to ensure both sides communicate effectively, differences of opinion can often escalate to detrimentally impact an athlete's career. In this scenario, the agent serves as the career-preserving advocate and spokesperson.

Another example of an agent's worth is when they serve as the chief marketing officer for the player when the player has produced results on the field. The decision makers of an organization generally have many factors that influence personnel moves as they evaluate the hundreds of players within the system. Given the number of players, accurate value judgments are challenging and special performances can go unnoticed.

> **The decision makers of an organization generally have many factors that influence personnel moves as they evaluate the hundreds of players within the system.**

Many statistical achievements in a single game or over the course of a season that are not flashy (like home runs or strikeouts) may easily be overlooked yet can be indicators of success. Examples include: hits with runners in scoring position, WHIP (walks and hits per inning pitched), OPS (on-base percentage plus slugging), or pitches that elicit a swing and a miss, to name a few. These successes must be brought to the attention of the organization or a media outlet to create maximum exposure and drive value and income opportunities in the forms of playing time, promotions, endorsements, appearances, and personal branding opportunities.[42]

AGENT MARKET

The agent market has expanded tremendously with the increase in

BRAMHALL: *As an example of the impact of agent representation, when I was in my first season back after consecutive Tommy John surgeries and in AA with the Miami Marlins, I had pitched 20-plus consecutive scoreless innings. I was at the top of the Southern League in ERA, with a 1.29, yet remained at the same minor league level from April to June. Within one week of hiring a new agent, Jonathan Maurer of MSM Sports, Inc., I was promoted to AAA New Orleans. Without the agent in my corner, I would have remained in AA, where I had spent the previous months waiting for an opportunity. In professional baseball, an athlete must capitalize on the streaks of success, because throughout the course of a season, there will be many ups and downs. A good agent, like Maurer, is key to communicating the value that a player has to an organization.*

MLB player salaries, growing revenue streams, and international popularity of the game. The MLB minimum salary increased from $68,000 to $570,500 in the past 30 years, and the average MLB salary is currently $4.36M/year.[43] Thus, there is a growing need for representation in negotiation, resolving player issues on and off the field, and identifying financial opportunities during and after the player's career. This is especially true with the limited time available for a player to devote necessary attention to these important matters during the season.

During a prospect's junior and senior years of high school, or any year during a college player's career, an agent/advisor generally initiates contact to form a relationship and persuade a commitment from a prospect prior to the MLB Draft. Agents and professional talent scouts evaluate prospects in a similar manner, and are often in attendance at the same showcases or games because of their shared interest in the top players.

If an athlete is high on an MLB organization's prospect list, agents are usually aware of it and will initiate contact. For the athlete who develops prospect status later in the season, an agent may recognize their value based on raw talent or proven performance. This could serve as a marketing tool to generate interest with MLB organizations that have yet to identify the player as a prospect. Professional athletes succeeding in the minor leagues may hear from agents who may be interested in representing them based on current trajectory and success.

Understanding whether your athlete is in need of representation depends on many factors such as physical stature, statistical measurements, and prospect status. While the majority of players do not have advisors entering the draft period, dominant performance at the professional level after the draft may warrant representation as their notoriety increases with career success.

there is a growing need for representation in negotiation, resolving player issues on and off the field, and identifying financial opportunities during and after the player's career.

If the athlete is unaware of their prospect status or is not receiving interest from advisors, it is likely that they are not in need of representation at the current time in their career. Alternatively, simply because an agent makes contact does not mean that it is guaranteed to benefit the athlete. Agent representation should be determined on a case-by-case basis based on many factors.

For many of the prospects entering the final phase before becoming a college or professional athlete, important questions arise and assistance is beneficial and necessary to maximize their opportunities. Many agents receive numerous inquiries from prospects who would benefit from either representation or receiving answers to questions.

However, every prospect may not have the economic market value to retain representation from an interested agent at a particular moment in their career. As a result, an athlete in this situation is unfortunately not able to receive guidance and valuable insight. This does not mean the prospect does not deserve the information they are seeking; the agent simply may not be the best resource or have the scheduling availability to provide answers. It is a business.

In these instances, seeking a sports consulting group or sports law practice to provide expertise, career advice, and answers to your many questions can be incredibly beneficial. These companies often have a network of relationships with industry professionals in every area of the game, including but not limited to coaches, agents, scouts, parents, players, and instructors.

FEES AND SERVICES

Fees for representation vary across the professional baseball industry. However, most agencies collect a percentage of the player's initial signing bonus and between 4-5% of a player's Major League Baseball earnings. Some may charge a yearly free agency negotiation fee to minor league players that can range from $2,000-$5,000. Service fees can reach 10% for foreign contracts with agents working in Taiwan, South Korea, and Japan. This is due to many factors such as communication expenses, overseas travel, and access to valuable overseas relationships. In the United States, 4% of contract salary is most common.

For off-the-field engagements, such as commercial sponsorships, media broadcast, and public appearances, agent fees may reach up to 20% of gross profit for generating these additional financial opportunities. Regardless of the fee structure, a player's agency, large or small, typically collects comparable fees over the course of a player's career for the many expenses incurred from travel, administration, counsel, apparel and equipment, and negotiating on their behalf. This demonstrates the need to wisely invest in an agent as the athlete earns status and service time to build a reputation and a brand as a professional.

RULES FOR ADVISORS AND AGENTS

There are many rules that distinguish amateur and professional athletes and the involvement of an agent may impact that status. Advisors, who have no legally binding agreement, are able to consult with high school and college players in an "advising" capacity before the MLB Draft while the player is still an amateur. This means the advisor may only provide information regarding a player's fair market value, evaluate a proposed professional contract, and give information about the draft process.[44] Only after the player signs a professional contract for immediate or future benefit or compensation (e.g., with an agent, a commercial sponsorship, or playing contract) will the athlete lose their amateur status.[45]

As discussed previously, a high school level athlete must remain as an amateur to protect collegiate eligibility if they plan to pursue an education as a student athlete. Their amateur status could be jeopardized by accepting benefits or favors without paying for the services. As previously stated, an advisor is permitted and so is an agent or attorney during negotiations with professional sports organizations. However, they must pay "the going rate" for the representation.

Further, the relationships must be terminated before enrolling in college.[46] Agreements for formal representation that do not terminate before college enrollment will compromise an athlete's amateur status and prevent any future collegiate opportunities. However, the decision to become a professional and subsequent reversal of that decision otherwise has no consequences to a high school baseball player's eligibility prior to college enrollment. You will notice a great deal of flexibility with high school athletes because this scenario applies to such a small percentage of them.

At the collegiate level, an athlete must be even more careful to preserve their amateur status and eligibility when receiving counsel on professional opportunities that are tied to their athletic ability. "NCAA rules forbid an athlete from accepting expenses or gifts of any kind from an agent or anyone else wishing to provide services to the student. Such payment is not allowed because it would be compensation based upon athletic skill and preferential benefit not available to the general student population."[47]

On May 31, 2019, The NCAA released a memorandum to DI baseball student athletes with remaining eligibility. The memorandum illustrates how student-athletes are not permitted to receive any benefits from an agent. "Examples of material benefits include money, transportation, dinner, clothes, cell phones, jewelry, etc."[48] Further, the memorandum lists 6 points to remember that will compromise an athlete's eligibility and amateur status:

1   You agree orally or in writing to be represented by an agent, distinguished from "advisor," or any individual acting on behalf of the agent (e.g., runner).

2   You accept any benefits from an agent, a prospective agent, or any individual acting on behalf of the agent (e.g., runner).

3   If an advisor markets your athletics ability or reputation to a professional team on your behalf.

4   If an advisor contacts a professional team on your behalf.

5   If an advisor negotiates on your behalf.

6   If you use an advisor and do not pay for the advising service.[49]

A permissible benefit from an advisor is receiving information on activities such as tryout arrangements with a professional team and coordinating tryout schedules.

The NCAA DI Manual provides additional information to student athletes to navigate these relationships in great detail. Read carefully because without proper translation and context, the application of the content can be difficult to interpret. Articles 11 and 12 provide the information surrounding the use of agents, legal counsel, and the utility of a Professional Sports Counsel for athletes at an NCAA member institution.

Most 4-year institutions do not have adequate resources for a truly effective Professional Sports Counsel in lieu of a personal advisor. This is due to factors such as the financial resources available at the institution, the number of sports that an athletic department oversees at the collegiate level, and the needs of each individual athlete during this decision period. However, whether the Professional Sports Counseling Panel consists only of the athlete's head coach, or includes several faculty and staff members, this committee may serve a beneficial role. It may offer guidance and/or bridge the gap between players and their families, and prospective agents and professional sports organizations.

Because of the questions that may arise surrounding these relationships, and the NCAA rules that govern them, we provide, and translate in plain language, the most important NCAA rules that impact the athlete at the collegiate level when engaging with agents, advisors, and the Professional Sports Counsel.

• BYLAW 12.2.4 states, "An individual may inquire of a professional sports organization about eligibility for a professional league player draft or request information about the individual's market value without affecting his or her amateur status." TRANSLATION: There will be no effect on the athlete's college career if they request information from a team or league about the possibility of playing at the next level.

• BYLAW 12.2.4.3 expands on this bylaw clarifying negotiations, ". . . Further, the individual, his or her family members or the institution's professional sports counseling panel may enter into negotiations with a professional sports organization without the loss of the individual's amateur status. An individual who retains an agent shall lose amateur status." TRANSLATION: The athlete, the athlete's school, or the athlete's family may negotiate and discuss a professional playing contract with a team, but may not use an agent for the negotiations.

• BYLAW 12.3 addresses the use of agents and the effect of entering into an agreement with an agent, "An individual shall be ineligible for participation in an intercollegiate sport if he or she ever has agreed (orally or in writing) to be represented by an agent for the purpose of marketing his or her athletics ability or reputation in that sport. Further, an agency contract not specifically limited in writing to a sport or particular sports shall be deemed applicable to all sports, and the individual shall be ineligible to participate in any sport." TRANSLATION: **An athlete may not agree to have agent representation to market athletic ability in any sport without losing the ability to play at the collegiate level. This applies to oral and written agreements.**

• BYLAW 12.3.2 permits an athlete to obtain legal counsel for the purpose of receiving advice. "Securing advice from a lawyer concerning a proposed professional sports contract shall not be considered contracting for representation by an agent under this rule, unless the lawyer also represents the individual in negotiations for such a contract." TRANSLATION: **An athlete may obtain a lawyer to help translate and explain a professional sports contract, but that lawyer may not participate in negotiations about that contract.**

• BYLAW 12.3.2.1 expands on the permission of legal counsel, "A lawyer may not be present during discussions of a contract offer with a professional organization or have any direct contact (in person, by telephone, or by mail) with a professional sports organization on behalf of the individual. A lawyer's presence during such discussions is considered representation by an agent." TRANSLATION: **A lawyer will be considered an agent if they are present, or have any contact with a team or league on behalf of the player. This is the specific point in time where an advisor or legal counsel becomes an agent. (Agents or attorneys may provide advice to prospective future clients, but remain advisors, and preserve an athlete's amateur status by following this bylaw).**

• BYLAW 12.3.4 permits an athlete's educational institution to provide a Professional Sports Counseling Panel to assist college athletes in various aspects when navigating professional sports opportunities. If the athlete's institution has such a panel, it is wise to consult with them prior to engaging in any lawyer or advisor relationship. If the institution does not have a Professional Sports Counseling Panel, a head coach may, ". . . contact agents, professional sports teams or professional sports organizations on behalf of a student-athlete, provided no compensation is received for such services," and, "shall consult with and report his or her activities to the president or chancellor [or an individual or group (e.g., athletics advisory board) designated by the president or chancellor]."[50] "It is permissible for an authorized institutional professional sports counseling panel (or head coach) to:

A Advise a student-athlete about a future professional career;

B Assist a student-athlete with arrangements for securing a loan for the purpose of purchasing insurance against a disabling injury or illness and with arrangements for purchasing such insurance;

C Review a proposed professional sports contract;

D Meet with the student-athlete and representatives of professional teams;

E Communicate directly (e.g., in person, by mail or telephone) with representatives of a professional athletics team to assist in securing a tryout with that team for a student-athlete;

F Assist the student-athlete in the selection of an agent by participating with the student-athlete in interviews of agents, by reviewing written information player agents send to the student-athlete and by having direct communication with those individuals who can comment about the abilities of an agent (e.g., other agents, a professional league's players association); and

G Visit with player agents or representatives of professional athletics teams to assist the student-athlete in determining his or her market value (e.g., potential salary, draft status). TRANSLATION: A group of employees or the head coach at an institution may: give advice to a student athlete regarding a professional sports career, assist with insurance against injury possibility, review contracts, meet with professional sports organizations with the athlete present, assist and schedule tryouts with professional sports organizations for the athlete, assist the athlete with selecting an agent, assist the athlete in determining their possible earnings from salaries, draft slots and signing bonuses, and marketing endorsements.

When encountering and evaluating ethical conduct in agent-athlete relationships and member institution involvement, the NCAA supports the Uniform Athlete Agents Act (UAAA) and Sports Agent Responsibility and Trust Act (SPARTA).[51] Reference these acts if your collegiate athlete is a potential early-round draft pick with significant agent interest and involvement.

It is important to discuss candidly the reality about the written rules and boundaries. Rules are rules, and it is important that you remain informed of the letter of the law. However, this sport is about relationships. Many of the NCAA bylaws were drafted based on the need for football athletes and the drastic spike in the marketable value of football players and revenue generated from the sport by athletic departments in recent decades. In reality, for baseball athletes, after forming a relationship with the player and their family, an agent most often works for them during high school or college, the MLB Draft, and throughout their professional career.

> **Most high school and college coaches welcome the presence of agents who take care of their athletes and provide communication for the prospective professional athletes.**

Most high school and college coaches welcome the presence of agents who take care of their athletes and provide communication for the prospective professional athletes. Additionally, MLB organizations frequently communicate through agents and advisors to the athletes throughout the athlete's career. Each member of the baseball industry communicates and collaborates much more closely than the "rules of compliance" may pretend to restrict. Sorry, compliance crew. It is probably time to re-work the rules regarding agent and professional team engagement with athletes to reflect the current reality of how the industry already operates.

As a final note on this topic, with the granting of name, image, and likeness (NIL) rights for collegiate amateur athletes, and the NCAA's decision to relinquish control, athletes are now permitted to have representation for NIL purposes as long as they are not directly tied to the athlete's involvement in a sport. While this new line between obtaining representation for NIL or competition purposes may appear blurry, athletes with NIL income opportunities may, and should, engage representation to manage the coming chaos and optimize well-deserved revenue streams.

As previously discussed, ALC www.athlete-licensing.com is a leading market resource for NIL opportunities, placing the athlete at the center of the NIL ecosystem. ALC recognizes the need to assist athletes in realizing their commercial NIL potential and the importance of keeping their interests protected. ALC provides a tech-enabled platform for:

- monetization (merchandise, NFTs, and ticketed events)
- IP protection
- facilitation of deals
- transparent accounting
- royalty statements
- tax withholding
- NCAA, state, and federal compliance, and
- required reporting

ALC partners with universities, agents, athletes, and booster clubs, and commercial sponsors to manage the back-office, while protecting the athlete's brand and keeping the athlete eligible for play. In addition to ALC's back-office NIL management benefits, our monetization platform creates custom merchandise, NFTs (non-fungible tokens), and ticketed event opportunities for the athletes and groups we represent.

AGENT CERTIFICATION

An agent is not required to be MLBPA-certified to represent a player signing a minor league contract, in the MLB First-Year Player Draft, to represent a non-40-man roster player, or to negotiate a minor league contract for an international player. MLBPA certification is mainly aimed at MLB 40-man roster contract representation. However, we recommend selecting an agent or agency certified with the MLBPA to ensure expertise and future value in the relationship. You want your athlete represented by an agent or agency that represents 40-man roster players and negotiates MLB contracts. There are three types of MLBPA certification.

1 GENERAL CERTIFICATION - required to represent a player as defined by §2(B) of the Agent Regulations including:

- Any player who is a party to a Major League Uniform Player's Contract, who is listed on a Major League 40-Man Roster, Major League Reserve List, or a Major League Voluntarily Retired, Emergency Disabled, Military, Restricted, Disqualified or Ineligible List;

- Any player who is a Major League free agent by operation of the Basic Agreement, the Major League Rules, or his Major League Uniform Player's Contract;

- Any player who is a professional free agent most recently employed by either a foreign or U.S. professional baseball league or club (e.g., a minor league, independent league, Japanese league free agent), and who is engaged in negotiations of, or preparing to negotiate terms to be included in, a Major League Uniform Player's Contract;

- Any other player engaged in negotiations of, or preparing to negotiate, any agreement or "side letter" concerning terms to be included in any future Major League Uniform Player's Contract

2 **LIMITED CERTIFICATION** - A Limited Certified Agent may recruit and/or provide client maintenance services on behalf of a General Certified Agent but may not communicate with a Major League Club on behalf of a Player.

3 **EXPERT AGENT ADVISOR CERTIFICATION** - May represent, assist and advise a General Certified Agent on behalf of a Player.[52]

"The Major League Baseball Players Association ("MLBPA") is the exclusive bargaining agent for all Major League Baseball Players and individuals preparing to negotiate a Major League contract. To be eligible for MLBPA Certification, a previously uncertified agent must:

Read, understand and agree to the MLBPA Regulations Governing Player Agents;

- Complete the Application for MLBPA Certification;
- Submit a non-refundable Application fee of $2,000;
- Submit a signed "Declaration by Applicant" and, in the case of an applicant for General Certification, a copy of the Agency's Representation Agreement;
- Provide permission for the MLBPA to conduct a background investigation;
- Successfully complete the background investigation;
- Pass the written examination; and
- Be designated as the Agent of a Major League Player, or

designated by a General Certified agent as a Recruiter, Client Maintenance Service Provider, or Expert Agent Advisor." [53]

MLB DRAFT PROCESS AND AGENT INVOLVEMENT

The Major League Baseball First-Year Player Draft ("MLB Draft") is generally held in the first week of June. With the exception of the 2020 MLB Draft ("The Pandemic Draft"), it is currently a 3-day event with up to 40 rounds. In recent years, the draft has received extensive media coverage due to public demand and increasing commercial value of the industry. This has led to additional promotion opportunities and real-time coverage online and on major sports broadcasting networks.

As of 2012, the Major League Baseball Players Association (MLBPA) and the Major League Baseball team owners signed a collective bargaining agreement that limits the signing bonuses newly drafted players can receive, according to slotted recommendations. This put guardrails on signing bonuses to protect small market teams with less money to spend and controlled inflated signing bonus negotiations. Prior to 2012, these recommendations from the MLB Commissioner's office were not required to be accepted. However, the MLB organization was required to provide an explanation if the team exceeded the slotted bonus value. Now if a club exceeds the total of the allotted spending amount for those rounds, a penalty is assessed.

"Each pick in the first 10 rounds of the Draft has an assigned value, with the total for each of a club's selections equals what it can spend in those rounds without incurring a penalty. If a player taken in the first 10 rounds doesn't sign, his [draft position] value gets subtracted from his club's pool. Any bonus money above $125,000 given to an individual player selected in rounds 11-40 also counts against a team's allotment."[54] "Teams that outspend their allotment by 0-5 percent pay a 75 percent tax on the overage. At higher thresholds, clubs lose future picks: a first-rounder and a 75 percent tax for surpassing their pool by more than 5 and up to 10 percent; a first- and a second-rounder and a 100 percent tax for more than 10 and up to 15 percent; and two first-rounders and a 100 percent tax for more than 15 percent."[55]

Generally, each MLB team receives one pick per round, with the exception of penalties for different violations such as exceeding slot value on a previously drafted player, exceeding the MLB salary cap, or other punishments imposed by the MLB Office of the Commissioner. There are also compensation rounds following rounds 1-3, which provide additional picks to organizations that may not have signed drafted players in the previous year for various reasons, such as failed negotiations.

The organization with the worst overall record from the previous season receives the first pick, and the World Series champion receives the last pick of each round.[56] Contrary to popular belief, with the exception of drafted players who have scholarships in other sports, all drafted players who do not return to amateur baseball, regardless of signing bonus, must sign a minor league contract with the drafting organization by the signing deadline of August 15th.[57] This deadline is also the same for the free-agents or graduated seniors who go undrafted but are also offered a minor league contract by an MLB organization.

"We can better understand how teams will negotiate if we can understand the situation from the team's perspective," said advisor/agent Jonathan Maurer of MSM Sports, Inc.

Many drafted players do not have representation during the draft process due to the unpredictability of signing bonuses or the projected future market value of the athlete. Because for many athletes, agents and advisors are not able to determine whether representation will result in compensation until the athlete has begun to perform at the professional level. This is not always the case, but can be detrimental to the athlete's outcome in the draft, future opportunities, and ultimate career success. The players who do have representation receive information prior to the draft about projected signing bonus, draft round, and teams that have shown interest in drafting the player.

Teams receive information from advisors about signability and expected benefits for the upcoming negotiations. "We can better understand how teams will negotiate if we can understand the situation from the team's perspective," said advisor/agent Jonathan Maurer of MSM Sports, Inc. This is what makes agents and advisors so valuable. For the players who do not have a representative for the meetings beforehand, it is crucial to communicate with scouts to create leverage and generate awareness of the athlete's ability to boost value. This potentially helps to raise draft selection position, signing bonus, and opportunities going forward as a professional.

Ultimately, the investment that an organization puts into a player is directly correlated to the opportunities a player has to fail, develop, and be promoted to higher levels of professional baseball. Organizations always provide more opportunity to the players who are selected earlier in the draft and/or who are compensated higher. This reinforces to fans, ownership, and staff that the administration made wise selections and that organizational development decisions are leading to success in these investments.

AMATEUR AND PROFESSIONAL SCOUTING

INTRODUCTION

Major League Baseball scouting is divided into two branches: **1** amateur and **2** professional. Each branch is essential to their respective organizations by focusing either on evaluating potential future players for the MLB Draft (amateur) or identifying the value and abilities of current professional players within the 30 MLB organizations (professional). Scouts in each branch travel within their designated geographic regions and form relationships with administrators, parents, coaches, and players.

Scouts evaluate players using the 5 tools of running speed, arm strength (throwing velocity), hitting for power, hitting for average, and fielding. A 6th tool is a combination of mental makeup, character, baseball IQ, and competitiveness. These tools are graded on a 20-80 Major League level scale. 20 is the lowest rating and 80 is the highest rating among MLB players for a particular skill. For example, a high school pitcher throwing 100 mph would receive a grade of 80 in the arm strength category, regardless of whether they are playing high school or professional baseball competition. This is because very few MLB players are able to throw 100 mph.

AMATEUR SCOUTING

Amateur scouts endure a rigorous travel schedule to evaluate high school and college talent. This consistent evaluation effort grades prospect status and potential signability of players with the goal of building a talented draft class, which is an investment in the organization's future.

THE AMATEUR SCOUTING HIERARCHY:

- **ASSOCIATE SCOUT** ("Bird Dog") - Unpaid part-time scout who covers a designated geographic area and is incentivized with commission payments when a prospect they identify is drafted or promoted within a minor league system.

- **AREA SUPERVISOR** - Full-time scout who is responsible for a designated geographic area. Their reporting responsibility is to the regional scout when evaluating a potential prospect.

- **REGIONAL SCOUT** - Full-time scout who covers a specific region in the country and is responsible for the area supervisors in that region.

- **NATIONAL CROSSCHECKER** - Full-time scout with influence over many important MLB Draft decisions for an organization. They are responsible for identifying high-round picks, and communicating with scouting directors and the organization's front office regarding player selection.

- **ASSISTANT DIRECTOR OF SCOUTING AND DIRECTOR OF SCOUTING** - Oversees an organization's entire scouting operation, and works closely with front office staff on all matters related to selecting prospects. The Director of Scouting generally has the final say in where a player is selected in the MLB Draft.

- **GENERAL MANAGER OR DIRECTOR OF OPERATIONS** - Controls player and coaching staff transactions and contract negotiations. This position is responsible for the hiring and firing decisions of all personnel.

Amateur scouts evaluate well-known players on the immediate national or regional radar to make early reports of draftability and performance evaluations. As other talented players compete against those early identified players, and as the season progresses, scouts have the opportunity to evaluate other athletes that demonstrate professional potential. Scouts send letters to many of these players to gauge draft expectations and collect contact information for the organizations' databases as the scout follows the athletes' playing careers.

Scouting letters often consist of a greeting and request for general information such as graduation year, contact information, summer baseball team, and desire to be drafted. For potential draft picks in the top few rounds, scouts conduct one-on-one interviews to discover signability and mental makeup, based on the organization's talent evaluation and the character of the individual.

Whether the amateur athlete is ready to play at the professional level that particular season or not, it is beneficial for the athlete to maintain communication with amateur scouts, provide the requested information, and appear in several MLB databases. When a professional team has a high level of interest in a high school player, leverage is created for the athlete when negotiating with college programs for scholarship money, playing time, and leadership opportunities for greater team impact.

Amateur scouts often conduct a "scout day" that features a pro-style workout and/or scrimmage to evaluate players. The scouts then

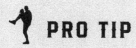

PRO TIP

When your athlete engages with a scout, they should treat the conversations as they would when speaking with a college coach. Scouts evaluate how athletes play the game and how they carry themselves on and off the field.

conduct interviews and collect information from the potential prospects for their respective organization's draft database. As with the high school prospect, pre-draft conversations are important to understand an athlete's projectability, signability, and overall makeup.

PROFESSIONAL SCOUTING

Professional scouting responsibilities are intense as they serve the purpose of evaluating current professional baseball players across all levels of unaffiliated independent leagues, international leagues, the minor leagues, and Major League Baseball. The reports generated by professional scouts contribute to scouting reports, searching for potential assets, trade considerations, and future projections for the organizations.

THE PROFESSIONAL SCOUTING HIERARCHY:

- **PROFESSIONAL TALENT SCOUTS** - Responsible for evaluating talent within the organization in addition to players in the 29 other organizations to assist the front office in identifying potential players for release, promotion, trade, free agency, and any other transaction.

- **ADVANCED SCOUTS/SPECIAL ASSIGNMENT** - Responsible for future game planning for their respective organizations, typically scouting opponents in advance for the upcoming two or three series.

- **ASSISTANT DIRECTOR OF SCOUTING AND DIRECTOR OF SCOUTING** - Oversees an organization's entire scouting operation, working closely with front office staff on all matters related to identifying and selecting future players for the organization.

- **GENERAL MANAGER OR DIRECTOR OF OPERATIONS** - Controls player and coaching staff transactions and contract negotiations. This position is responsible for the hiring and firing decisions of all personnel.

At the minor league level, professional scouts are responsible for analysis of players across all 30 organizations. These scouts generate comprehensive reports on strengths, weaknesses, and tendencies for future matchups, trades, and acquisitions. Lance Zawadzki, former big leaguer and current Double-A Hitting Coach in the Boston Red Sox organization, said, "The information available on players, including analytics and video, at the minor league level now is greater than what was available in the big leagues ten years ago."[58]

At the MLB level, professional scouts perform similar duties to those required at the minor league level, however, the depth of research, and financial and time resources devoted to the reports increases exponentially. Many MLB teams have graduated from scouts in the stands to advanced, in-house scouting departments to incorporate technology into player evaluation and upcoming series preparation through use of video and computer software. The video and electronic reports provide pitcher tendencies, defensive alignment, pitch sequencing, spray charts, and other analytics to develop strategies for upcoming series. Nevertheless, professional scouting roles at the MLB level focus on assisting the team in strategic game plans, preparation for upcoming opponents, and player analysis for future acquisitions.

PROFESSIONAL BASEBALL

"At each higher professional level, the physical talent doesn't significantly jump. The players just have better plans, more discipline, and make fewer mistakes."

♦ SCOTT CENTALA, *SVP AT TEAMALYTICS - performance development consultant for several MLB organizations*

INTRODUCTION

This chapter will undoubtedly shed new light and challenge what you think you may know about the inside experience for professional baseball players. Because our goal as formers players is to educate and provide truthful information, we discuss the good, the bad, and the ugly in this transition from high school and college. Without a firm understanding of the future landscape until after a contractual agreement is reached, fans and athletes alike often misunderstand much of professional baseball. You will notice a different tone in this chapter because at the pro level, it is not the same team sport you watched your athlete play for years. It is a business focused on individual achievement until the playoffs when the team unites to compete for a ring.

We've included descriptions about each level from the minors to the bigs, as well as independent and international leagues, as they currently exist in the progression of a professional baseball career.

This will help prepare your athlete mentally and provide context for the journey from a minor leaguer's first spring training to "The Show." Each level carries its own unique challenging and exciting experiences that a ballplayer needs to know to give them a leg up before the journey begins.

It is beneficial to be successful out of the starting blocks and avoid the many possible pitfalls your athlete may fall victim to from lack of information. Figuring it out alone is a harrowing challenge. Within this insider's view, we also discuss the hardships of the minor leagues and propose positive changes. We raise questions for you, current players, administrators in the industry, legislative bodies, and the general public to consider, and welcome additional solutions and future discourse on the topic.

Finally, we conclude this chapter with the pinnacle of professional baseball, the Major Leagues. Former big leaguers recount first-hand experiences of everything from the first call-up to everyday responsibilities and expectations that come with the biggest stage. These current and former stars provide priceless insights on general differences between the big leagues and the lower levels, how to stay at the top, and the special moments that shaped their baseball careers.

---

360 DEGREES OF PROFESSIONAL BASEBALL

JESSE WINCHESTER - "A Showman's Life"

(*Listen to George Strait's cover of this song here: youtu.be/HJLeouIUJyg*)

A showman's life is a smokey bar
And the fevered chase of a tiny star
It's a hotel room and a lonely wife
From what I've seen of a showman's life
Nobody told me about this part

They told me all about the pretty girls
And the wine and the money and the good times
There's no mention of all the wear and tear
On an old honky tonker's heart
Well I might have known it
But nobody told me about this part

A boy will dream as children do
Of a great white way, until the dream comes true
And a phony smile in a colored light
Is all there is to a showman's life
Nobody told me about this part

They told me all about the pretty girls
And the wine and the money and the good times
There's no mention of all the wear and tear
On an old honky tonker's heart
Well I might have known it
But nobody told me about this part

And nobody told me about this part

They told me all about the pretty girls
And the wine and the money and the good times
There's no mention of, all the wear and tear
On an old honky tonker's heart
Well I might have known it
But nobody told me about this part
Well I might have known it
Nobody told me about this part[59]

As a baseball player becomes a professional, Jesse Winchester's "A Showman's Life" depicts many of the emotions experienced on the road by entertainers of every kind, unknown to fans.

REALITY CHECK

The transition from a high school or collegiate athlete to a professional has many adaptations and adjustments required to survive and succeed at the next level. Not only does the trade become a full-time devotion to skill improvement, the lifestyle also shifts from team-focused and achievement-oriented to individual development, marketable value, and outright survival to stay in the game. Prior to professional baseball, players compete and refine their skills for their entire careers to earn roster spots at each level based on incredible performances, inarguable statistics, or contributing to their teams in some valuable way.

> **If an athlete's father was a Major League Baseball player, their chances to play in the big leagues improves 800 times over other players whose fathers did not.**

Yet, at the professional level until the big leagues, performance is not the only factor that determines whether the athlete will receive an opportunity to advance. In fact, if an athlete's father was a Major League Baseball player, their chances to play in the big leagues improves 800 times over other players whose fathers did not.[60] This is due to the many beneficial factors that result from the relationship including: athletic genes, network, exposure and name recognition, intimate exposure and knowledge of the game and the industry, and correct information about how to be a better ballplayer.

This supports the notion that opportunities and promotions are often dependent on factors that are not as black and white as statistics, performance, grit, and character. Instead, in addition to these factors, opportunity is often also a result of network, subjective evaluation, and raw skill measures for projectibility and development purposes by each system's administration. Despite these realities, even the unlikeliest of players beat the odds.

WELCOME TO THE PROS

The expected level of the athlete's initial performance will determine their initial professional team assignment, whether they are a high school draft selection or college veteran coming straight from the postseason. For most high school draft selections and college players who sign immediately after the MLB Draft, the players report to the MLB organization's Spring Training headquarters in either Arizona or Florida. These facilities house all minor league personnel, medical staff, and rookie development programs.

The players who sign later, due to extended contract negotiations or an extended run in the college postseason, may be sent directly to their initial assignments. Regardless of the starting place, the first orders of business are physicals and medical clearance before the athlete is permitted to participate in physical activity. Once players are medically cleared and rosters have been set, the players officially begin their professional baseball careers.

The first day as a professional baseball player is likely to open the athlete's eyes in many ways. Professional baseball is generally thought to be years behind other professional sports regarding lifestyle accommodations, performance and nutrition, and overall skill and psychological development practices. This will be apparent upon

BRAMHALL: *Before our first road trip in my first week of rookie ball, I laid my mesh duffel bag full of clean clothes next to the team bus while I went into the unairconditioned locker room to pack my baseball gear. When I came out, a teammate from the Dominican Republic backed over the duffel bag in a borrowed car and dragged it over 200 yards down the gravel and dirt parking lot before I could stop him. My whole bag was filled with dirt and rocks, and I spent my first night on the road rewashing a week's worth of laundry at the hotel laundromat.*

the player's arrival to their first assignment, with the biggest reality check in their career to date. Players must fend for themselves, and without a motivated mindset, they will fall severely behind. At the lower levels, a player may not even have a dry uniform before the game or a clean shower towel at the end of a long day.

Many would argue that, overall, Major League Baseball has been slowly improving the well-being of minor leaguers in recent years due to external pressures. While this is true, there are proven methods that have been used in many other professional sports for decades that, if adopted, would immediately enhance the performance and well-being of these employee-athletes.

Along with the lifestyle challenges, outside of the special loyal few, the fan base becomes less supportive than in college because there is no direct relationship and players are viewed as entertainers. This is because fans are revenue-generating customers of the organization, rather than school supporters, friends, and/or family.

Further, the player must become individually career-focused because the organization has no primary interest in whether the team wins or loses. Organizations need the prospects to receive playing time for skill development, and for minor league teams to appear philanthropic in the community to appeal to the fan base.[61]

In the next series, we arrived at the unairconditioned visitor's locker room to one more reminder of our place in the pecking order. This locker room had only two toilets without stall walls or doors, 3 showerheads for 30 players and staff, and a clogged shower drain. The clubbie had stacked all of the towels on the floor by the entrance to the shower, which became soaked as the water flooded out onto the locker room floor. We dried off with the clothing we had worn to the stadium.

In the minor leagues, team camaraderie is low compared to high school or college. The focus for each player shifts toward promotion to the next level. Rosters change frequently, and wins, losses, and performance are only contributing factors toward promotions and demotions. In fact, a roster can completely change over the course of a couple of months.

EMOTIONAL STABILITY = LONGEVITY

At the upper levels of the minor leagues, AA and AAA, every player is talented. The mission here is less about development and more about the refinement and performance of skills capable of translating to a big league diamond. Aside from the obvious fast-track prospects who are not required to grind or prove consistent production, most who endure the minor league ladder and successfully prevail almost always have a support system to believe in them and support their journeys. It takes a special support system for a player to maintain the emotional strength to combat loneliness, find purpose, persevere, and bounce back from disappointments. General anxiety is common, and personal struggles are difficult to process away from a safe and trusting community.

As for romantic relationships, the saying "the woman makes the man" is never truer than when a player has a dependable partner in their corner through thick and thin. Disappointments are always more bearable and celebrations more meaningful in a shared journey. For those who quickly move through the minor leagues, this may not be as much of a factor. But for those who must prove themselves and earn promotions, which is most players, the support system strongly correlates to survival and success. This is plainly clear in the performances, mood, and longevity of fellow teammates.

On this note, we have witnessed prospects' careers be wrecked by romantic interests or relationships that did not have their best interests at heart. As challenging of a task as this may seem, it is critical that the athlete be counseled to avoid relationships with leeches or gold diggers who are destructive rather than supportive. In a vulnerable state on the road for months on end, an athlete needs to be surrounded by those who bring positive energy to the relationship and who understand the commitment required.

As Winchester might have said, there is "no mention of the wear and tear on an old [ballplayer's] heart." This "fevered chase of a tiny star" will wear even the best players down. It's no wonder that alcohol and drug addiction, performance enhancing drugs, anxiety, and depression are problems that plague many players. Without the balance of community or quality of life, the grind is endless and life remains on pause in search of the call that could change it all.

Professionalism should provide an athlete the freedom to dedicate passion and energy to their career, and find physical and emotional balance.

So, why does it have to stay this way? Becoming a professional athlete in other sports does not render athletes isolated, destitute, and poverty stricken. Rather, it is a privilege that is rewarded by an improved quality of life. Professionalism usually increases an athlete's overall health, well-being, and community connection, rather than depleting all of those. Professionalism should provide an athlete the freedom to dedicate passion and energy to their career, and find physical and emotional balance.

A DAY IN THE LIFE

Prior to the charm of pregame warm-ups and the stadium experience with hot dogs, beer, and popcorn on summer nights nationwide, players have a full work day prior to the game to prepare their bodies and minds. With the exception of morning or day games, which are most commonly scheduled on the last game of a series and Sundays, here is a typical itinerary of a professional baseball player.

8 am - 11 am - Most players wake up and have breakfast with their

roommates, girlfriends, wives, and/or children at home, the motel, or at a local restaurant. Local coffee shops and diners are frequented often by the early risers. A few times each week, players have scheduled strength and conditioning sessions after breakfast. When playing at home, most ballparks have a small but sufficient weight room for the home team. On road trips, the team bus taxis players to the gym in the morning for workouts but generally not on travel days.

11 am - 1 pm - Players grab lunch and make their way to the ballpark for treatment and early work. Typical team stretch is a minimum of 4-5 hours before the first pitch. Position players require more preparation time than pitchers with hitting sessions and defensive work with coaches and other development staff from the MLB organization.

1 pm - 3 pm - Depending on whether the game is at home or away, the team participates in stretching and warm-up routines, and practice begins. Practice for pitchers consists of long toss, bullpens, and other throwing work, followed by conditioning, arm care, and treatment for some players.

3 pm - 6 pm - Team practice consists of team defensive work consisting of bunt coverages, cuts and relays, pick offs, fly balls, and ground balls. This is followed by batting practice. The home team has the field first to allow for travel and arrival for the visiting team.

6 pm - 7 pm - Grounds crew prepares the field while players eat a meal and change into game uniforms. At the lowest minor league levels, the pregame meal is generally peanut butter and jelly with bananas on value brand bread. As the player rises up the ranks, a hot pre-game spread may be served by the clubhouse managers. At the big league level, pre-game meals are tailored to the nutritional needs of a professional athlete, with specific requests filled for players by a team of clubhouse managers.

7 pm - 11 pm - Game time.

11 pm - 12 am - Post-game spread is provided for additional cost in

most organizations, but not all. Pitchers and position players who played in the game have strength and conditioning workouts when the team is at home.

11 pm - 2 am - Travel to the hotel or player's apartment, wind down, and lights out.

At the Major League level, teams schedule off days each month for rest and travel, usually every 8 days. Whereas, in the minor leagues, there are generally 1-2 off days each month. For perspective, this amounts to 12-14 *total* off days scheduled in the 150-plus day season! Even more surprising, those off days are often used for rainout makeup and overnight travel to and from away series. There are no weekends or holidays off for celebration, friends, or family for professional baseball players. This is the showman's life.

February through September are completely blocked for baseball, without the ability to schedule a weekend, vacation, attend a wedding, or visit with friends and/or family who are not able to travel. Upon special request, an organization allows a player bereavement leave or permission to attend a funeral or wedding of a close family member. Aside from the physical demands over the course of a season, the emotional toll this takes on players and their families is often heavy, which makes the big league call-up and subsequent lifestyle change even more special.

SPRING TRAINING

Aside from the first season following the MLB Draft, each season begins with Spring Training. Major League Spring Training, which is invite-only, begins in early to mid-February. Pitchers and catchers report first, and full squad workouts start roughly a week later. Many minor league players receive big league camp invitations and are later sent to Minor League Spring Training. Minor League Spring Training generally begins later than big league camp, in early March.

Due to protections from the MLBPA and collective bargaining

agreements, Major League Spring Training invitees are the only professional baseball players to receive compensation for their labor during Spring Training. Minor leaguers receive a shared hotel room, breakfast and lunch at the stadium, and meal vouchers or per diem for dinner. Yes, 3 to 6 weeks of unpaid work, no days off, and only a bed and meals provided.

A typical Spring Training schedule consists of breakfast[62] followed by team warmup and stretching around 8 am. After warm ups, morning and afternoon workouts cover all skill aspects used during a professional season. This includes bullpens, individual and team defensive drills, fielding practice, batting practice, and strength and conditioning. After lunch, intrasquad games within the organization or scheduled exhibition games versus other organizations are played. Because there are no off days during Spring Training, rest and recovery each evening is critical to remain strong and healthy.

For the players who are not veteran big leaguers or high round selections with prospect status, an increased demand to focus and earn a job during camp becomes critical to continue their careers. This makes camp about producing results and displaying talent rather than serving as a warm-up in preparation to play a full season. Positions are not guaranteed. The effort is often described as more demanding and intense than during the regular season because each opportunity is life or death for a player's career. Each performance is under heavy observation and analysis. (Bramhall: I needed 3-4 days without any throwing after Spring Training to recover before the regular season.)

As Spring Training closes at the end of March, players are released, rosters are finalized, and coaches and players begin to arrange travel and housing for April opening day assignments across the country. When camp breaks, players have 3-4 days to travel independently or with the team, secure housing, practice, and begin the 132-162 game "marathon of daily sprints" season over the next 6-7 months.

EXTENDED SPRING TRAINING

Extended Spring Training is a period unassociated with full-season competition, hosted at the Spring Training site for each organization. In this period, training continues with workouts and simulated intrasquads for injured players who require additional treatment or rehab and are not in full-season form. This period also provides additional development for players who do not make a full-season squad, but are maintained by the organization. Many young players in "Extended" are there for position changes, poor performance, or additional competition evaluation by the front office or development staff.

REGULAR SEASON LEVELS

In February 2021, Major League Baseball reorganized the minor leagues. The new organization consists of two Triple-A leagues and three leagues each for Double-A, High-A, and Low-A. Additional clubs are permitted to assemble at the Spring Training and Dominican Republic training complexes for each organization, but the former rookie leagues were eliminated in the reorganization. Triple-A will be the only league to play 144 games, which was previously the regular season game count required of all full-season levels. Double-A will play 138 games, and both A-ball levels will play 132 games.[63]

ADDITIONAL CLUBS/ROOKIE BALL

There are introductory leagues for a young professional baseball player prior to joining a full-season squad.

DOMINICAN SUMMER LEAGUE (DSL)
The DSL is the only Latin-American rookie league and is hosted in the Dominican Republic at development complexes that are owned or leased by MLB organizations. This league consists of a 72-game

season composed of Dominican prospects who require additional development before arriving at the Spring Training headquarters in Arizona or Florida. Many of these players are either under age 18 or recently signed and in their first experiences with high-level organized competition.

GULF COAST LEAGUE (GCL)/ARIZONA LEAGUE (AZL)

These 50-60 game short season rookie leagues are the lowest rung of the minor league ladder. Rosters primarily consist of high school draft picks, late round or free agent college players, and young international players. Many of the players making up these rosters were kept for additional development in Extended Spring Training.

This is the first official level of professional baseball where athletes accrue career statistics. It is not uncommon for a well-developed college player to face a young athlete who may be physically capable, but have low baseball IQ, low self-awareness, and lack of maturity. A common experience is for a hitter to face a pitcher throwing 90-plus mph, with no accuracy. Thus, moving beyond the GCL and AZL is a relief for many but also a developmental necessity for others.

CLASS A

Class A, also known as "Low-A," is the first full-season of professional baseball affiliated with Major League Baseball. This level consists of approximately 132 games, with playoffs following the regular season. Travel demands are intense, spanning over large geographic regions and requiring overnight bus trips. Players sit doubled-up in the seat next to another teammate on the bus, and play up to 30 games in a single month. There are three regional leagues:

- East

- Southeast

- West

This level of full season competition is the first taste of the grind for a player and possibly the most mentally challenging experience on the journey. A player's mental fortitude is tested with many facilities and playing surfaces grading worse than many Division I surfaces. This is in addition to poor meal quality, low pay, below average overnight accommodations, and tough travel. A player who succeeds at this level can earn prospect status within the organization and move up quickly.

AA

Double-A contains a higher number of prospects than other levels, with players on the brink of a Major League call-up. Competition is elevated and the stars of tomorrow frequently spend time at this level prior to making their MLB debut. A player will rarely reach AA without at least one specific skill that grades out at the MLB level. Aside from temporary fill-ins, AA starting positions require results to maintain playing opportunities. There are three Double-A leagues that each play a 138-game regular season schedule:

- Central
- Northeast
- South

Travel and nutrition improves as organizations invest more in the players who prove their ability. Additionally, MLB roster players frequently make rehab appearances in AA prior to rejoining the team after an injury. Different from the lower levels of Minor League Baseball, AA is a level where hitters often feel more comfortable at the plate. Most pitchers have an understanding of their tools and have better command of pitches. The jump in maturity and baseball IQ is evident in the overall makeup of players, defensively and offensively.

AAA

Triple-A is the highest level of the minor leagues with the best overall talent, facilities, and a number of players with previous MLB service time. Many players are on the organization's MLB 40-man roster and are regularly sent up or down from the big leagues, which makes this level highly competitive. The polish of players at the Triple-A level is noticeable compared to Double-A, which houses more future prospects who are continuing to improve but may not yet have reached Triple-A or the big leagues. There are two Triple-A leagues:

- West

- East

Each league plays a 144-game schedule, which is the most games played of any minor league level. This is the first level where teams frequently travel by air, more often in the West than the East. The West is generally known as a hitter's league because many of the destinations have higher elevation and low humidity.

MINOR LEAGUE PLAYOFFS

Traditionally, the best record winners of the first half of the season in each league automatically qualify for a playoff berth. The second half winners, or next best overall record, capture the remaining spots. However, in Triple-A, the full season record is considered for each team. There are generally no more than four teams to qualify for the playoffs, whether that be the top two in a two-division league, or the four winners in a four-division league. The semi-final winners advance to the finals for the league championship.

The Triple-A format, where the overall season winners qualify for the playoffs, is more logical due to the continuous roster turnover of minor league teams throughout the season. The first-half rosters are rarely made up of the same players when September comes, which defeats the purpose of awarding the first-half winner a playoff berth.

The players actually playing in the playoffs months later may have been in leagues below or above during the previous months of the regular season. Team dynamics change dramatically throughout the season. In leagues below Triple-A, the first-half winner could lose all games in the second half and still qualify, or the team with the overall best record in the league could miss the playoffs by not winning either half of the season outright.

For minor league players, the playoffs matter very little. It is simply an extension of games tacked on to the end of a long season and as discussed previously, promotion to the next level is an individual, rather than team pursuit. Compare this to the end of a special achievement in a team environment, such as at the college or big league level, where losing is devastating and the individual pursuit is secondary to a player's devotion to the success of the team.

ARIZONA FALL LEAGUE

The Arizona Fall League, commonly referred to as the "Fall League," is an invite-only prospect league, with teams composed of the selected few from each MLB organization. Played in the greater Phoenix area each fall following the end of the MiLB (Minor League Baseball) season, this highly advanced league of MLB prospects competes in a 30-game season. Each MLB team sends 6 of its top prospects to play for one of six teams:

- Glendale Desert Dogs - White Sox, Reds, Dodgers, Brewers, and Cardinals

- Peoria Javelinas - Red Sox, Astros, Pirates, Padres, and Mariners

- Surprise Saguaros - Orioles, Royals, Yankees, Rangers, Nationals

- Mesa Solar Sox - Cubs, Indians, Tigers, Angels, Athletics

- Salt River Rafters - Diamondbacks, Rockies, Marlins, Twins, Rays

- Scottsdale Scorpions - Braves, Mets, Phillies, Giants, Blue Jays

MINOR LEAGUE HARDSHIPS

"All truth passes through three stages. First, it is ridiculed. Second, it is violently opposed. Third, it is accepted as being self-evident."

ARTHUR SCHOPENHAUER

There are several important topics that were formerly hidden from the public view but have been exposed with the impact of social media, articles written by sports journalists or former minor leaguers, and lawsuits brought against Major League Baseball and MLB clubs regarding labor laws. Sharing these truths is intended to provide clarity regarding this part of a player's career and serve as a call to action to improve the integrity of the industry.

These changes should not simply be better than yesterday, but fair going forward, because the current state never should have been permitted.

Similar to the way the bright lights and glamour of Hollywood conceal many injustices, marketing dollars and stories of the successful few hide much from the public light in the business of professional baseball. This reality is an opportunity for the general public, and Major League Baseball, to look at all of the facts and hardships created by the treatment of minor leaguers, from credible sources with firsthand experience, and make fair changes.

These changes should not simply be better than yesterday, but fair going forward, because the current state never should have been permitted. Career opportunities outside of baseball are spoiled for these athletes who have invested in identities as professionals and succeeded at each progressive level. Further, it creates significant life-altering challenges off the field, while dangling an obscure carrot without fair wage compensation. There is no choice for these athletes but to continue in pursuit of a passion that has always been rewarded by measurable success as the rules of the game are often replaced by by abuses of power and employee exploitation.[64]

If you don't agree, maybe a shift in perspective is warranted, rather than a denial of reality and fair business practices. Those speaking out through social media, journal articles, lawsuits, and this book are lifetime supporters of the game seeking to improve the industry.

PAY

Minor league salaries per month are determined by level, with a slight increase for each year of service and up to a maximum allowed for that level. As of the latest 2021 MiLB reorganization, minimum salaries are:

- Rookie - $400/week ($9,600/year)
- Low/High A - $500/week ($12,000/year)
- Double A - $600/week ($14,400/year)
- Triple A - $700/week ($16,800/year)

As is evident above, the current pay for most professional baseball players who have not signed MLB contracts, or are not on the 40-man MLB roster, are well-below the federal minimum wage of $15,080/year.[65] Additionally, these player-employees do not receive overtime or compensation for mandatory off-season training. On a paystub, the salary only accounts for 3 hours per game played, rather than necessary compensation for the hours of training, practice, travel, and extended games, which amount to 9- to 12-hour days in the regular season and 4- to 6-hour days in the offseason, on average.

According to JC Bradbury, author of *The Baseball Economist*, minor league salaries remained fairly consistent and unchanged over the past 70 years, without adjustment for inflation. The consequence of this omission by Major League Baseball to compensate its player-employees appropriately with the rate of inflation, translates into shocking annual figures when comparing current salary equivalents to those in the 1950s as shown below.[66] This also disregards the other variables that should contribute to player-employee income such as exponential revenue growth, increased cost of living, year-round training demands, and talent expertise that makes the current game an entirely different endeavor than it was more than 70 years ago.

LEVEL	1950	2017
AAA	$43,170	$10,750
AA	$30,470	$8,500
High A	$17,775	$7,500
Low A	$17,775	$6,500
Rookie	$8,380	$3,300

As an example, look at the AAA figures. AAA players, in the level immediately prior to the Major Leagues, consisting of multi-year, highly-skilled veterans, made the equivalent of $43,710 in today's dollars in 1950. Yet, in 2017, the same level of players, in a much more robust revenue-generating business, with greater year-round demand and talent expertise than in 1950, made just $10,750. This is grossly inadequate compensation in a line of employment that demands year-round dedication and refined physical and mental performance of the highest order. Especially in a market that has grown to $10.7 billion and increased $9 billion over the past 25 years.[67] The marginal $6,000/year salary increase from 2017 to 2021 is a far cry from fair according to current labor standards, or proportional compensation to the 1950 figures.

Further, this pay is only for the regular season, without compensation for Spring Training, and only the standard daily compensation rate is provided when a team makes the playoffs. This disparity in pay for the value provided and commitment required of minor leaguers leads to a lifestyle that is nearly impossible for many athletes.[68] Frequently, athletes must give up on potential and retire, or work a second job in the off-season just to make ends-meet while continuing to devote time and money to training for the upcoming season. These athletes are considered to be the 1%, the greatest in the world in their sport. Yet, they are expected to fuel and train their bodies and minds with little to no income, and outperform players in the MLB who are making a minimum of $570,500 per year, with the MLB average salary reaching $4.4 million per year.[69]

In comparison to the average $6,000 per year minor league salary in 2018, the NBA compensates its G League "minor league" players $35,000 per year.[70] While no G League player is getting rich by American standards, a professional basketball athlete can meet costs of living and provide for minimum needs. This is a legitimate parallel request for the players of the "developmental" leagues of MLB organizations.

A market that has grown to $10.7 billion and increased $9 billion over the past 25 years.

How is this compensation to baseball player-employees legally permitted? Excellent question. In 1922, the Supreme Court decided that professional baseball was an "exhibition affair" and not considered to be a business or trade engaged in interstate commerce.[71] Therefore, Major League Baseball was exempt from antitrust laws under the Sherman Antitrust Act of 1890, which prevents monopolies and supports the view that the interstate economy of the United States is better with more innovation and competition in the marketplace. This decision would unequivocally be decided differently today because courts then focused only on the production and distribution of physical goods, such as the petroleum trade, across state lines when interpreting "interstate commerce" under the Commerce Clause.[72]

In 1953, this ruling was challenged and heard again by the Supreme Court. The Court, rather than reversing the ruling to bring Major League Baseball current and subject to the more broadly interpreted Commerce Clause, and subject to antitrust legislation as a result, instead deflected responsibility to Congress by concluding, ". . . if there are evils in this field which now warrant application to it of the antitrust laws, it should be by legislation." Thus, the Court shrugged off the responsibility to politicians who are not professional athletes, who only understand baseball from the romantic and highly marketed fan perspective, and who are lobbied by the effort of millions of dollars per year by Major League Baseball. This led to further one-sided deals, and permitted mistreatment of its player-employees. All the while, all other professional sports with similar models do not have the exemption to do the same, which is the most obvious evidence that this abusive exemption must be lifted.[73]

> **In fact, in 2018, MLB spent $2.6 million lobbying Congress in the Save America's Pastime Act to ensure continued exemption from fair labor standards, to avoid paying contracted players minimum wage and overtime pay, and to avoid a cap on the maximum number of hours each player could work per week.**

In fact, in 2018, MLB spent $2.6 million lobbying Congress in the Save America's Pastime Act to ensure continued exemption from fair labor standards, to avoid paying contracted players minimum wage and overtime pay, and to avoid a cap on the maximum number of hours each player could work per week.[74,75] In this bill, buried on page 1,625 inside the 2,232 page Omnibus Appropriations Act, the class action lawsuit brought by Garrett Broshius on behalf of minor leaguers to request minimum wage and overtime pay was effectively quashed at the federal level by this so-called "vote" of Congress.

The Supreme Court exemption of all minor league players from the Sherman Antitrust Act in 1922, reaffirmation by Congress in the Curt Flood Act of 1998,[76] and recent endorsement of the exemption from the Fair Labor Standards Act by Congress in the Save America's Pastime Act,[77] allows MLB and its constituents to be exempt from compliance with nationally recognized and enforced employee protections and federal wage standards, such as meeting minimum wage and overtime pay requirements. This allows MLB to continue to "conspire and adopt anti-competitive wage rules that would normally run afoul of federal antitrust law, that stifle minor league opportunities to negotiate market-based compensation."[78]

This allows MLB to continue to "conspire and adopt anti-competitive wage rules that would normally run afoul of federal antitrust law, that stifle minor league opportunities to negotiate market-based compensation."

Competing businesses and all other privately owned sports teams who do not receive these exemptions can't collude in ways that unreasonably restrict competition or underpay their employees. For non-exempt businesses, "If restraints on competition adversely impact the wages, hours, and other working conditions . . . of a unionized labor group, those restraints must be collectively bargained with that labor group."[79]

Nevertheless, due to the exemptions and lack of political lobbying influence to lift them, that is not the case for minor league player-employees. This leaves the standard-form and largely non-negotiable contract offered unilaterally by MLB teams as the only employment rights received by a player, without the federal labor protections or oversight afforded to other professional athletes.

Notwithstanding the past, minor league player-employees should be covered employees under President Biden's effort to increase the federal minimum wage to $15 per hour, whether they are currently exempt by outdated and politically motivated policies or not. While this wage increase will unfairly stress small businesses, Major League Baseball is a flexible, multi-billion-dollar corporation that should not be exempt from socially demanded change. Let's call it both ways.

Major League Baseball organizations have improved and updated many workplace conditions such as increasing player support staff and nutrition benefits, and agreed to marginally bump the minimum salary for minor leaguers beginning in 2021. However, while these changes are appreciated and seemingly altruistic, the recent reorganization cut dozens of lower-level rookie and short-season teams across multiple leagues resulting in fewer roster opportunities and less expenditures by the organizations.

> **It is our opinion that such a servitude should never be part of a multi-billion-dollar business in the United States of America.**

Further, it has been stated that increasing the pay of minor leaguers "puts undue burden on the minor league teams by requiring minimum wage and overtime pay. What MLB has conveniently left out is, the Major League organization [with revenue streams in the hundreds of millions] pays the wages to the minor league players, not the minor league teams."[80]

Congress's removal of the exemption would free up the market to advocate for – and fairly compensate – minor league players. MLB could use a portion of the millions spent lobbying in opposition to this fair change and defending fair wage class action lawsuits. It is our opinion that such a servitude should never be part of a multi-billion-dollar business in the United States of America.

HOUSING, HOTELS, AND TRAVEL EXPERIENCE

This portion of the chapter was completed prior to any changes in housing that were proposed in 2021 by MLB. We chose to leave this section in its original form to preserve the quality and content of the section.

In September of 2021, MLB owners approved a policy that requires housing to be provided by the teams for minor leaguers. This is a step in the right direction and a long time coming. More information can be found here: whosonfirstbook.com/housing. Our hope is that MLB will implement our other suggestions, as they have with housing, for the betterment of the industry and its athlete-employees.

The lower minor league levels commonly have host families that support local teams and offer housing to players at affordable rates. This generosity helps young players adjust to a new city, especially those who did not attend college and learn to live away from home. While this community outreach is very helpful, on the whole, MLB and its affiliate MiLB organizations do a poor job of assisting players with basic house hunting.

After Spring Training, a player is typically given 3 days in a hotel to find housing and sign a lease, rent or buy a bed, set up utilities, shop for groceries, and attend mandatory practice sessions prior to beginning the season. Due to the insufficient pay, players are forced to live together in groups of 4-5 in unfurnished housing, share a car, and "survive" the Minor League season, often sleeping on air mattresses. These professionals are grown men, often fathers, and college graduates. The public view of an MiLB player is that of a "young man," however, the vast majority of players who reach a full season team are in their mid-twenties, many with wives and families to provide for.

Either a living stipend or fair salary should be provided for players to find reasonable housing, independent of roommates, if desired. After all, MiLB coaches are provided living stipends and are no more economically important to a club than a future MLB superstar. An organization could easily task these needs to a human resources department to bring continued housing improvements and cost of living to a reasonable baseline.

PER DIEM

"Per diem" is the monetary allowance given to players for meals, travel expenses, and incidentals when a team is on the road. Unfortunately, the actual amount rarely covers the costs associated with adequate nutrition and mandatory clubhouse dues during travel. As a result, players must come out of pocket for basic necessities.

In the last five years, the daily allowance was raised from $25 to $30 per player for each away game. This amounted to a total expense increase for MLB of $50,000 across all levels. This increase was certainly appreciated by the players. But while it seems satisfactory and benevolent, mandatory clubhouse dues still consume almost all of the funds that are intended to be used by the player for personal needs and adequate meals.

At each level, the Major League affiliated organization requires players to pay a daily fee for the clubhouse manager (the "clubbie") to provide laundry service and a pregame meal. At the higher levels, a post-game meal is also provided for an additional fee. Clubbie performance varies widely in the minors, and there are many excellent and poor clubbies alike. The good ones are never forgotten and become friends with players.

Generally, rookie level clubhouse dues are in the $5-10/day range, progressively increasing to as much as $17-25/day at the AAA level. A clubbie, like a coach or a trainer, is necessary staff for players, and players are not required to pay coaches or trainer salaries. So why are clubhouse dues not a covered expense by the employer? Players enjoy tipping a clubhouse manager for good service, but wouldn't it seem odd for a player to pay dues out of their salary to a coach for pitching or hitting instruction? Pre-game nutrition and laundering of uniforms and underwear should not be at the expense of the player. This is even more true if MLB continues to hold the position that minor leaguers are in an "apprenticeship" rather than in full-time professional employment.

At the Major League level, clubhouse dues are $80-$90/day, not including tip. However, MLB clubbies provide multiple meals, often 5-star post game meals, and players receive a daily per diem of $100-plus on the road. Combined with the minimum MLB salary of $570,500 per year, clubhouse dues are not burdensome. Compare the relative dent of additional expenses of a big leaguer to the total available income for the minor league athletes with a total income of $3,000-$16,800 per year.

HOTELS

Hotels generally improve as a player moves up the ranks. The home team is responsible for arranging hotel accommodations for the visiting team, which results in varying quality across the many minor league cities. At the lowest levels, the hotels tend to be a typical 2-star chain hotel such as a Red Roof Inn, Super 8, or Days Inn. In Double-A, hotels improve to a Holiday Inn, Fairfield Inn or Courtyard by Marriott. In Triple-A, accommodations may be similar to a Renaissance or Embassy Suites.

Hotel quality at the lower levels may come as a surprise to college players, who likely stayed in the AA- and AAA-quality hotels on road trips prior to professional baseball. Nevertheless, a low-quality hotel that covers the basics is not a major issue. Minor leaguers appreciate a somewhat clean and convenient location for meals options and easy access to the stadium. Whenever an organization makes the effort to provide acceptable accommodations, players are more likely to respect the MiLB franchise and focus on baseball, rather than "having the ass" all series.

Finally, an interesting note about travel rewards. Unlike other professions that require and fund employee travel, players do not receive credit or points from hotels and airlines. The MLB organizations recoup the frequent flyer miles and hotel points and put them back in their coffers. Preventing and recouping a professional's earned points and miles on business travel is blatantly disrespectful. A neutral or pro-employee industry is better for employers and employees.

PROPOSALS FOR POSITIVE CHANGE

While the purpose of Part I: Development and Competition is to present the path to success for parents and athletes at each level by sharing proven wisdom for success and presenting the independent facts of the experience that are most applicable, you have unquestionably been exposed to the mistreatment and hardships of the minor league athletes in this section. This is true whether you consider it justified on some level, severely corrupt, or somewhere in between.

Regardless of your stance on these topics, it is important to propose a handful of specific equitable solutions to inform your conversations and advocate to improve this level of the journey. If adopted, these solutions would give athletes the best opportunities to succeed on account of their on-the-field impact. Love for the game by the fans and players alike must include awareness of the entire picture. A paradigm shift often occurs when the collective consciousness and public conversation reforms an old pattern of belief after new truths are exposed to reveal a more realistic depiction. As an example, the food industry's mistreatment of animals and inhumane farming practices were exposed in the 70s and 80s. This sparked the vegan, cage free, and grass-fed movements.

Whatever the injustices may be, increased awareness of the facts and positive democratic action promotes a beneficial shift for justice and equality to be delivered with the newfound understandings. If a change is unwarranted or without merit, it will quickly lose credibility and revert back to previously accepted methods. In this case, however, it is unlikely that bringing MiLB treatment up to fair economic standards is not a worthy revision.

Positive change will, without a doubt, promote a healthy existence and improve the lives of players and their families for as long as the organizations deem their employment worthwhile. Perhaps, the public appetite will crave an ethically excellent sport to represent our passions and future aspirations for the stars of tomorrow. It would be beautiful to see professional baseball operated as it should, and to never be thought to be anything but the way it has always been.

SOLUTION #1: CONTRACT REFORM

Initial MiLB contracts are for a non-negotiable 7-year term. This is a long time. A more reasonable and equitable agreement for a college drafted player is for a 4-year contract term, or the option to become a free agent upon reaching age 25 if they have not been promoted to the MLB 40-man roster.

College drafted players are generally 22 or 23 years old and more developed than high school draft picks upon entering professional baseball. Locking a player in a "black hole" contract until they have passed their prime with no leverage is not a fair agreement for two reasons.

1 There is no incentive for a team to speed the player's development, promote the player, or protect the player with the many additional benefits afforded to 40-man roster players. The player has no leverage or opportunity to excel with another organization in such a long contract, especially as the player reaches "old" baseball age.

A recent example occurred when Chicago Cubs third baseman Kris Bryant was sent down to AAA in 2015. Going into 2015, Bryant was one of the best overall players in baseball, and more importantly, one of the best in the Chicago Cubs organization. However, Bryant

"That's the way it has always been" is certainly an unacceptable statement in current politics, and it should not be acceptable in fair labor standards for professional baseball players either.

was still under his original 7-year contract. Rather than keeping Bryant on the big league roster where he had been dominant all of Spring Training, he was sent to AAA to avoid free agency qualification following the 2020 season.

This move ultimately saved the Cubs one year on Bryant's initial contract by one day and preserved a fourth arbitration year for the Cubs to retain Bryant at a much lower cost. The Cubs cited "defensive play" as the reason for Bryant's 8-day demotion, which kept his service time under the threshold, and does not appear to have been done in good faith.[81]

2 A player who is in a system deep with talent could potentially move up the ladder or play in the Major Leagues quickly with another organization. Upon reaching age 25-26, if not before, a player with the requisite talent is physically and mentally capable of competing at the Major League level. Restricting this player from other opportunities prevents the player from exiting the minor league "apprenticeship."

An MLB club should have the right to decide personnel decisions but not for an unconscionable period of time that effectively expires a player's chances elsewhere. We do not argue the same for high school drafted players who may need 6 or more years of development to reach full potential, demonstrate results on the field from the investment by the MLB organizations, and are still in their mid-twenties upon expiration of their initial contracts. These athletes still have valuable shelf-life and the organization uses vast resources developing these former high school athletes.

SOLUTION #2: FAIR PAY AND BENEFITS

Many solutions have been mentioned regarding fair pay previously, but to reemphasize the most important changes that are needed: fair hourly wage with overtime pay or comparable salary; reimbursement of travel expenses; removing fees for essential clubhouse management and pre-game nutrition; team-arranged housing and/or housing stipends; and offseason pay and gym membership stipends for returning players.

These bare minimum solutions would provide the basic necessities required by professional athletes. Further, the benefits would allow a player to choose the minor league lifestyle as a career that could potentially grow in profitability, impact, and competition level as one would in any other industry, rather than enduring a necessary servitude of poverty to potentially reach lifelong goals.

An easy way to accomplish this is to incentivize compensation for making a full-season team. Each level, beginning with A ball, endures a similar physical demand and season length as at the MLB level, give or take a few weeks on the front and back end. A progressively increasing salary could be awarded with respect to each level when a player "makes the cut." This would be similar to a promotion from area to regional manager in a sales industry. More responsibility equals increased expectations, demand, and salary.

While each minor league level currently receives a step up in pay at each level, the pay even at the highest level is far below compensatory for the hours worked and expertise of the athletes. If an athlete is cut mid-season or not signed for the upcoming season, the athlete would naturally not be paid through the offseason.

The NBA has a minor league developmental structure where players in the G and D leagues receive a living wage. The fact that MLB houses more total MiLB players than the NBA is of no argument. MLB organization payrolls ranged from $64 million-$230 million in 2019, which is roughly 1.5% of the total 9.9 billion in gross revenue generated that year.[82] Similarly, the NBA generated gross revenues of 8.76 billion with payrolls ranging from $87 million-$145 million in the 2018-2019 season, roughly 1.1%.[83]

The NBA's enterprise is not limited by fairly compensating its minor league players, and neither would MLB's. There are numerous negotiable solutions for owners, front office personnel, and MLB to make MiLB salary payment expenses equitable between the clubs, regardless of the market size or revenue figures of a particular organization.

Ultimately, Congress should become educated, and take matters out of Major League Baseball's hands to make fair changes, regardless of the lobbying money present. The MLB corporation is far too large, politically motivated, and entirely oblivious to the struggle and hardships of the lifestyle. "That's the way it has always been" is certainly an unacceptable statement in current politics, and it should not be acceptable in fair labor standards for professional baseball players either. Required compliance with fair labor standards on par with all other American employment is the only way to change and improve conditions for the professionals who have not received a 40-man roster spot.

SOLUTION #3: RESPECTABLE HOUSING, PROFESSIONAL TRAVEL, AND PERSONAL CARE

Our final solution centers around boosting quality of life and overall morale in accordance with the type of work performed. As professional athletes who grind over many months consecutively, greater care should be provided to accommodate for appropriate housing, travel, and individual improvement measures over the course of the season. A common saying in the industry is, "Don't like it? Play better!" If you have gained anything from this section, you know that playing better does not always improve circumstances or speed the duration of the MiLB experience.

Teams should provide housing options in the area, whether the responsibility be placed on the MLB organization or the independently-managed minor league teams. If this requires a room block paid by players who have indicated interest in advance, great.

If it requires providing a list of move-in ready and furnished options prior to player arrival, this is also acceptable. For a player to search Craigslist from a mobile device from a hotel with no furniture arrangements and 3 days before the career-determining season begins, is simply unacceptable.

Further, many players do not have vehicles due to the distance traveled from home or because they are not in a financial position to afford one. This leaves these players dependent and somewhat burdensome on other teammates to provide transportation not only to work but also to grocery stores, restaurants, and entertainment. While this may seem insensitive, consider a comparable ratio of professionals outside of baseball who are obligated to provide rides for co-workers for months or years on end. Very few.

Teams could arrange for rental cars to be shared among players, as is the case when Americans travel to foreign countries to play in international professional baseball leagues. Teams could also designate front office personnel, such as an intern, to be a dedicated shuttle service driver for athletes without a vehicle. It should never become the responsibility of a teammate, and no teammate should be without transportation.

Another solution is for the well-being of the player. One three-day leave of absence should be granted in advance, at the player's travel expense, for each full-season player. The minor leagues are different from the big leagues where an organization is dependent on name, image, and likeness of players for ticket sales of a particular game, or when win and loss records impact organizational profits and losses, or playoff berths.

MiLB players should be able to choose one personal weekend away, just as an American worker may take a day away from work or a weekend to recharge or cope when challenging personal circumstances arise. This option will benefit the mental well-being of a player in countless ways and bring the player back recharged or in a better place. One period away, once per season, will not financially hurt the MiLB team or development of a player.

Much of the emotional and financial instability is a result of these issues. When there are many hardships, it is easy to expect and be overcome by the next hardship. This changes the attitude individuals have about themselves and the treatment they give to their teammates and families.

The fight or flight response is one of humanity's oldest protective mechanisms, and it is used in almost every encounter. Our autonomic nervous systems make the subconscious decision to either trigger a fight response in words or actions during encounters or trigger the flight response to leave a situation, withhold response, etc.

Utilizing or releasing these emotions when activated is a natural response and can be handled appropriately with the proper outlet. In most professional positions, acceptable options are available such as an approved brief departure to collect oneself (flight). In minor league baseball there are not. A player can't leave and exit a poorly managed situation or a difficult week on the job.

This difficult predicament often induces destructive coping behaviors common in pro baseball. Burn out, substance abuse, anxiety, depression, and emotional outbursts often result. If there was an acceptable outlet, or a weekend off, these situations and emotional health issues would improve.

Finally, three designated team breaks, with a full 48-hour period between games not used for rainout make-ups or travel, should be scheduled each season, and gym membership stipends should be provided. Extending the season by 6 days, or shortening Spring Training by the same, would have a low impact in the course of a year, and pay incredible physical and emotional dividends to the athletes. Further, an athlete must train in a gym and baseball facility in the offseason to maintain strength and conditioning, improve, recover from injuries from the previous season, and prepare for the upcoming season. Spring Training is no longer a warm up, but an intensely competitive period to make or break a career, which requires months of preparation. An offseason training stipend is an investment in the organization's future. It is time that these players be treated as professionals.

INTERNATIONAL AND INDEPENDENT PROFESSIONAL BASEBALL

Similar to international playing opportunities in other sports, there are professional baseball leagues outside of the United States that are not affiliated with Major League Baseball organizations. Many of these leagues provide better salaries than those offered to MiLB players and are more competitive. We don't cover every league, but the ones listed provide the best financial and competitive opportunities for a professional baseball player, apart from Major League Baseball.

The Asian leagues are played in the spring through fall during the traditional baseball season. Newcomer salaries in South Korea and Japan often surpass MLB minimums in the United States, which makes the opportunity attractive.[84] With the exception of the Mexico Baseball League, the leagues in Australia and Latin America are considered MLB affiliate "winter" leagues. Their seasons are played October through January, concluding prior to Spring Training. The champions from Mexico, Venezuela, Cuba, and Puerto Rico compete in the well-known Caribbean Series each year. Some of the best Latin American talent is showcased on this international stage.

American and European independent baseball leagues are not typically as competitive but are full-season opportunities for players to continue their careers and potentially find a path back to an affiliated baseball contract within Major League Baseball, or land an overseas opportunity.

- TAIWAN - The Chinese Professional Baseball League (CPBL) is played on the island of Taiwan and consists of 5 teams. The CPBL is considered the lowest level of the three major Asian professional baseball leagues.

- **SOUTH KOREA** - The Korean Baseball Organization (KBO League) consists of 10 teams and is a highly competitive, full-season league in South Korea that generates tens of thousands of fans each game. Many players find their way to Japan or the MLB after having success in this league.

- **JAPAN** - Somewhat comparable to the MLB, the Nippon Professional League has the highest salaries, fan attendance (30,000-47,000 average fans per game), and competition level among the Asian leagues. Ichiro, Daisuke Matsuzaka, and Hedeki Matsui are household names in the United States who had careers in Japan prior to Major League Baseball. Current Seibu Lions star Zach Neal describes every regular season game as, "wild, and the playoffs are on a completely different level. There's nothing like the fan support in Japan."

- **PUERTO RICO** - Played in the late fall and winter months, La Liga de Béisbol Profesional Roberto Clemente (LBPRC) consists of 5 teams across the island of Puerto Rico and is an MLB affiliated winter league. The league champion competes in the Caribbean Series.

- **MEXICO** - Liga Mexicano de Beisbol (LMB) is an MLB affiliated league, consisting of a 114-game regular season. The league champion competes in the Caribbean Series.

- **VENEZUELA** - Liga Venezolano de Béisbol (LVB) consists of 8 teams and is played in the late fall and winter months. The league champion competes in the Caribbean Series. As of August 22, 2019, Americans have been banned from playing in this league based on the socialist rule of Nicolas Maduro.

- **DOMINICAN REPUBLIC** - Liga de Béisbol Profesional de la República Dominicana (LIDOM) consists of 6 teams competing from October through January. The league champion competes in the Caribbean Series.

- **AUSTRALIA** - The Australian Baseball League (ABL) is a

winter league played from November to February. The league consists of 7 teams in Australia and 1 in New Zealand.

- EUROPE - The Confederation of European Baseball (CEB) currently has 38 member countries who compete across Europe.

- AMERICAN INDEPENDENT BASEBALL LEAGUES ("Indy Ball") - Despite popular belief that all professional teams feed into MLB organizations, there are a number of professional baseball leagues in the United States who are independent of any Major League Baseball affiliation. Salaries are low, with the average salary in the highest paying league of $2,000/mo., and there are no drug testing compliance programs for performance enhancing or recreational drugs.

   Many players in these leagues aspire to sign with an MLB affiliate or stay in shape for an opportunity with a foreign league. Not many players make long-term careers out of independent ball, although there are some who hang around for the love of the game with incredible commitment and performance. The top independent leagues are:

   - Atlantic League
   - American Association of Professional Baseball
   - Frontier League
   - Pioneer League

For more information about American Independent Professional Baseball, visit: whosonfirstbook.com/indyball.

MAJOR LEAGUE BASEBALL ALSO KNOWN AS "THE SHOW"

Welcome to the highest level of competitive baseball in the world. The biggest stage for the most talented players to realize lifelong dreams, perform at their peak to win games, and represent themselves and their tribes on the greatest stage. For our readers who are new to baseball, here's a quick overview before we discuss inside information that can't be found anywhere else. It's important to understand how league play operates at the highest level because Major League Baseball is what other parents and athletes will discuss, imitate, and admire.

MAJOR LEAGUE BASEBALL IS MADE UP OF TWO LEAGUES:

- National League - 15 teams
- American League - 15 teams

EACH LEAGUE IS SUBDIVIDED INTO 3 DIVISIONS:

- East
- West
- Central

Each MLB team has a roster of 40 players, with a maximum of 25 players on the active roster at any time. Each team plays a total of 162 regular season games beginning in April and ending in September. Post-season playoffs follow the regular season, which end in October and, on rare occasions, November.

The postseason consists of 10 total teams across the National and American Leagues, 5 in each league. The Wild Card Game decides the last team to compete in one of two Division Series. The Wild Card game consists of the two teams in each league with the best overall records that did not win their respective divisions but still have a chance to compete for the championship. This winner will face the team with the best overall record in the Division Series. Winners advance to the Championship Series (known as the ALCS and NLCS) to determine which team advances to the World Series to face the other league's Championship Series winner in a best-of-7 series to decide the world champion.

The regular season is emotional, grueling, and intense. It is similar to the previously similar to the previously described professional baseball section. At this level, however, the stakes are elevated and performance is everything. There are incredible luxuries to balance the physical and mental demands put on these athletes, but only for those who survive.

In this section, MLB players who have had the privilege of wearing a big league uniform share their experiences.

FIRST CALL-UP

A player's first call-up to the big leagues can come in different ways, but the ultimate result is the same, the player is going to "the Show" and reaching their dream. Call-ups can come at any point during the season for various reasons including:

- To replace injured players
- To replace players who are not performing well
- To replace players who are traded
- To provide depth at a position or in the bullpen after a taxing string of games
- September call-ups[85]

This moment, whether in April or September, will never be forgotten by these once minor leaguers, now instantly turned big leaguers. Here are a few stories from our MLB contributors on their first MLB call-ups.

MLB PLAYER'S GAME DAY ITINERARY

A game day itinerary is similar for most players at the big league level. These are professionals who carry themselves with purpose and who would not reach the highest level without a firm commitment to the process. Your athlete will follow and gain inspiration from the game day routines of the household names at this level.

Depending on bedtime the previous night after a game or travel, most players typically wake between 8 am and 10 am for coffee and breakfast and spend time with girlfriends, wives, or families. While on the road, players visit a local coffee shop or walk around the city in the morning to get out of the hotel. Following lunch, players arrive

💬 **JOE SAVERY:** *Joe Savery, former Phillies first-round draft pick and two-way All-American out of Rice University, may have one of the best September call-up stories of all-time and certainly one of the best overall stories of the 2011 season. After 3 developmental years as a pitcher in the minor leagues with typical highs and lows, which Joe describes as "average," the Phillies organization agreed to give him the opportunity to play first base. Joe was one of college baseball's top hitters and position players prior to being drafted as a pitcher.*

After a stellar performance in the High-A Florida State League at the plate to begin the 2012 season, he was promoted to the AA Reading, Pennsylvania squad in what he expected to be a shared role at first base for the remainder of the year. However, in an extra-innings game, he was asked to switch roles and pitch out of the bullpen. Joe had a lights-out performance, which raised the eyebrows of the Phillies personnel. After several successful outings in AA, Joe was promoted to AAA Lehigh Valley toward the end of the season and was back on the radar as a bullpen prospect. Fully expecting to finish the minor league season and make the drive home to Texas with his then girlfriend, Jennifer Wegmann, Joe had his truck packed. The Phillies had other plans.

After showering and dressing in a hurry to pick up Jen from the airport, the clubbie tapped him on the shoulder and let him know that his manager, hall of famer Ryne Sandberg, needed to speak with him. "I walked in there with 4 other guys and he raised a beer and said, 'This is for you guys, y'all are going to the big leagues.' I began crying instantly. After starting the season in High-A as a hitter, thinking I didn't have much longer as a player, I was going to finish the year in the Major Leagues as a pitcher."

at the stadium for treatment, stretch, workouts, and mental and physical preparation. There are comprehensive weight rooms for both home and visiting teams, hot and cold tubs, and ample support personnel for any other needs.

Over the next 24 hours during his MLB debut, the Phillies clinched the National League East Division Championship. More importantly, Joe proposed to his wife, Jennifer in the team hotel after his first day in the Show, immediately after popping celebratory champagne for clinching the division. Joe credits his brother Jack for transporting the diamond ring to Philadelphia and helping make the engagement happen.

CHASE HEADLEY: *Chase Headley, former San Diego Padres second-round draft pick, University of Tennessee All-American, 2012 Silver Slugger Award winner, and 2012 Gold Glove Award winner also has a unique first call-up story. Chase was playing for AA San Antonio when his first call-up to the Show came in his second full-season in the minor leagues.*

Kevin Kouzmanoff went down with an injury, which opened third base up for the highly touted young prospect in the Padres organization. Chase flew to his first game at Wrigley Field, which he described as intimidating because he did not know many of the players. He had spent both spring training and the beginning of the regular season in the minor leagues that year.

In his second game, Chris Young and Derek Lee initiated a bench clearing brawl, which he got in the middle of, all before his first hit in the big leagues. Headley had friends and family from all over the country travel to witness his big league debut and see his first hit off of Rich Hill, which is an experience he will never forget. In that game, Greg Maddux was on the bump. At three different times in his start, Maddux aligned Chase in the precise location where opposing hitters rolled over on ground balls directly at him.

MATT LANGWELL: *Matt Langwell, former Major League baseball player out of Rice University, played in the big leagues with the Cleveland Indians and the Arizona Diamondbacks. As a rookie, Matt struck out the batting title champions in both the National and American Leagues, Miguel Cabrera and Michael Cuddyer, respectively. Matt was asleep when he received a call at 2 am from his Triple-A manager for his first call-up. He spent the entire night packing and was on the road by 7 am to Cleveland.*

Thankfully, Ubaldo Jimenez threw a complete game that night, so he did not make his first appearance on little sleep. However, the next day he got his shot. On Matt's second pitch, he received a "welcome to the Show" home run at Jacobs Field by Evan Longoria of Tampa Bay. Following the game, the team flew to Yankee Stadium and were treated like royalty. Matt's first call-up experience lasted a few weeks and he was able to play in his home state to be greeted by friends and family.

Position players generally have a more strenuous preparation schedule with batting cage work, stretching, and treatment before team practice. Team practice includes dynamic warmup and offensive and defensive practice sessions on a daily basis. Following batting practice, pitchers and position players return to the clubhouse for meetings to discuss scouting reports of the pitchers and lineups of the opposing team. Reports on which opposing players are performing well and which players are struggling is important, especially in game-deciding situations.

Most relief pitchers understand their roles and when they will appear in the game, which dictates the individual schedule for each

ZACH NEAL: *Zach Neal's first call-up came when he was on the road with the AAA Nashville Sounds in Des Moines, Iowa. Oakland, his affiliate organization, was getting pummeled by the Red Sox. Zach had thrown a bullpen practice session after starting a game two nights before, and his arm was tired. Zach was in the dugout and the trainer's phone rang. In the minor leagues, the trainers are in charge of almost everything. They are essentially the operations directors, in addition to their many medical care responsibilities. The trainer handed the phone to his pitching coach who answered, "He did throw a [bull]pen, but I think he'd be okay to pitch tomorrow."*

Zach began to put the pieces together, and after the game the coaching staff asked if he could throw in relief tomorrow, except that he would have to do it in Fenway Park in Boston, rather than Iowa. Zach and his manager immediately began to cry, 6 years of hard work, getting passed over, and finally getting an opportunity to prove himself. After a 4:30 am wakeup for a flight to Boston, Zach was dropped off by a taxi with all of his bags and fans around in front of Fenway. That night he was called into the game and pitched against the Boston Red Sox.

to begin loosening up and expecting the bullpen phone to ring. Prior to appearing in the game, distractions cease and focus narrows in on establishing pitches, pitch sequencing, and plan of attack based on the scouting reports and upcoming hitters.

Post-game can often be the most important preparation period for the following day. Unlike other levels of professional baseball, where staff and players are ready to return home, it is not a rushed process at the MLB level. Players often eat a nutritious post-game meal provided in the clubhouse, lift weights to maintain strength and overall health, recover in ice baths, and recap the game or wind down with teammates in the locker room. If family or friends are in town, players may meet at a restaurant, team hotel, or bar after the game. Lights are turned out between midnight and 2 am. It is extremely important not to waste this window of recovery to rest and enjoy time away before giving it another best effort the following day.

Each of the big leaguers featured in this section want our readers to know how critical it is to separate work and home life for the sake of overall mental wellness and family relationships. The game can wear a player down, yet should not affect the way a player treats his family, girlfriend, spouse, or children. In fact, Savery and his wife made a rule to wait until settling at home before discussing any events from the game or the "work day" as a period to diffuse and process the day. This practice helped their relationship immensely over his multi-year career.

Another excellent approach to separate work and home life was used by Chase Headley's former teammate. After each game, he would stand in the mirror prior to leaving the stadium and boldly declare to himself, "I will see you tomorrow." This declaration created a boundary between baseball at the stadium and his personal life at home. It helped separate the two and give him the best chance of success as a father and husband at home, and a player when he arrived back to work the following day.

JUGGLING FAMILY AND WORK DURING BASEBALL SEASON

With the lack of time available to dedicate to family life during a professional baseball season, how a player manages relationships, commitments, and family responsibilities in season often determines career success and the health of their support systems during and after their playing career. While everyone does the best they can, many families struggle during this time, and it is no secret that divorce rates are higher among professional athletes than the national average. This should raise the attention of the athletes and organizations to continually improve the ways that relationships are fostered, and keep one from sacrificing the other, all in the name of success.

The player's home base, whether as a temporary call-up or as an established contract player, allows for family to be together and establish permanent living arrangements. Travel arrangements are the major logistical priority for families. Most players have their partners and families present for home series as often as possible. For most of Headley's MLB career, his children were not at schooling age, which made travel and extended family time more feasible. When the children began school, his wife was tasked with traveling back and forth, often from their off-season home, which could be a challenge.

Reports on which opposing players are performing well and which players are struggling is important, especially in game-deciding situations.

For players who are not established or in a long-term contract, the planning logistics can be much more complicated. Most wives and girlfriends visit when schedules best match, especially those who are working separate jobs during the season. Langwell's wife, Stephanie, maintained a full-time career throughout Matt's baseball career thousands of miles away, and would spend holidays and summers with Matt during the season.

A player whose significant other makes friends easily helps to ease the stress and dependency on the player alone to be available for support. This is especially true when the team is on the road. Overall, players view the presence of significant others as a benefit to provide emotional support, ease distracting temptations, and share experiences with their loved ones. This creates a healthy separation from the ballpark.

Zach Neal, former American big leaguer currently playing in the Japanese big leagues, said that he is fortunate to have his wife, Kianna, with him throughout the season in Japan. Otherwise, it would be difficult to lean so heavily on technology, as they must, to communicate with their extended families while overseas.

In a game that presents many failures and inconsistencies, and grueling travel schedules, a structured and stable environment with relationships away from the game can be a positive balance and allow a player to be their best mentally and physically with the emotional stability off the field.

CLUBBIE DIFFERENCES FROM MILB TO MLB

The clubhouse manager, known as the "clubbie," is responsible for all matters inside the locker room for coaches, players, and support staff. Responsibilities include meals, snacks, cleaning, shower supplies, travel arrangements, locker organization, golf tee times, dry cleaning, player-guest accommodations, special favors, and any other needs. Clubbie personalities and roles are similar at all levels of professional baseball. Except in the Show, there is an elevated expectation of performance, similar to the increase in expectations for MLB players. In the bigs, however, there are many more clubbies than at other levels, and both the hospitality and care provided for each player are on another level. Clubbies are paid well, eligible for playoff bonuses, and on the receiving end of generous tips. These individuals truly make a difference in the lives of professional athletes and can make or break a locker room atmosphere.

> For players who are not established or in a long-term contract, the planning logistics can be much more complicated.

GENERAL DIFFERENCES IN MILB AND MLB

Excluding the obvious and previously discussed compensation differences, there are still many differences that exist across professional baseball between the minor leagues and Major League Baseball. There is a huge jump in the competition and level of consistency, which requires an adjustment period. The freshly-minted big leaguer must drink from the firehose, adapt to the pressures, and raise the competition bar or be quickly replaced. After adjusting and understanding expectations, it is a day in and day out effort to succeed and keep a job.

Additionally, the scouting reports are precise and teams know the strengths and weaknesses of a player, often more than young players know their own strengths and weaknesses. Overall, there is a professional mindset to play the game the right way because there are always players down the ladder waiting for opportunities. Ultimately, long-term contracted players are there to stay unless an injury occurs, therefore, the few roster spots available to seize are few and far between.

On a typical upper-level minor league team, there are a few guys with MLB talent who are dangerous and better than the rest of the competition. But in the Show, there are no free outs. A pitcher may face Bryce Harper, Anthony Rendon, Jayson Werth, and Ryan Zimmerman in the same inning. Whereas, in the minors, only one of those players is at the heart of the lineup. "Hitters in the big leagues are not only more talented, they have such a better feel for the strike zone than in the minor leagues," said Savery. "They take [rather than swing at] more close pitches and don't chase nearly as often. Big league hitters will chase down in the count 1-2 or 0-2, but they don't swing at 2-0 sliders in the dirt. Pitchers must learn how to get guys out."

It is a day in and day out effort to succeed and keep a job.

Aside from the challenges of competition, the amenities are exponentially different. Travel, hotels, clubhouses, ballparks, tailored uniforms, food service hospitality, food quality, size and quality of support staff, and union security are the best available. Teams charter travel privately, directly from the stadium to the plane, and then straight to the team hotel with concierge luggage service. This improves the experience and strain on a player's body. In the bigs, everything can be provided by someone in short order and personal attention is available and devoted to every player.

ORGANIZATION DIFFERENCES

You may be tempted to believe that all teams are as uniform in the Show as the marketing portrays. In truth, each independent organization has different priorities in the ways it approaches the game, builds teams for the season, and provides for its players. Joe Savery played for one of the top 3 market teams, the Philadelphia Phillies, and the lowest market team, the Oakland A's.

> **But in the Show, there are no free outs**

The Phillies jockeyed for the top free agents in the game year after year, spending money on the top players, facilities, performance psychologists, dieticians, and technology. All potential advantages were justified in the eyes of the organization. The A's had a different mentality regarding what they would spend on players and were always active on the tradewire looking for players who could produce but might have holes in their game. Facilities were run down and overall amenities were not comparable by design.

Similarly, Chase Headley played for the New York Yankees and the San Diego Padres in his career. He described the Yankees, the largest market team in MLB, as "providing a step up in every way from family hospitality to caring for players' performance needs and the way they go about it." Chase had only positive things to say about San Diego, but holds that New York was on another level.

Matt Langwell played for Cleveland and Arizona, both smaller market teams who rely largely on regional support and hometown communities, which made them similar. What was different in his experience was the manager who led the MLB club. With Cleveland, Tito Francona, one of the most infamous player's managers in the game, was always in his corner. With Arizona, Curt Gibson is not known to be as much of a player's manager, and that was apparent by his personal engagement. Nevertheless, treatment in both organizations were great from a player's standpoint and the professional experience was top notch.

MAINTAINING LONGEVITY AS A BIG LEAGUER

Maintaining longevity at the MLB level is one of the most challenging tasks in all of sports. The number of talented players, in a game riddled with failure, means that a player must show up and be the same guy each and every day. "Consistency is the key, which is why organizations will pay millions to "average" players who will perform as expected, without any major surprises," said Savery.

Similarly, Langwell said that work ethic and routine across all aspects are vital when a player has the talent. The guys who hang around are diligent in their routines, have well-structured off-seasons, and focus on the details to a T. This is a day in and day out process from Spring Training through the season and into the off-season. For Headley, a soft tissues specialist was utilized throughout the season for recovery and to keep him feeling as healthy as possible.

Further, paying attention to changes in the game will determine who gets to stick around. When Savery entered professional baseball in 2007, there was value in the "old baseball" culture of veteran players. The typical Hollywood locker room portrayal of players drinking beer and playing cards after the game was fairly accurate. Front offices were composed of former players, and traditional statistics such as batting average and ERA were most heavily weighted as performance measures.

By the time Savery retired from baseball, the front offices were increasingly managed by Ivy League graduates with no athletic experience but were in tune with modern analytics and newly accepted performance metrics. Organizations valued statistics such as slugging percentage, swing and miss rate, strikeouts, and spin rate, which made pitchers seek velocity and hitters swing for the fences. This shift in the determination of a player's value and impact changed the game and the types of players on a roster.

An example of a recent change in the game is that pitchers have been told to "keep the ball down" for years to avoid giving up extra-base hits. But with the rise in the strike zone back to its original location, pitchers now have to practice throwing high strikes because hitters have focused on launch angle. Swing paths focused on launch angle can create a hole in a hitter's swing that pitchers must take advantage of to be successful. Future players must continually be aware of how the game changes and where emphasis is placed to stay in the game.

OFF-SEASON AND PRE-SEASON PREPARATION

Off-season recovery and preseason preparation are both critical for success during the season. For Savery, the off-season usually began with a long drive home, which was important to unpack the many emotions of excitement, relief, and disbelief that would come from the end of an 8-month effort. "You go to the stadium every day for 8 months, and one day it is over. You will never again have the same team or season, and many of the coaches and teammates you had, you will never see again."

After arriving home, Savery would catch up with family and friends, and eat at his favorite restaurants before beginning off-season workouts. This downtime was important to digest the rights and wrongs of the season, and create a plan to deal with the results and improve or build on successes moving forward. New goals might include a plan for weight loss or gain, strength gains, learning new pitches, or changing a swing.

After a few weeks of recovery, which shrunk as he aged in his career, it was time to get to work. Joe was always competing for a spot, so there was no guarantee. This created the necessity to show up on Day 1 in mid-season form. "This is how it is for bottom of the roster players in MLB. There is nothing wrong with it, but it certainly requires a different mentality."

This period dedicated to weights and conditioning would last until Christmas, when he would begin a throwing program to build arm strength and work through any soreness or setbacks. Following the beginning of the new year, it was time to focus on pitching, achieving desired body composition, and preparing for Spring Training. Savery says one problem that some players run into is they forget they had to play the game again after the off-season training period. "Being strong and in shape helps, but making sure your sinker, slider, and cutter work is what is most important, otherwise, none of the rest matters."

Before leaving home for another season, Savery would make rounds with friends and family, service his vehicle, and secure a place to live at Spring Training. This period before camp was the best he ever felt, both physically and mentally, due to the hope and excitement of the season ahead, and the rest provided by the offseason.

Langwell took a different approach than most guys he played with. After his season, he would take only one week off before beginning his off-season routine, which consisted of weights and conditioning up to 4 days per week. He followed the program provided by the MLB organization's strength and conditioning staff.

More importantly for Langwell, he would continue throwing lightly throughout the off-season to maintain range of motion and arm slot. These workouts consisted of long toss and flat grounds, throwing all pitches almost daily by November. During this time, he would make adjustments and add pitches with consistency, if necessary. While pitching has power and conditioning elements, it is also about precision and execution. Getting hitters out is what keeps a player in the game.

Similar to Savery, Langwell needed to arrive at Spring Training in mid-season form. There are players who would take his job if he fell behind, and pitching is what he was paid to do. In fact, organizations commonly make decisions early into Spring Training. Arriving unprepared is asking for a release. Langwell's offseason routine paid off. Matt spent 0 days on the disabled list (DL) over the course of his 7-year professional career, which is a hell of an achievement.

Chase Headley would return home after the season for vacation and relaxation through the first week of November. Prior to Thanksgiving, Chase began his off-season strength and conditioning program, and waited on specific hitting and throwing workouts until after the New Year. Earlier in his career, he would begin hitting before Christmas. But with long holiday breaks and family commitments, the gap would leave him starting over after the holidays. Later in his career, he did less tee work to prevent wear and tear on his body, especially as a switch hitter. The most important aspect, especially for an established big leaguer like Headley, was to stay healthy and mentally prepare for the grind ahead.

Neal took 3 months off from throwing early in his professional career, a practice he believes is important for long-term health in young arms. However, as his seasons have extended at the higher levels, it's almost year-round throwing now. After the season, Neal definitely takes 2-3 weeks away from all workouts, but believes that getting back in the gym quickly lays a solid foundation for the upcoming season.

SPECIAL MOMENTS AND MEMORABLE CONVERSATIONS

No player reaches the Major Leagues without special moments and memorable conversations that inspire and change the course of their career. Anyone who has excelled in athletics owes the people who provided vision to overcome the humbling lows and steady the rollercoaster of emotions on the path to success.

Early in Langwell's career, his pitching coach, Tony Arnold, saw potential that he was not yet able to see for himself. Matt says this changed the course of his career. Arnold realized that Langwell was lacking confidence and identity, and asked him a series of questions:

Q "Where did you attend college?"

A "Rice University."

Q "Were y'all good?"

A "Yes, we were in the top 5 in the nation and appeared in back-to-back College World Series in my career."

Q "Did you play an important role in the team's success?"

A "Yes, I was a weekend starter on both World Series teams."

Arnold then responded, "Well, the guys you are facing here [in the minors] would not have even made the team at Rice and definitely would not have been key contributors like you. You are better than every hitter in this league and you need to show that when you are on the mound. You have the ability, but you need to stop trying to miss their bats and be aggressive in the strike zone. Start pitching offensively instead of defensively on the mound." Matt began to challenge every hitter he faced, regardless of the hitter's resume. This major change in mindset propelled his career through the minors to the big leagues.

The next conversation Langwell remembers most is skill-specific. On his drive to Cleveland for his MLB debut, he received a phone call from former MLB All-Star, Jason Bere, to congratulate him. Bere said, "If you make a mistake, miss in the dirt. MLB hitters make their careers by hitting pitcher's mistakes." This advice helped Langwell execute off-speed pitches and never take a pitch off mentally.

For Savery, there were two moments that changed his career the most, and for the better. After what Savery describes as "three average years" as a pitcher in the minor leagues, he asked to return to being a position player. In the same season, Savery went from a position

> "Being strong and in shape helps, but making sure your sinker, slider, and cutter work is what is most important, otherwise, none of the rest matters."

player and shortening his arm path to the resurrection of his career on the mound and receiving a call-up to the Show. Had he not gone back to playing a position in the field, he does not believe that he would have made it to the Major Leagues.

Savery also shared a conversation that was specific to pitching. In the Triple-A clubhouse weight room in Lehigh Valley, long-time big leaguer Scott Elarton asked Joe, "When you come in the game and the other team sees you running in from the bullpen, what are they telling the hitters about you?" Scott was asking Joe what his identity was as a pitcher, which Joe had no idea about at the time. That conversation started Joe on the path to finding his identity on the mound, which led to his best years.

Neal shared two moments that changed the course of his career. When he was in the minor leagues with the Miami Marlins, the organization wanted to send him back to A ball to repeat the same level. This move was unjustified based on his previous success at that level. He stood up for himself, took his release, and signed with Oakland.

Oakland eventually gave him his first MLB opportunity, which would never have been possible had he stayed with the Marlins. "In pro baseball, there is no one looking out for you but yourself. It becomes a very selfish game and you have to do what is best for you and your family." The second moment that changed Neal's career was his decision to play overseas. This decision was a huge turning point in his career and has paid off with his incredible success and an extended contract with the Seibu Lions.

> "If you make a mistake, miss in the dirt. MLB hitters make their careers by hitting pitcher's mistakes."

BIG LEAGUE ADVICE TO YOUNG ATHLETES AND PARENTS

For parents and young athletes, the most valuable advice is from the players who were once in your shoes. These are not coaches, parents, or friends, but players who found a way to achieve the dream that everyone reading this book has chased. Take this advice to heart and recognize its usefulness.

Headley wants you to know that specializing too early and giving up other sports to focus on one year-round is not the ticket to success. Playing different sports improves overall athleticism, helps promote positivity, and creates energy in the specific sport that the athlete participates in at the time. Overspecialization can lead to injuries and burnout, among other mental and physical problems. "Sometimes doing different things for a while really makes you love the game, or other activities much more."

> "Life in pro baseball will make a player more of what they already are. If they struggle with temptation, addiction, working hard, eating right, etc., the long, stressful season will only magnify those struggles."

Matt Langwell's advice for parents and young athletes is to keep your priorities straight. Langwell shared six priorities.

- PRIORITY #1: Take care of business in the classroom or your dreams will be over before they begin. A player doesn't have to love school but care about it enough to not limit their athletic potential.

- PRIORITY #2: Take breaks and enjoy time with friends, family, and playing other sports. "Too much focus on baseball can be detrimental to the success and career longevity of a player."

- PRIORITY #3: Do the right work in baseball and pay attention to the details within the game. There should be a purpose every moment you touch the ball.

- PRIORITY #4: Prioritize strength and conditioning, stretching, and recovery. The only way to have a long career is to stay healthy.

- **PRIORITY #5:** Carry confidence, regardless of who you are playing or what the results have been.

- **PRIORITY #6:** To parents specifically: stay supportive and give the athlete a break when you see they need it.

Langwell also has a message specific to relief pitchers, who generally have less innings in a season than starters: "Once you get to professional baseball, the seasons are very long but one bad night can mess up your stats for a month or more. Execute every pitch and never take a night off. If you limit the damage to less than 2 runs in an outing in the games where you don't have your best stuff, you will be okay.

If you fail to minimize the damage, you could pitch for months with a poor ERA that follows you from only a few bad outings. This mindset allows a player to lock down on tough nights, even without their best stuff. It is a goal within the larger goal. "This game takes a lot of mental toughness. You can beat opponents with better mental preparation than them."

Neal believes parents and their athletes need to realize the probability of not making it to the Major Leagues. Everyone assumes that with all of the travel baseball and lessons that this will lead to the big leagues. But the percentages are not in anyone's favor. "Kids need to go camping at the lake. A 10-year-old playing baseball all summer gets no life experience besides baseball, and there is more to life than just trying to play in the big leagues."

On the other hand, throughout life you will be presented with decisions and you must keep your end goal in sight. Ultimately, you must base your answers on that end goal. "If your friends are interested in late night partying when you have an early morning workout, what is your end goal? If it is to be the best you can be, it should be an easy decision to stay back. Make the best decision in each situation and dedicate yourself to what you really want in life, whether that is in baseball or anything else. Never look back and wish you had given more time or investment toward your goals or had taken them more seriously. If you give it your all and it doesn't work, that's okay, but the people who do everything they can to be ready to play, to win, and perform their best have the best chance to reach their goals."

Savery's advice speaks directly to the athlete about doing an introspective evaluation. "Life in pro baseball will make a player more of what they already are. If they struggle with temptation, addiction, working hard, eating right, etc., the long, stressful season will only magnify those struggles." Savery said that many guys he played with should have made it but were more worried about the "lifestyle" rather than performance to achieve their goals.

Professional sports present a tiny window, and everyone is replaceable. A player must dominate to stick around. Take the decision out of the coaches' and administrators' hands and perform above and beyond. "There will always be other prospects and more talented players, but the game does not care about your feelings or your situation. Results matter and it is the only controllable factor. Athletes these days must know that being a good 'showcase' player will get you an opportunity, but it won't get you a career. Dominating is the only option."

"Baseball will end for everyone, and for the large majority, not on our terms. It is the game that tells you that you are done," says Savery. Therefore, exploit every opportunity to improve and have

"There will always be other prospects and more talented players, but the game does not care about your feelings or your situation. Results matter and it is the only controllable factor. Athletes these days must know that being a good 'showcase' player will get you an opportunity, but it won't get you a career. Dominating is the only option."

the foresight to recognize the opportunities and actions that could damage your chances at becoming your best.

PARENT ETIQUETTE IN PROFESSIONAL BASEBALL

Parents will have less involvement as the athlete becomes a professional. Offering support and understanding is beneficial as your athlete navigates the waters of professional baseball with a rollercoaster of emotions, failures and success, business opportunities, and agent selection. By this point, you should know to stay out of the way as the coaches and front office personnel evaluate many factors unknown to you. If parents are unstable or unsupportive, it can harm the athlete's reputation. Scouts and team administration may question the maturity and mental stability of the athlete, and whether they will be an asset to the organization. The more supportive you can be, the better.

PART TWO

FOUNDATIONAL ESSENTIALS

"How good we are when we start something is not related at all to how good we can become at anything."

♦ SCOTT KELLY, UNITED STATES ASTRONAUT[86]

INTRODUCTION

———————

Now that you understand the journey from youth baseball to the big leagues, let's discuss the foundational essentials that will lead to purposeful effort and more efficient hours. While Part I provided valuable insights into each level, Part II contains important information for overall approach and understanding how to succeed. This part will bring focus and direction to the commitments you have made to provide the best opportunities for your ballplayer.

As baseball fans, we often rush onto the ball field before making a game plan and considering the best courses of action required to generate the results we desire for our athletes. With a deeper understanding of: the priceless value of failure; knowing when or when not to specialize in baseball over other sports; knowing which instructors to trust nationwide for pitching and hitting instruction and where to find them; and the best books, podcasts, and research for further understanding of baseball skills, you will point your athlete in the right direction.

FAILURE AND ADAPTATION

"Intelligent people who embrace their mistakes and weaknesses substantially outperform their peers who have the same abilities but bigger ego barriers."[87]

🔻 RAY DALIO, FOUNDER, BRIDGEWATER ASSOCIATES

"In the midst of prosperity, the mind is elated; and in prosperity, a man forgets himself; in hardship, he is forced to reflect on himself, even though he be unwilling."

🔻 ALFRED THE GREAT, KING OF THE ANGLO-SAXONS

I know what you're thinking. Why is failure discussed in a book about how to succeed in baseball? Because failure, and our response to failure, is precisely the recipe for success. This is important. Let's restate this concept for clarity. Failure is the only experience that causes any living organism to process information, strengthen, overcome, and ultimately adapt permanently to survive and succeed.

Failure is the greatest teacher and directly complements, rather than opposes, success.[88] Failure encourages us to focus on our missteps, mistakes, and problems for the motivation to become better versions of ourselves. This biological wiring, although seemingly negative, can be immensely beneficial once we are able to recognize it as an opportunity to accurately redirect our focus towards improvement. Without addressing our failures, we cannot develop the awareness to understand our mistakes, seek solutions for change, and evolve. As author Nasim Talib says, "We need the light of experience gained by disaster."[89]

While a constantly negative mindset may inhibit progress, a balanced view of our mistakes, problems, and failures, coupled with potential solutions and aspirations for future success, is the recipe for improvement and achievement in any endeavor. Understanding our missteps allows us to: **1** proactively avoid future mistakes; **2** adapt into mentally and physically stronger individuals; and **3** make strides in the right direction. Often, a rude awakening from a failure is a necessary motivator to develop the drive and determination to succeed that is strong enough to surpass expectations. It is often invaluable to our development to gain the awareness necessary to anticipate similar situations.

The concept of embracing failures translates to mentally challenging tasks such as repetitive problem solving, biomechanical body movements, or physiological healing from an intense physical demand, injury, or illness. In baseball, failure is guaranteed, and how a player embraces and adjusts determines outcomes in the short-term and career longevity in the long-term. Heck, as much failure as this game brings, ballplayers must constantly believe they are good, when they may actually suck over a given period of adaptation. Few people understand this lesson, but ultimately, it is what buys an athlete enough time to return to performing well again.

Although time pressures can be a positive force for adaptations in physical strength and cognitive understanding, the narrowing gap of opportunity and increased competition of today's youth sports incorrectly insinuates that short-term failure is a reliable indicator of long-term ability. While failure may be the factor that prevents a player from receiving opportunities, or making a desired team in the short-term, a series of mistakes is actually an indicator of growth because of the adaptation and information processing that occurs as a result.

As such, we must not view mistakes as unerring evidence of long-term success potential. Viewing failure as a part of growth, while adapting to demands and expectations, will allow your ballplayer to rise to the challenge(s) and adapt to the mental and physical pressures associated with training and performance. Similar to bamboo, which builds 80% of its root system over the course of four years before shooting ninety feet into the sky in a matter of weeks, so is a player who is diligently learning, believing, improving, and waiting for the opportunity to make an impact.[90]

As coaches, teachers, and parents, we must be careful to assign a final value to short-term failures and successes. Failure is imminent and should be welcomed. Determining an athlete's ability from a single success or failure only prevents our athletes from preparing for the next challenge and opportunity to improve. This can negatively impact the athlete's ability to respond to failure, and limit future opportunities. Let those roots mature.

Two thousand years ago, the Roman philosopher Seneca eloquently explained the value of failure. His words remain true today:

"For our powers can never inspire in us implicit faith in ourselves except when many difficulties have confronted us on this side and on that, and have occasionally even come to close quarters with us. It is only in this way that the true spirit can be tested, – the spirit that will never consent to come under the jurisdiction of things external to ourselves. This is the touchstone of such a spirit; no prizefighter can go with high spirits into the strife if he has never been beaten black and blue; the only contestant who can confidently enter the lists is the man who has seen his own blood, who has felt his teeth rattle beneath his opponent's fist, who has been tripped and felt the full force of his adversary's charge, who has been downed in body but not in spirit, one who, as often as he falls, rises again with greater defiance than ever."[91]

Failure, and our response to failure, is precisely the recipe for success.

Those who have fallen and rise again find a way to improve themselves or win by learning the weaknesses of the opponent. We must recognize those who take it on the chin, improve to meet the challenges and demands required to succeed, and keep coming back for more. Failure separates the players with "potential" from the players who come for blood and who come to win.

As a parent, set aside time for unemotional performance evaluation. Have a conversation with your athlete to discuss how they handled a failure and positively redirect focus towards improvement. Proper timing is key. Before initiating this conversation, you should consider the athlete's emotional state. Moreover, there is no universally-correct way to have this conversation. Trust your gut and stay true to the dynamic of your specific parent-athlete relationship. When the athlete fails to meet expectations, allow them to process such a failure with the hope of another opportunity.

A positive outlook and renewed self-esteem will enable your athlete to rise to the next challenge with more knowledge and increased mental strength. By having this conversation, they will be better equipped to handle inevitably difficult learning experiences, ultimately providing the toolkit they need to prepare for a future in baseball. You never know when something discouraging will ultimately work out in their favor. Young athletes are not made of glass, thus, focusing on the ability to overcome facilitates future progress.

It is vitally important for the athlete to understand that a box score or batting average is not the ultimate measurement of success. We like to refer to this concept as "Keep the Calculator Out of Your Pocket." Measuring success cannot always be done by statistics, especially in the short-term, or when new physical and mental skills are in the development process. An athlete can hit a ball on the screws and not be rewarded with a hit, throw a great pitch and have a defensive mistake in the field, or have a blooper fall in for a hit – all unavoidable parts of the game.

We must reevaluate our message to the athlete if we are statistically obsessed. By focusing more on the box score and less on the consistent development of the athlete's mental focus and resiliency, you are sending the wrong message. Do your best as a parent to step away from the fan zone. Become an advocate, teacher, or counselor. Become whatever is necessary to encourage their consistent development.

In fact, several recent studies have shown that grit and fortitude are the greatest predictors of long-term success more than raw talent and ability measures, such as an SAT academic score or a 40-yard dash time. Not surprisingly, failure is necessary to the development of these qualities. Grit, as defined by Angela Duckworth, University of Pennsylvania psychologist, is "passion and sustained persistence applied toward long-term achievement, with no particular concern for rewards or recognition along the way. It combines resilience, ambition, and self-control in the pursuit of goals that take months, years, or even decades."[92]

Duckworth further explains: "Grit is about having what some researchers call an 'ultimate concern'—a goal you care about so much that it organizes and gives meaning to almost everything you do. And grit is holding steadfast to that goal. Even when you fall down. Even when you screw up. Even when progress toward that goal is halting or slow. Talent and luck matter to success. But talent and luck are no guarantee of grit. And in the very long run, I think grit may matter at least as much, if not more."[93]

For more on the topic of grit, we highly recommend watching Duckworth's TED Talk: Grit: The Power and Passion of Perseverance and listening to Angela Duckworth discuss grit on the Intangibles podcast. They are available here:

- TED TALK: whosonfirstbook.com/ted

- INTANGIBLES PODCAST: whosonfirstbook.com/duckworth

As coaches, parents, mentors, and teachers, we have a responsibility to create a safe space to allow our youth to stumble and fall. This allows them to process and experience the pain of failure without humiliation, and rise up to meet the challenges and demands the next time. Risks and failures encourage athletes to make adjustments needed to reach new limits, as well as overcome misunderstandings or mechanical issues, which require muscle memory development and attention to detail.

If a player does not sense that they have the space to make adjustments, the same mistakes will be made in the future. If they are bombarded for a mechanical mistake, the negative feedback limits that player's ability to learn and grow. By fixating on mechanical errors, we encourage our athletes to place more importance on succeeding in the moment than on proper development without restraint.

The journey to a goal worthy of our commitment consists of millions of steps – forward, backward, and to the side. Success is not a one-shot leap rooted in current skill level. Therefore, let us remember, it is the journey that provides opportunities for growth with every challenge. It is the journey that determines the effect this sport will have on the life of your athlete.

Humans adapt and improve with experience and understanding. When in doubt, return here. Continually remind yourself that what you do with this information today affects the opportunity for growth tomorrow. Failure is not the enemy – it is the catalyst for growth and great achievement. Allow your athlete "to be willing to fail, to be wrong, to start again with lessons learned."[94]

OVERSPECIALIZATION AND OVERALL ATHLETICISM

In baseball, overspecialization earlier than necessary is not always the path to success. In other words, outright devotion and commitment is not necessarily enhanced by single-sport specialization, especially during athleticism development in childhood and adolescence. Baseball is one of the most specialized games in the world. Success depends on years of skills practice beyond generally recognized athleticism. However, skill specialization alone will not lay the proper foundation for elite talent development. A well-rounded athletic approach that develops raw athletic ability, spatial awareness, understanding of the rules, and mental fortitude, while the foundations of baseball skill specialization are laid, is most effective.

Playing baseball at a young age is necessary for teaching the concepts of the game, including learning proper mechanics, teamwork and communication, and repetition. Overall athletic development should be prioritized along with baseball skills practice during the early years. This will develop rotational explosiveness, flexibility, and proper sequencing in various activities.

Parents are frequently led to believe that specializing in sport at an early age is necessary to ensure future opportunity for their children. In 2014, The Journal of Clinical Sports Psychology disproved this common misconception in "Patterns of Specialization in Professional Baseball Players." In this study of 708 minor league professional baseball player participants, results revealed that most players participated in many different sports, with only 25% specializing in a single sport before age twelve. Interestingly, the players who specialized later were more likely to receive college scholarships.[95]

Consider this question: how often do you see a young athlete develop into their full potential before puberty and dominate the competition, only to have the others catch up in the years to come? The rise of athletic prowess during puberty is typically not the result of physical/mental skill as much as strength and hormonal changes in the transition from child to adult. The early bloomers are not always better baseball players in the long run when their competitors undergo physical change and catch up. Accordingly, don't let your young athlete's early knack for a sport (or lack thereof) dictate their future success, especially if they are maturing at a normal pace. It is okay during the pre-teen and teenage years to leave room for growth and improvement, especially as your child grows into their frame.

Therefore, before puberty, continue to involve your athlete in all sports that bring enjoyment. Let the athlete decide which sport(s) they wish to pursue development instruction and discipline in, encourage a winning and fearless mentality, and don't rush the development process. Once the athlete approaches prospect age, it may be beneficial to single out a specific sport. Nevertheless, we know many athletes who might have been better off in the long-run keeping doors open for other sports, because specializing early does not guarantee success. The timing of each athlete's decision will be different due to individual biology based on physical and mental maturation.

Prospect age may differ for each athlete based on their skill set at a particular point in development. While some high-level programs may begin showing interest in prospects as early as eighth grade, many athletes may not physically develop into a prospect until later in their high school career, and that is okay. There are plenty of examples of eighth grade athletes choosing one sport and committing to NCAA Division I programs.

On the flip side, there are also plenty of examples of elite-level athletes, such as Kyler Murray, who made a college decision later in high school and didn't pigeonhole themselves into a specific sport until participating in multiple sports at the collegiate level. Kyler went on to be the 9th overall pick of the Oakland Athletics in the 2018 MLB Amateur Draft before winning the Heisman Trophy at the University of Oklahoma. Then, in 2019, Kyler was the first overall pick in the NFL Draft and received the Offensive Rookie of the Year award. Allow the athlete's specific situation to determine when sport specialization is necessary.

Intuitively understanding how to compete and win in any sport is the keystone for future success.

Oftentimes, the multi-sport athletes are those with the most toughness, grit, and competitive fire. Intuitively understanding how to compete and win in any sport is the keystone for future success. Additionally, becoming a multi-sport athlete also assists the athlete in cultivating relationships, gaining knowledge, and developing awareness by interacting with many athletes who would never be in a baseball dugout.

By playing different sports, the athlete will learn to adapt to unique roles, positions, teammate personalities, and levels of competition. This will translate to better baseball performance. Scouts and recruiters from baseball's elite levels are not searching for baseball-specific mechanics alone. They are also observing an athlete's grit and competitive nature, while using speed, explosive power, body awareness, and perception to enhance the raw tools to predict whether a player will succeed in baseball.

The most well-rounded baseball prospects have a generalized athletic awareness and use this learned intuition to find a way to win, regardless of the sport. These are the players who despise losing in any competition. Those who are disgusted by losing should work to understand what caused the loss as motivation for future success.

Nevertheless, in this overall athletic development period, continue to involve the player in as many baseball-specific activities as they desire and seek the highest level of competition and instruction based on the current stage of their physical and mental skill. Feed the athlete when the athlete is hungry. On that note, it is critical to understand the importance of an intensely focused devotion to become the best in baseball at the proper age or stage of athletic development. In the words of Derek Jeter, "there may be people who have more talent than you, but there's no excuse for anyone to work harder than you do."

If you're looking for inspiration or to better understand what "devotion" means to many of the athlete's future teammates and opponents, take a baseball trip to Latin America or search for articles or documentaries on the career development of your favorite Latin baseball star. These athletes exude outright hunger, passion for the game, and sheer drive to achieve the dream of becoming a professional athlete. In Latin America, there are fewer opportunities and greater rewards for achieving the goal of becoming a professional athlete. Compared to the typical American baseball prospect, the rising talent from Latin America lives, breathes, and dreams baseball more passionately and at a much younger age.

To summarize, athletic development is crucial to maximize the skill development from the passionate pursuit and devotion to become a great baseball player. Specialization will come naturally as the athlete matures. Understand the difference. Practicing baseball, alone, will not miraculously provide the athlete with all of the raw tools necessary to compete at the highest level possible.

The best way to ensure success is to incorporate a well-rounded approach to athletic competition while maintaining a focused devotion to becoming a better baseball player with overall athletic awareness and training. Multi-sport athletes gain invaluable understanding through conditioning, mental and physical endurance, and overall exposure to other sports, activities, and hobbies. By encouraging the athlete to play other sports, they will gain the athleticism, understanding, and well-rounded approach they need to become a successful ballplayer.

SPORT SPECIALIZATION STUDIES

For a more in-depth understanding of how early specialization may lead to increased rates of burnout, overuse injuries, and a decrease in performance due to overtraining, please see detailed studies of sport specialization below. These studies emphasize the importance of well-rounded athletic development.

Overuse Injuries, Overtraining, and Burnout in Child and Adolescent Athletes

whosonfirstbook.com/burnout

A case of early sports specialization in an adolescent athlete

whosonfirstbook.com/specialize1

Sports Specialization in Young Athletes, Evidence-Based Recommendations

whosonfirstbook.com/specialize2

THROWING INSIDER

INTRODUCTION

This chapter will not address specific baseball mechanics because of the multitude of resources available. Instead, it will direct you to the essentials needed to succeed. It is our purpose to provide you with the most accurate and current information and best resources to improve your athlete's opportunities to fully develop as a ballplayer. This inside look identifies important developmental considerations involved with throwing, while spotlighting and directing you to many of the best coaches and instructors available to assist in your athlete's journey.

OVERVIEW

As our world becomes increasingly accessible through the Internet and social media, access to high-level instruction is becoming more widespread. Baseball-specific influencers are now sharing credible information at a much higher rate than in the past due to social media's evolving user-friendly platforms. Identifying the philosophies and techniques that best complement the athlete's physical makeup, tools, and body type is of utmost importance when implementing these training methods.

For example, renowned throwing specialist Tom House encourages budding athletes to focus on consistent throwing repetition between the ages of 7 and 12 to train the shoulder's major fast-twitch muscle fibers. According to Coach House, this activation is necessary to generate elite-level throwing velocity later in one's career.[96] During this period, maximum intensity repetition creates throwing-specific strengthening in the rotator cuff and shoulder capsule. After the age of 12, it is difficult, and possibly detrimental, to alter the way an adolescent has trained their biomechanics to repeatedly perform a full body movement, such as throwing.[97]

Accordingly, the athlete must take advantage of this window of opportunity to learn correct technique and practice. Between the ages of 7 and 12, the athlete will also develop shoulder flexibility and habits concerning grip, rhythm, generation of momentum, arm action and release point. Therefore, it is imperative to recognize the importance this window has on the development of throwing mechanics.

Moreover, it is equally as important to perform these movements properly so as to train the kinetic chain from thought process through release point. Efficiency and agility are every bit as important as brute strength in athletic movements, if not more so. Brute strength alone does not generate maximum power.

Efficiency and agility are every bit as important as brute strength in athletic movements, if not more so.

One must combine that strength with proper movement in order to generate velocity through rotational explosiveness, which starts from the ground and travels through the core, and out of the extremities. There are many examples of pitchers who are far from impressive in the weight room, but who throw with a higher velocity than one would expect due to trained fast twitch fibers and efficient kinetic chain movement patterns.

It is imperative to ensure the athlete repeatedly practices throwing with purpose during these early years. Doing so is invaluable to the development of rhythm and mechanics, as well as the necessary muscular physiology to sustain and improve future performance. As mentioned in Foundational Essentials, trial and error is a necessity in refining an athlete's skill set as they adapt and learn from repetition, success, and failure.

If you are not convinced, search on YouTube to find any NBA player throwing out the first pitch of an MLB game. Compare this to any high-level arm action of an MLB pitcher. In doing so, you'll find that even the most developed and athletic NBA players struggle with a baseball-specific throwing motion, despite elite athleticism, hand-eye coordination, and fast-twitch fibers that are among the best in the world. This is because baseball-specific throwing is a learned skill refined by repetition and intentional, purposeful movement at an early age.

SAFE BALANCE

With the necessary repetitive throwing and refinement required to reach advanced competition levels, we must balance the drive to succeed with safety measures, such as pitch counts, to protect young arms. An ongoing issue, especially at the high school level, is a coach requiring or allowing an athlete to throw too many pitches in a game, too early in the season, or over the course of a season. This often results in inflammation and soreness or injury.

We recommend communicating with the coaches about pitch count limits. This can either be initiated by the athlete or the parent depending on the age of the ballplayer. If there are protective measures to protect throwing arms in place, you will more likely avoid risking an athlete's future until those few moments when rules go out the window and the stakes are higher, such as in a high school, collegiate, or professional championship situation. Athletes committed to colleges are in a good position to discuss concerns with their high school coach because the athlete's future successes or failures may reflect back on the coach in some way.

Perfect Game www.perfectgame.org, one of the leading authorities in competitive youth baseball, has pitch count limits and rest requirements for athletes who compete in tournaments under its control. Let their chart serve as a guide for your athlete's competition season or tournament schedule.

PITCH COUNT LIMITS

AGE	OUTS	OR	PITCHES
7/8U	15	OR	50
9/10U	18	OR	75
11/12U	18	OR	85
13/14U	21	OR	95
15/16U	21+	OR	95
17/18U	21+	OR	105

REQUIRED REST (PITCHES)

AGE	0 DAYS	1 DAY	2 DAYS	3 DAYS	4 DAYS
7/8U	1-20	21-35	36-50	N/A	N/A
9/10U	1-20	21-35	36-50	51-65	66+
11/12U	1-20	21-35	36-50	61-65	66+
13/14U	1-20	21-35	36-50	51-65	66+
15/16U	1-30	31-45	46-60	61-75	76+
17/18U	1-30	31-45	46-60	61-80	81+

ACCESSIBLE THROWING INSTRUCTORS AND RESOURCES

In this section, you will find resources to assist you in better understanding which tactics may work for your ballplayer, given their specific skill set. You do not need to spend a lot of money to effectively and properly develop your young, aspiring athlete. Many of the facilities and individuals we discuss have a national presence; however, some do not, and that is okay because credible instruction trumps popularity.

Our goal is to provide you with a wide selection of credible resources. We strongly recommend you use these resources and improve your game locally to save valuable time and money. While online training and education is a valuable substitute to live instruction, it is beneficial to pursue on-site training with one or more of these resources to guarantee improvement in your athlete's game. This will lead to levels of mental and physical development beyond what they would achieve without hands-on exposure and dedication to these programs.

 **PRO TIP** ——————————————————

There are countless throwing programs available for building arm strength and improving pitching mechanics but none of them work unless your athlete fully commits. Do your research on the best options and encourage your athlete to follow through. Most failure to improve is from a failure to follow the process.

DRIVELINE BASEBALL

WWW.DRIVELINEBASEBALL.COM

Kyle Boddy and his staff based in Washington state create custom-built programs, designed for players who want to gain the most out of their careers. Driveline's comprehensive programs offer youth development for pitchers and hitters, software, live or remote workouts, and much more. Additionally, Driveline offers online courses, live training camps, research and training-specific literature, as well as a paid subscription forum containing weekly articles and helpful, industry-leading videos. If you are not interested in the subscription service, Driveline publishes a free, weekly newsletter called Sunday Thunder Nuggets.

f	Driveline Baseball	**⊙**	@drivelinebaseball
🐦	@drivelinebb	**▶**	Driveline Baseball

BEN BREWSTER

WWW.TREADATHLETICS.COM

Ben Brewster is a former MLB player, published author, and strength and conditioning coach. Follow Tread Athletics for excellent, credible content.

f	Tread Athletics	**⊙**	@tread_athletics
🐦	@treadathletics	**▶**	Tread Athletics

JAEGER SPORTS

WWW.JAEGERSPORTS.COM

Alan Jaeger is one of the early pioneers of shoulder and arm care, and well-known for his "Jaeger Bands." He incorporates components of psychological performance into his programs with self-awareness education during and in between physical activity. He has trained, and "raised," some of the greatest names in college and professional baseball today. Not only are the bands an incredible maintenance and strengthening tool for career longevity, the exercise programs and processes he has developed for in-season maintenance, post-season recovery, and pre-season training have withstood the tests of time.

 Jaeger Sports

 @jaegersports

 @jaegersports

 Alan Jaeger

PITCHING NINJA

The Pitching Ninja, founded by Rob Friedman, is a fantastic resource on Twitter. Pitching Ninja provides an easy-to-use Dropbox website to assist your athlete's understanding of technique, drills, arm care, and more. Pitching Ninja also provides video content of the best practices from some of the greatest pitchers in the world.

 PitchingNinja

 @PitchingNinja, @flatgroundapp

 @pitchingninja

 pitchingninjavideos

ROBBY ROWLAND

WWW.THEROBBYROWSHOW.COM

Robby Rowland's podcasts and social media platforms provide insight into the most current and beneficial technology for hitting and pitching instruction, as well as all-around skill development. Follow his life and career while also enjoying the all-star cast of special guests on his podcast.

f Robby Rowland

O @robbyrow12

y @RobbyRow_12

▶ Robby Rowland

 The Robby Row Show

EUGENE BLEECKER

WWW.108PA.COM

"Bleeck" is one of the game's sharpest minds for hitting and pitching development. His book Old School vs. New School not only dives into the science and biomechanics of hitting and pitching, but also provides an in-depth look at how the game has evolved with the availability of new technology used to measure and compare athletes' statistics. Bleek provides information on the best ways to develop athlete-specific training programs that are catered to each athlete's specific deficiencies. If you don't have the time to read his book, follow him on Twitter for a tremendous amount of credible information with practical content.

f 108 Performance

O @108.performance, @108_pitching

y @THE108WAY, @108_pitching

▶ 108 Performance

TEXAS BASEBALL RANCH

TEXASBASEBALLRANCH.COM

The Texas Baseball Ranch, founded by Ron Wolforth, is a baseball camp that teaches players how to generate velocity, increase arm health and durability, and improve command of all pitches.

 Ron Wolforth's Texas Baseball Ranch   @txbaseballranch

 @TXBaseballRanch   TXBaseballRanch

RECOMMENDED THROWING AND PITCHING LITERATURE

In addition to the resources above, many of the greatest teachers of the game have published books and comprehensive throwing programs worth your time and investment. Let these books accompany this career guide as you continue to improve your understanding of the throwing essentials necessary to give your athlete the edge.

- Hacking the Kinetic Chain – Kyle Boddy
  whosonfirstbook.com/boddy

- Ball Four – Jim Bouton
  whosonfirstbook.com/bouton

- Building the 95MPH Body – Ben Brewster
  whosonfirstbook.com/tread

- The Art and Science of Pitching - Tom House, Gary Heil, and Steve Johnson
  whosonfirstbook.com/tomhouse
- The Complete Guide to Pitching - Derek Johnson
  whosonfirstbook.com/johnson
- The Arm: Inside the Billion-Dollar Mystery of the Most Valuable Commodity in Sports - Jeff Passan
  whosonfirstbook.com/passan
- The Physics of Baseball - Robert Adair
  whosonfirstbook.com/adair

THROWING STUDIES AND ARTICLES

To conclude this chapter, we provide select scientific throwing studies on our website that are beneficial to add to your arsenal of knowledge and tools. While some of these studies are offered free to the public, others require purchase. We can't overemphasize the importance of understanding the balance between developing velocity, proper throwing mechanics, and arm care and injury prevention. To access, please visit our website at: whosonfirstbook.com/research.

HITTING INSIDER

"You can tell a man that his wife is ugly, and he will laugh. But tell him that he doesn't know anything about hitting, and he will want to fight you in the parking lot."

♥ TED WHITMER

INTRODUCTION

It's exciting to start a new construction project but, shouldn't you consult the experts who design buildings instead of following your own lead? You must rely on the blueprints and schematics. If you don't know where the pieces are meant to go, you run the risk of accidentally drilling the wrong holes or making improper connections. This is how we feel about repairing a broken swing. Our goal in this chapter is to provide you with the best information available to assist your athlete with the development of their swing before you attempt a "DIY" without the proper guidance.

OVERVIEW

We are all fans of the game, and probably have been since childhood. However, you may not know as much as you think you do about the art of hitting, especially with the major changes which began to evolve in the early 2000s. The competition will outgrow the athlete if they stay attached to certain patterns they learned in the past. The old formulas are continuously changing and adapting to the new levels of competition.

Hitting a baseball is arguably the most difficult accomplishment in any sport and can be a mentally taxing process. Becoming an elite-level hitter entails properly sequenced movement patterns, a combination of physical attributes including strength, flexibility, bat speed, vision, pitch selection and a well-planned approach at the plate. Optimizing these attributes will put your athlete in a great position to succeed.

 PRO TIPS

1 Your athlete should train at levels more difficult than they face in a game. Hitters who are afraid to fail in the cage with high velocity or high spin batting practice are unprepared for good pitching in a game.

2 Composite bats are meant for warmer climates, generally above 50 degrees Fahrenheit. Alloy or aluminum bats are recommended for playing in cold climates.[99]

Past at-bats against a specific pitcher, game situations, and scouting reports all play major roles in determining what the approach will be for a hitter pitch by pitch. Good hitters make adjustments at-bat to at-bat, but the greatest hitters in the world make adjustments pitch to pitch.

One of the most difficult aspects of training to become an elite-level hitter is the difficulty of simulating live at-bats in practice situations. Pitching machines, while helpful in simulating pitch pressure

> **Good hitters make adjustments at-bat to at-bat, but the greatest hitters in the world make adjustments pitch to pitch.**

and different types of off-speed pitches using spin manipulation, often do not accurately represent the same pressure and environment that a hitter experiences when facing a live arm in a game situation. Thus, training with a specific purpose behind every swing and in every practice-situation becomes even more important to create the best chance at success in games.

BATS AND SIZING

There are new and used bats available in all sizes to accompany your financial budget and the athlete's interest in competition level and quality. Ebay.com, justbats.com, and a number of other new and used bat distributors online or on social media provide adequate options. Unfortunately, bats have a "shelf life" and may break with time and use, which makes it important to know your purchasing options when the time comes.

The term "drop" is the difference between the length of a bat in inches, and the weight of a bat in ounces. Example: a bat 33 inches in length that weighs 30 ounces is a drop 3. Many athletes are capable of swinging a drop 8 by 6th grade and drop 5 for 7th and 8th grades, however, this will depend on the size and strength of each individual. We highly recommend no lighter than a drop 10 in 6th grade, drop 8 in 7th grade, and a drop 5 in 8th grade. This helps provide a smooth transition for the drop 3 requirement in high school and some pre-high school leagues.

💬 **HEADLEY:** *As the owner of Redstitch Baseball Institute (RBI), a premier baseball and softball training organization with facilities across middle and east Tennessee, I am involved in bat sizing conversations with parents on a daily basis. With so many options available, the most important aspect is for* the hitter to choose a bat that they are confident swinging. It is more about the Indian than the arrow.[98]

I provide a chart below of the hitters I coach to give you the range of bat sizes hitters should swing, based on age. Remember that there are always outliers and exceptions, because young athletes grow and mature at different rates.

AGE	LENGTH (IN)	WEIGHT (OZ)
6U	25-27	14-16
7U	26-27	14-17
8U	26-28	16-18
9U	27-30	17-22
10U	28-30	18-22
11U	28-30	18-22
12U	29-31	19-23
13U	29-31	20-28
14U	30-32	22-27
15U	30-33	27-30
16U	30-33	27-30
17U	31-34	28-31
18U	32-34	29-31
COLLEGE	32-34	29-31
PROFESSIONAL	33-34	30-32

Additionally, Louisville Slugger provides a Baseball Bat Guide for sizing, information about the governing bodies' regulation sizes for youth, high school, college, and USSSA, and an FAQ section to answer commonly asked questions. Visit: whosonfirstbook.com/slugger.

ACCESSIBLE HITTING INSTRUCTORS AND RESOURCES

While there are likely experienced baseball instructors in your local area, below are a few of the top instructors in the country. These professionals are leading the charge by providing the highest quality instruction with state-of-the-art technology and understanding of the rapidly evolving game. Their efforts are producing results and manufacturing tomorrow's big leaguers. If you have not heard of these incredible baseball minds through word-of-mouth, research, or personal contact, do your ballplayer's career a favor and get to know who they are and what they teach. Trust us and trust them!

If you are unable to visit one of these instructors or facilities, tell your player to tune in through social media and online outlets to mimic the skills taught by these instructors. Above all, you must remember and understand that the game is constantly changing. Players adapt, new technologies lead to performance improvement, and training techniques constantly evolve. That said, we guarantee that it has changed dramatically since you played youth sports. By following the leads of these baseball experts, you will avoid paying for and developing skills fit for a version of the game that is now a ghost of history.

Absorb the years of experience these experts communicate through their social media platforms. All of it is free. This is the best investment of time you can make before your athlete steps into the practice arena. Utilize social media outlets to access the advice of these elite instructors to correctly mold the way the athlete approaches the art of hitting. The world has changed. Modernize your practice by tuning in to these instructors to make the best use of the athlete's time and development.

DOUG LATTA

WWW.BALLYARD.NET

🐦 @lattadoug   📷 @lattadoug

                                ▶️ Ballyard

DRIVELINE BASEBALL

WWW.DRIVELINEBASEBALL.COM

f Driveline Baseball   📷 @drivelinebaseball

🐦 @drivelinebb   ▶️ Driveline Baseball

JASON FERBER

📷 @coachferber

JASON OCHART

*Minor League Hitting Coordinator for the Philadelphia Phillies and
the Director of Hitting at Driveline Baseball*

🐦 @JasonOchart

ROB BENJAMIN

New York Yankees Baseball Organization

🐦 @riothitting   📷 @riothitting

BASEBALL REBELLION

WWW.BASEBALLREBELLION.COM

Chas Pippitt, Founder

f Baseball Rebellion   **◉** @baseballrebellion

🐦 @BRrebellion   **▶** Baseball Rebellion

CRAIG HYATT

🐦 @HyattCraig   **◉** @hyatt_craig

                        ▶ Craig Hyatt

EUGENE BLEECKER

108PA.COM

f 108 Performance   **◉** @108.performance
                                   @108_pitching

🐦 @THE108WAY   **▶** 108 Performance
     @108_pitching

JOEY CUNHA

WWW.THESYSTEM.FARM

MLB Hitting Consultant, Co-Host & Co-Founder of The Farm System

f The Farm System   **◉** @_joeycunha, @thefarmsyster

🐦 @_joeycunha, @thefarmsystem   **▶** The Farm System

CHAD LONGWORTH

WWW.CHADLONGWORTHONLINE.COM

f Chad Longworth

○ @clongbaseball

𝕏 @clongbaseball

▶ Chad Longworth

NATE HEADLEY

WWW.RBIHFA.COM

f Nate Headley

○ @nheadley14

𝕏 @nheadley14

CARLTON SALTERS

WWW.CARLTONSALTERS.WORDPRESS.COM

f Carlton Salters

○ @coachsalt

𝕏 @CoachCSalt

▶ Carlton Salters

ZBI

WWW.ZONABASEBALL.ORG

Trent Otis, Founder

f Zona Baseball

○ @zona_baseball_instruction

𝕏 @Zona_Baseball

▶ Trent Otis

JEFF LEACH
WWW.HITFORTH.COM

f Hitforth

Instagram @coachjeffleach, @hitforth

Twitter @coachjeffleach, @hitforth

YouTube Hitforth

BOBBY TEWKSBARY
WWW.TEWKSHITTING.COM

f Tewksbary Hitting

Instagram @tewkshitting

Twitter @TewksHitting

YouTube TewksHitting

EUGENE BLEECKER
108PA.COM

f 108 Performance

Instagram @108.performance
@108_pitching

Twitter @THE108WAY
@108_pitching

YouTube 108 Performance

ENGLISHBEY PERFORMANCE
WWW.ENGLISHBEYHITTING.COM

Steve Englishbey, Former first-round draft pick

f Englishbey Hitting

Instagram @senglishbeyperformance

Twitter @SteveEnglishbey

YouTube Englishbey Hitting

CASEY SMITH
WWW.OUTFRONTHITTING.COM

f Out Front Hitting

🐦 @outfronthitting

⊙ @outfronthitting

NATE HEADLEY
WWW.RBIHFA.COM

f Nate Headley

🐦 @nheadley14

⊙ @nheadley14

STANCE DOCTOR
WWW.STANCESWINGS.COM

f Stance Doctor Baseball &
Softball Academy

🐦 @StanceDoctor

⊙ @stancedoctor

▶ Stance Doctor

DO DAMAGE HITTING

Hunter Mense Minor League Hitting Coordinator, Toronto Bluejays

⊙ @dodamagehitting

HIPRO HITTING

WWW.HIPROHITTING.COM

f HiPro Hitting   **◎** @hiprohitting

𝕏 @HiProHitting   **▶** HiPro Hitting

THE HIT LAB LLC

WWW.THEHITLABTN.COM

Joey Lewis, Founder

f The Hit Lab   **◎** @thehitlabllc

𝕏 @TheHitLabLLC

FULLER HITTING

WWW.FULLERHITTING.COM

Ryan Fuller, Founder, Minor League Hitting Coach, Baltimore Orioles

f Fuller Hitting   **◎** @fullerhitting

𝕏 @FullerHitting   **▶** Fuller Hitting

CATALYST SPORTS LLC

WWW.GOCATALYSTSPORTS.COM

f Catalyst Sports   **◎** @gocatalystsports

LINE DRIVE PRO

Tim Gibbons, Founder, Minor League hitting coach, Baltimore Orioles

f LineDrivePro Baseball   **◎** @linedrivepro

𝕏 @LineDrivePro

BRAD MARCELINO

f Coach Marcelino   **◎** @marcelinobaseball

𝕏 @CoachMarcelino

YOUGOPROBASEBALL

WWW.YOUGOPROBASEBALL.COM

John Madden, Founder

f Yougoprobaseball.com   **◎** @yougoprobaseball

𝕏 @yougopro   **▶** YouGoProBaseball

PODCASTS

If you are unfamiliar with podcasts, they are akin to the "radio shows" of years past. Fan engagement and reviews dictate a podcast's success without the need of large corporate funding. Podcasts are a great and convenient way to tune-in from your mobile device. For the purposes of this book, we recommend these podcasts for road trips, to and from practice, or simply for the athlete's free time.

AHEAD OF THE CURVE PODCAST

WWW.AOTCPODCAST.COM

Hosted by Jonathan Gelnar

 AOTC_Podcast

GOING YARD PODCAST

WWW.GOINGYARDPODCAST.COM

 @GYPodcast   @goingyardpodcast

DUGOUT CHATTER PODCAST

POWERED BY STICK & BALL TV

Jeremy Sheetinger, Host

 @DugoutChatter_

HITTING LITERATURE

For a deep dive into hitting, these are our favorite books:

OLD SCHOOL VS. NEW SCHOOL - *Eugene Bleecker*

whosonfirstbook.com/oldnew

THE SCIENCE OF HITTING - *Ted Williams*

whosonfirstbook.com/ted

HITTING BIOMECHANICS - *Bob Keyes*

whosonfirstbook.com/keyes

THE CATAPULT LOADING SYSTEM - *Joey Meyers*

whosonfirstbook.com/meyers

ELITE SWING MECHANICS - *Bobby Tewksbary*

whosonfirstbook.com/tewkshitting

HITTING STUDIES AND RESEARCH ARTICLES

The following studies on hitting contain scientific research that will educate and lead your athlete to a better overall understanding of kinematic sequencing and biomechanics, vision training, and bat speed velocity.

RSO ROTATIONAL STRENGTH ON ANGULAR HIP, ANGULAR
SHOULDER, AND LINEAR BAT VELOCITIES OF HIGH
SCHOOL BASEBALL PLAYERS
whosonfirstbook.com/torso

"HITTING A BASEBALL: A BIOMECHANICAL DESCRIPTION"
whosonfirstbook.com/biomechanics

"CONTRIBUTING FACTORS FOR INCREASED BAT SWING
VELOCITY"
whosonfirstbook.com/batspeed

When researching social media, articles, and other online
development resources, apply the buffet line rule. Choose the right
courses for a complete meal to nourish your swing and keep it as
healthy as possible. It is okay to try something new on occasion but
always consume a full helping of what keeps you at your best. Try
different offerings from time to time, and understand that you may
keep what works and discard the rest.

PART THREE

PERFORMANCE AND WELLNESS

INTRODUCTION

Distinct from mechanical training and skill development, there are many ways to maximize an athlete's performance and overall wellness to improve on and off the field. At the conclusion of Part III, you will be able to:

1 Understand and implement optimal nutrition programs;

2 Research and adopt workout and training regimens that are most beneficial for your athlete's baseball strength and conditioning development;

3 Understand the best psychological tools and practices for enhanced information processing to develop and maintain your athlete's mental edge;

4 Understand common baseball injuries and how your athlete can prevent and/or manage them;

5 Return your athlete from injury or surgery through proper rehabilitation and recovery techniques; and,

6 Utilize the latest performance aides to boost performance, enhance body awareness, and improve overall athletic development in your athlete.

As we dive deeper into each category, ask yourself:

1 where can my athlete improve; and

2 where do they already have the best opportunity to succeed?

The more you utilize this performance and wellness information, the more likely your athlete's career will be successful in both the short- and long-term.

Medical advice should be evaluated on an individual basis. The content in this book should never be used as a substitute for direct medical advice from your doctor or other qualified clinician.

NUTRITION, FUELING
THE FIRE

————

"What a player puts in their body is shown in their overall health and performance."

♥ DANNY LEHMANN, WORLD SERIES CHAMPION MLB COACH

"Let thy food be thy medicine."

♥ HIPPOCRATES, 460-375 B.C.E.

INTRODUCTION

In this chapter, we collaborated with Taylor Stolt, RDN plateandcanvas.com, and Jenna Waters, RDN JennaWaters.com, two of the most competent and passionate registered dietician nutritionists in their fields, about the fundamentals of nutrition specifically related to athletic performance and recovery.

It is important to note that the opinions and recommendations contained herein should not serve as a substitute for professional medical advice. While there are general guidelines and proven methods for a nutritional approach to performance improvement and recovery, they do not take into account necessary individual adjustments prescribed in a clinical setting. Individual nutritional recommendations vary widely. Therefore, view this information generally as an educational approach and cornerstone to guide the research of your individual nutritional needs.

INITIAL ADVICE

There is a direct link between nutrition and longevity, injury prevention, performance, recovery, attitude, and overall health. Our desire, from a baseball perspective, is to provide the necessary information on how to prime your athlete for peak performance and recover from the demands of the sport. Nutrition is a critical, foundational component for every swing your athlete takes and every game they play. In fact, "It is the position of the American College of Sports Medicine that physical activity, athletic performance, and recovery from exercise are enhanced by optimal nutrition."[100]

We must treat an athlete's fitness and nutrition habits as seriously as we do their performance and our desire to facilitate their success. Investing in the health, performance, recovery, and wellness of your athlete's body is just as important as skill development and the mental aspects of the game. They go hand in hand. Without proper nutrition, the athlete has a comparable disadvantage to playing with outdated gear or training in an unfocused environment. If the athlete is not improving every aspect of their game, they might as well not care about the results.

Talent will only take an athlete so far, and there is less room for failure at each successive level. Sometimes, even the best performances do not turn out as planned. Nutrition is one of the few

> Investing in the health, performance, recovery, and wellness of your athlete's body is just as important as skill development and the mental aspects of the game.

variables we, as athletes, have within our control. Regardless of your athlete's career accomplishments or longevity in the game, attention to proper nutrition is critical. The benefits, both mind and body, will continue paying dividends even after their athletic career is over.

ADVANCES IN SPORT NUTRITION

American football, with its wide array of financial resources, is light years ahead of other sports when it comes to practicing proper nutrition. In football, recent years have produced an astounding level of athleticism and speed of play. It is well known that this increase in performance is directly linked to proper nutrition, weight lifting, and conditioning. There is an ever-increasing demand on elite athletes to constantly evolve to keep up with the competition.

Collegiate and professional baseball have only recently begun to capitalize upon the effectiveness of sport-specific nutrition. In the short amount of time since this realization, baseball has seen tangible effects in throwing velocity, running speed, endurance, bat speed, exit velocity, and overall performance.

In addition to the workout-recovery supplements provided by many college and professional teams, pre- and post-game meals are becoming commonplace collegiately and are available for purchase in the clubhouse by players in professional baseball. Collegiate and professional teams are also beginning to hire full-time dietician nutritionists to counsel athletes on optimal nutrition for training, competition, recovery, hydration, and more. Because nutrition is finally receiving the attention it deserves in the world of professional athletics, athletes are sleeping better, recovering more efficiently, and gaining strength and speed thanks to the "all in" approach of the comprehensive nutrition, and strength and conditioning programs.

FUELING THE ATHLETE

The three principal macronutrients ("macros") in food are: protein, carbohydrates, and fats (triglycerides). We will break down each macronutrient group for a better understanding of the dietary purposes and functions for each.

PROTEIN

The tissues in the human body are made up of proteins, i.e., amino acids. Proteins are essential for facilitating muscle repair, muscle remodeling, and immune system responses. To maximize muscle building and recovery (anabolism) and stimulate muscle protein synthesis, athletes should consume 0.4 grams of high-quality protein per kilogram of body weight with each meal.[101] No food scale? No problem. As a good rule of thumb, this is the equivalent of a meat or fish serving slightly larger than the palm of your hand.

However, each athlete is different. There are more individualized approaches to calculating the amount of protein an athlete needs to consume to maximize muscle development. For example, an athlete focused on optimal exercise performance and recovery can divide their weight (in pounds) by 2.2 (to convert pounds to kilograms), then multiply by 1.6 to calculate the exact amount of protein recommended for daily anabolism.[102]

For athletes focused on fat loss while maintaining muscle mass, or athletes who are undergoing periods of high frequency and/or high intensity training, protein consumption as high as 1.8-2.0 grams per kilogram body weight may be necessary. In addition to an individualized dietary regimen, high-quality protein and composition of meals will greatly influence athletic development.

Studies show that athletes are able to obtain necessary amounts of protein through meals alone. However, supplementing diet with protein shakes or protein-centric snacks is an easy way to ensure adequate protein consumption. This is especially true during travel and competition season. We also provide a "Protein Powder Guide," and several high-quality protein sources and total protein content with regard to serving size in our "Protein Content of Foods" on our website at: whosonfirstbook.com/extra-innings/. Ultimately, a balanced diet requires many protein sources, and many sources are equally beneficial for strength and mass gains.

CARBOHYDRATES

Carbohydrates support both the nervous system and muscles. The current research supports that the majority of daily calories for athletes should come from carbohydrates, although this concept is challenged with strong scientific evidence by proponents of a ketogenic diet, which we will address. Carbs are essential for priming the body for high output performance and recovery. For athletes, daily carbohydrate recommendations range from 6-10/grams per kilogram of body weight. This amount of carbohydrates maintains blood glucose levels during exercise and replaces muscle glycogen both during and after exercise to optimize recovery.[103]

For athletes undergoing periods of high intensity training and/ or long duration exercise, it is especially important to pay attention to carbohydrate intake. For sustained (45-75 minutes) high intensity exercise, small amounts of carbohydrates can stimulate parts of the brain and central nervous system to increase work output. A lightly sweetened sports drink like Pedialyte is a good option in this case.

During endurance exercise, including "stop and start" sports, 30-60 grams of carbohydrates per hour is recommended. During ultra-endurance exercise (>2.5 hours) up to 90 grams per hour is recommended. Sports fuel products that contain both glucose and fructose achieve especially high oxidation levels, which is helpful for quick fuel. When recovery time between workouts is limited (<8 hours), an athlete should consume 1-1.2 grams per kilogram of body weight each hour for 4 hours after their first workout, then resume daily fuel needs until the next workout. It is important to note, well-balanced meals generally provide adequate carbohydrate intake for low-to-moderate-intensity exercise, or when there is ample recovery time between games or exercise events.

An athlete's diet should mainly consist of unprocessed, nutrient-dense carbohydrates such as sweet potatoes, butternut squash, quinoa, lentils, beans, oats, brown rice, and fruit. This will optimize nutrient intake and positively impact recovery and performance.

FAT (TRIGLYCERIDES)

Fats get a bad rap. Generally speaking, public misinformation has led us to believe that consuming any type of "fat" contributes to increases in body fat. In reality, fats are essential for hormone production, nutrient absorption, blood sugar regulation, and body temperature maintenance. In many cases, body fat increases are actually due to the consumption of sugar and refined carbohydrates.

Athletes should consume a high amount of healthy fats to supplement energy needs and assist with the metabolic demands of elite athletic performance. Healthy fats improve the body's ability to fight inflammation and improve performance.[104] Examples include avocados, seeds, nuts, nut butters, medium chain triglyceride (MCT) oil,[105] avocado oil, olive oil, coconut oil, and minimally processed meats, fish, and dairy products.

Unhealthy fats, i.e., those found in fried foods or inflammatory oils such as canola oil, palm oil, and soybean oil should be avoided at all costs. These types of fats will not only negatively impact athletic performance now, but they are linked to long-term health consequences and chronic disease.

Both Omega-3 and Omega-6 fatty acids are critical to minimize inflammation, support brain, liver, heart and bone health, support blood sugar balance, and optimize both exercise performance and recovery. But we're eating more omega-6's than ever before and our omega-3 intake is dangerously low. Medical professionals recommend a ratio of between 1:1 and 4:1 omega-6's to omega-3's, and most Americans consume a ratio of 20:1. Not good!

A great way to increase the ratio of Omega-3 to Omega-6 fatty acids is by regular consumption of fish such as salmon, barramundi, mackerel, herring, sardines, and anchovies. These all contain high amounts of Omega-3 fatty acids and low levels of mercury. If regular fish consumption is not feasible, try to supplement your athlete's diet with high-quality fish oil that contains both DHA and EPA.

Comprehensive nutrition is a key component for athletic success.

MAKING THE CONNECTION

"Proper nutrition promotes muscle regeneration, glycogen restoration, reduces fatigue, and supports physical and immune health, which helps the athlete prepare for the next competition or training session throughout the duration of a season."[106] All athletes should adopt a nutrient-dense diet with adequate caloric intake to create the energy needed to fuel the demands of a sport. But bear in mind, all calories are NOT created equally. Individual athletes will process calories differently based upon their unique physiological needs.

Three of the largest determinants of athletic performance and recovery are:

1 the sources of the proteins, fats, and carbohydrates we ingest;

2 when we ingest them; and

3 how often we eat.

The proper macronutrient ratios of carbohydrates, proteins, and fats ultimately depend on which method provides the best energy needs and performance outcome for each individual athlete. However, a few of the most popular diets for athletes that endorse varying macro ratios include:

ZONE DIET – This diet is focused on minimizing diet-induced inflammation and optimizing insulin levels. This can help to diminish undesirable weight gain, sickness, and premature aging, which results in efficient loss of excess body fat, long-term wellness, better performance, and optimal cognitive function. The Zone Diet recommends a balanced plate with 1/3 of the plate coming from a protein source, 2/3 from colorful vegetables and a small amount of fruit, and the remainder of calories from a small amount of monounsaturated fat such as olive oil, avocados, or seeds.[107] The basic rules are:

- Eat a meal or snack within 1 hour of waking up in the morning.

- Start each meal or snack with a low-fat protein, followed by foods containing healthful carbs and fats.

- Eat small, frequent meals during the day, every 4–6 hours after a meal or 2–2.5 hours after a snack, whether hungry or not.

- Consume plenty of Omega-3 and polyphenols.

- Drink at least eight 8-ounce glasses of water a day.[108]

KETOGENIC DIET – Growing in popularity, this low-carb diet commonly referred to as "Keto," consists of virtually no carbohydrates and instead relies on high fat and moderate protein intake for fuel. A low-carb diet often results in weight loss and improved blood sugar levels, cholesterol, triglycerides, and blood pressure.[109]

Before allowing your athlete to undergo a low-carb diet, we strongly suggest obtaining advice from a licensed physician or dietician nutritionist to ensure that proper caloric and nutritional needs are met. That said, there is growing research to support this type of diet for athletes, when keto-adaptation is managed properly. This may be especially true for baseball players, who frequently undergo short bouts of high intensity activity, such as swinging or throwing, and are less frequently stressed over long durations without frequent recovery periods.

When the body is in ketosis, the liver converts stored body fat and ingested fat into ketones, and ketones are released into the bloodstream.[110] Ketones become a viable energy source [with fat as the largest available stored energy source of more than 20X that of carbohydrate storage] for the brain and body, rather than carbohydrates and glycogen as the primary energy source. Furthermore, keto-adapted athletes experience improvements in insulin sensitivity, overall fatigue, and lactate metabolism.[111] Benefits of a ketogenic diet include:

- extended energy and avoidance of "sugar crashes" or need for carbohydrate intake for energy
- benefits against cancer, diabetes, epilepsy, and Alzheimer's disease
- body fat reduction
- decreased hunger pains

A MAJORITY OF MEALS SHOULD REVOLVE AROUND THESE FOODS:

- meat: red meat, steak, ham, sausage, bacon, chicken, and turkey
- fatty fish: salmon, trout, tuna, and mackerel
- eggs: pastured or Omega-3 whole eggs
- butter and cream: grass-fed butter and heavy cream
- cheese: unprocessed cheeses like cheddar, goat, cream, blue, or mozzarella
- nuts and seeds: almonds, walnuts, flaxseeds, pumpkin seeds, chia seeds, etc.
- healthy oils: extra-virgin olive oil, coconut oil, and avocado oil
- avocados: whole avocados or freshly made guacamole
- low carb veggies: green veggies, tomatoes, onions, peppers, etc.
- condiments: salt, pepper, herbs, and spices

FOODS TO AVOID INCLUDE:

- sugary foods: soda, fruit juice, smoothies, cake, ice cream, candy, etc.
- grains or starches: wheat-based products, rice, pasta, cereal, etc.

- fruit: all fruit, except small portions of berries

- beans or legumes: peas, kidney beans, lentils, chickpeas, etc.

- root vegetables and tubers: potatoes, sweet potatoes, carrots, parsnips, etc.

- low fat or diet products: low fat mayonnaise, salad dressings, and condiments

- some condiments or sauces: barbecue sauce, honey mustard, teriyaki sauce, ketchup, etc.

- unhealthy fats: processed vegetable oils, mayonnaise, etc.

- alcohol: beer, wine, liquor, mixed drinks

- sugar-free diet foods: sugar-free candies, syrups, puddings, sweeteners, desserts, etc.[112]

40/30/30 DIET - This diet is the most effective and predictable way for athletes to reach their training, performance, and recovery goals. It is best for the majority of athletes who do not have dedicated personal nutritionists or are not adequately educated to monitor their personal fuel intake needs. The target 40/30/30 macronutrient approach means that 40 percent of an athlete's diet should come from carbohydrates, 30 percent from protein, and 30 percent from fats.

To assist with practical implementation, we have included a calorie calculator, courtesy of Jenna Waters here: whosonfirstbook. com/calories. This interactive tool allows your athlete to enter individual variables to generate an accurate caloric intake estimate, based on their training goals. Not only does the Personalized Nutrition Report indicate the total recommended calories, it also provides a breakdown of each of the three macro groups (in grams) and water (in ounces) that should be consumed on a daily basis for proper nutrition and hydration.

Remember, baseball has long seasons replete with many games requiring repetitive, explosive, and powerful movements. For optimum recovery, an athlete must replenish their glycogen stores within the first hour following a workout or practice. Accordingly, it is a beneficial practice to bridge the gap between practice/training and dinnertime with a snack rich in protein and carbohydrates.

There are many macronutrient tracking apps available that are useful tools to indicate where an athlete's macro intake is incomplete, and provide information regarding the proper nutrition necessary to meet their needs. Our favorite macronutrient tracking app is My Fitness Pal: www.myfitnesspal.com/.

DIGESTING THE INFORMATION

If you have never encountered this information before, it may seem overwhelming. A great place to start when developing a nutritional plan is to focus on the produce section at the grocery store. This section contains the greatest number of unprocessed foods in their natural state. It may come as a surprise that most foods on the store shelves contain only a select few ingredients: corn, sugar, wheat, soy, and their processed derivatives.

The norm is to bypass whole foods directly from the earth and fill our pantries with processed, "cheap" foods. These highly-marketed foods lack vital nutrients necessary for overall wellness, disease prevention, and peak cognitive and physical performance. Remember, large quantities of empty calories typically do not result in healthy weight gain just as caloric restriction is not always the best path to healthy weight loss. "Empty calories are those that provide energy but very little nutritional value. The parts of food that provide empty calories contain virtually no dietary fiber, amino acids, antioxidants, dietary minerals, or vitamins."[113]

Be realistic with your athlete about where they are with their nutrition. In the current political

> For optimum recovery, an athlete must replenish their glycogen stores within the first hour following a workout or practice.

climate, a coach walks a fine line when discussing a player's outward appearance and diet. However, as a parent, you are in a beneficial position to strategically plan for your athlete's future in a positive way. Follow the experts and feed your athlete accordingly to instill positive habits that will persist years after baseball has finished.

MEAL TIME

We understand how difficult it is to plan several proper meals each day. It is easier and more convenient to go to a restaurant and simply eat what tastes good.

To assist in your grocery shopping and meal choices, we included a grocery list of nutritious foods on our website at: whosonfirstbook. com/extrainnings that should make up the majority of your pantry and refrigerator/freezer. By committing to utilize these foods in replacement of other options, regardless of culture or family tradition, you give your athlete the best opportunity to succeed and to promote a healthy lifestyle.

At the above website, we also provide an example of a common popular meal that utilizes nutritious substitutes to increase the overall benefit without sacrificing taste, macronutrient content, or satisfaction. Allow this excellent recipe to inspire you - take your favorite dishes and modify them with healthier ingredients while maintaining, or even improving, taste and quality.

Nutrition should adequately accommodate energy expenditure needs. Minor adjustments may be necessary depending on whether you are feeding your athlete after light, moderate, or intense training and/or competition days. Players have different total energy requirements that may vary by position, number and length of games in a day, whether the athlete participated in strength and conditioning training, and the unique physiological demands.

To assist in building a plate with your pantry and refrigerator/ freezer full of excellent choices, we provide examples of complete meals for different energy expenditure and recovery demands available at: whosonfirstbook.com/extrainnings.

MEAL TIMING

Remember these important considerations when choosing meals or snacks before practice or competition:

1 Fluids, fluids, and more fluids.

2 Fats and fibers tend to lead to bloating. By selecting foods relatively low in fat and fiber, the athlete will facilitate gastric emptying to avoid gastric distress.

3 Select foods relatively high in carbohydrates to maximize blood glucose maintenance which will satisfy the body's short-term energy needs.

4 Select foods with moderate protein levels.

5 Opt for familiar foods. This is not the time for experimentation.

6 Keep your athlete in mind. Some individuals will tolerate certain foods better than others.

HYDRATION AND REHYDRATION

Don't forget to provide plenty of water! Adequate hydration is key to performance long before the first pitch. Proper hydration begins 24-48 hours before any type of physical activity. Dehydration affects explosive physical movements, as well as endurance, cognitive processing, and recovery after exercise. Dehydration results in increased muscle tension, which increases your athlete's risk for muscle sprains, muscle tears, and bone fracture.

Dehydration also increases the risk of heat exhaustion, which can lead to a life-threatening heatstroke and cause permanent damage to the brain and other vital organs. Athletes should consume 16-24 ounces of fluid per every pound of body weight lost during exercise to avoid dehydration. There are many sugary beverage options available to replace fluid loss, such as Gatorade, which can replenish muscle glycogen and electrolytes during intense exercise for adequate hydration. However, there are plenty of lower sugar fluids, such as unflavored Pedialyte or coconut water, which are typically preferable on non-competition days.

An athlete can perform a "urine check" to determine their body's hydration level at any given point in time. The hydration chart available here: whosonfirstbook.com/hydration is commonly posted in locker room bathrooms and provides a urine color to hydration comparison. Clear urine (or close to it) is the best indicator of adequate hydration prior to competition or performance. This also occurs after mealtime, which is a sign the body is utilizing greater amounts of water, and that it is time to consume more fluids. Beware that overconsumption of water resulting in clear urine and frequent urination could result in electrolyte dilution. Stick to the chart!

Proper hydration begins 24-48 hours before any type of physical activity.

BODY COMPOSITION

As your athlete advances in their career, they will be exposed to body composition testing, which provides measurements of total body tissue composition for baseline testing. This allows the athlete to evaluate changes over time. Body composition measurements can indicate nutrient deficiencies and provide markers for nutritional goal setting to reach targeted body tissue composition, such as increasing lean muscle mass and/or decreasing total body fat. This scientific field is vast and heavily-researched, therefore, we will narrow the focus to the testing methods that are the most common and accurate for baseball athletes.

METHODS OF TESTING

DUAL-ENERGY X-RAY ABSORPTIOMETRY (DEXA) - This is the most precise and comprehensive body scan available. It utilizes X-ray absorptiometry to determine bone mineral density, total body fat percentage, total fat mass, and total fat-free mass in regional areas (trunk, arms, legs, pelvis) and the entire body.[114]

WHOLE BODY PLETHYSMOGRAPHY (BOD POD) - This is considered the gold standard for fast, accurate, and repeatable body fat assessments. The Bod Pod uses air displacement plethysmography to determine body composition. Additionally, "this method also eliminates the invasiveness of Dual Energy X-Ray Absorptiometry (DEXA) and is therefore suitable for frequent, longitudinal tracking of body composition and metabolic changes over time."[115] The subject is required to fast for 2 hours prior to testing inside the Bodpod chamber.

SKINFOLD CALIPERS - This is one of the most accessible and affordable methods for determining body composition. The target measurement areas are: triceps, shoulder blade, above the top of the pelvis, abdomen and calves. The test administrator pinches the skin, and holds firmly while the measurement device measures the thickness of the skin fold.[116]

HYDRODENSITOMETRY (UNDERWATER WEIGHING) - Body volume, density, and fat mass vs. fat free mass are accurately determined by comparing normal body weight to body weight while completely submerged in water. The subject remains motionless, expels all air from the lungs while submerged, and repeats the process several times to ensure accurate measurements.[117]

LET'S TALK SUPPLEMENTS

A supplement is "a food, food component, nutrient, or non-food compound that is purposefully ingested in addition to the habitually consumed diet with the aim of achieving a specific health and/or performance benefit."[118] The most common supplements take the form of macronutrient-[119] or micronutrient-enriched foods. Foods that are rich in micronutrients take many forms. They can be: **1** specifically formulated for nutritional support before, during, or after exercise; **2** isolated or concentrated single nutrients; or, **3** multi-ingredient products intended to address a specific issue, such as:

- Managing nutrition deficiencies;

- Supplying convenient, short-term energy;

- Directly improving performance; and/or

- Indirectly supporting intense training or recovery by increasing specific nutrient concentration in the body.

Supplements are also a beneficial substitute when time or location constraints render mealtime impractical. Common examples include during long tournaments, double- or triple-headers, or travel competition. There are many situations that can result in an inability to store or consume nutrient-dense, well-balanced meals. Whether we like it or not, convenience is often the name of the game.

Before ingesting any supplement that is not part of a balanced diet, we recommend a complete nutritional assessment by a licensed professional. You should also perform a careful cost-benefit analysis to determine whether the benefit is worth the expense. These methods of analysis will protect your athlete and your wallet. Many dietary supplements on the market are no more effective than a well-balanced diet.

Surprisingly, in the multi-billion-dollar supplement industry, there are only a few legal, isolated single-nutrient supplements that actually enhance athletic performance. We have listed these below. You should only consider purchasing these supplements if it is safe, legal and effective to introduce them into your athlete's diet. When consuming dietary supplements, we recommend choosing products that have a third-party testing verification label, such as NSF, to verify that the products are not contaminated. This is because the FDA does not require supplements to undergo the same quality testing procedures as other foods. Supplements contaminated with banned substances could cost an athlete their career. To ensure safety and optimal results, please consult a licensed physician or registered dietitian to discuss dosage and/or whether supplements are right for your athlete.

- CAFFEINE - A stimulant beneficial for endurance or short workouts. Caffeine increases alertness, stamina, and endurance. When consuming a low-moderate dose, pair with fluids and a carbohydrate. High doses are linked to negative side effects such as nausea, restlessness, anxiety, and insomnia.

- PROTEIN - Protein supports increases in lean muscle mass when consumed in conjunction with resistance training due to the presence of amino acids, i.e., the building blocks of muscle tissue. For individuals who can properly digest whey protein, the amino acid leucine triggers a rise in muscle protein synthesis and suppresses muscle protein breakdown. Generally speaking, the body typically absorbs whey protein faster than other protein sources, making it the most beneficial for fast recovery and increased muscle protein synthesis. In addition to retention of lean mass, whey protein also encourages the loss of unhealthy bodily fat. However, individuals suffering from autoimmune disease, gut issues, or dairy-intolerance should consult their physicians before consuming whey protein. Alternative options include collagen protein, egg white protein, and plant-based protein powders. *We have included a Protein Powder Guide as a reference for high quality protein sources and alternative options to whey protein for individuals with dietary restrictions or different preferences, available at: whosonfirstbook.com/extrainnings.

- NITRATE - High nitrate levels are beneficial for longer duration exercise below maximum intensity and the ability to perform repeated bouts of high intensity effort. These foods are high in nitrates: leafy greens, root vegetables, celery, and beetroot.

- SODIUM BICARBONATE - This supplement enhances extracellular buffering capacity to potentially provide benefits for sustained high intensity exercise performance, which means the ability of a cell to perform more efficiently. Please note that this supplement may cause gastric distress.

- CREATINE MONOHYDRATE - Creatine can result in acute increases in performance by facilitating greater gains in lean mass, muscular strength, raw power, and enhanced adaptive response and recovery to exercise.

- VITAMIN D - This vitamin is an essential nutrient known to influence many aspects of mood stability, as well as electrolyte metabolism, immunity, nerve, bone, muscle, and cell function. Vitamin D supplementation is especially beneficial during winter months to combat low levels of available sunlight. Vitamin D is a fat-soluble vitamin, which means it is stored in fat tissue and can accumulate over time – it is important to get vitamin D levels tested on a regular basis (annually or biannually) to avoid vitamin D toxicity. Research suggests vitamin D levels of at least 40 ng/mL should be maintained for optimal performance, and the Vitamin D Council suggests maintaining levels between 50 and 80 ng/mL for overall optimal health.

- OMEGA-3 FATTY ACIDS - These types of fatty acids improve cognitive processing, reduce delayed onset muscle soreness, and increase muscle protein synthesis. Consumption will also decrease inflammation by improving the ratio of Omega-3 to Omega-6 fatty acids in the body.

NSF International Certified for Sport has a comprehensive database of unharmful and approved supplements available here: whosonfirstbook.com/nsf. Purchasing supplements that have been independently tested and approved will ensure no harmful effects to your athlete's body or to their career due to a failed drug test.

You can order supplements that are NSF Certified for Sport here: whosonfirstbook.com/thorne. Thorne produces safe and effective supplements, with the largest number of pre-screened NSF Certified for Sport products on the market.

The NCAA and MLB both have banned substances lists to prevent confusion on which substances may result in suspensions and other consequences. Be aware that these lists are continually evolving and changing with the introduction of new information. Your safest bet is to rely upon your organization's approved substances lists to avoid potential consequences. The banned substances lists for the NCAA and MLB are available here:

- whosonfirstbook.com/substances
- whosonfirstbook.com/prohibited

Finally, for your reference, we have included a link to the complete Joint Drug Prevention and Treatment Program for Major League Baseball. This program governs all MLB-affiliated baseball players. Available here: whosonfirstbook.com/prevention.

STRENGTH AND CONDITIONING

"Adapting to a true performance lifestyle isn't about what you do during the 1-2 hours of strength training, it's about what you do during the remaining 22-23 hours away from the gym."

♥ HERMAN DEMMINK III, M.S. BIOMECHANICS, RSCC-D*, CSCS, USAW, CROSSFIT L-2

INTRODUCTION

This chapter was written in direct collaboration with one of the most knowledgeable and talented strength & conditioning coaches in the country. Herman is a former NCAA Division I and professional athlete. He is the owner of 3D Performance Training and holds his Master's degree in Biomechanics from the University of Tennessee. As a former TEAM USA Sports Performance Director (Baseball), he also holds a Registered Strength and Conditioning Coach with 15-year Distinction (RSCC*D) honor as one of the premier performance coaches in the country. With Herman's background and expertise in overhead athletes and baseball specific conditioning, there is no more valuable contribution to your athlete's future than from the knowledge and insight he shares in this chapter.

BEFORE WE BEGIN

Hear this: strength and conditioning will facilitate gains in strength, speed, agility, flexibility, and explosiveness, improve skills on the field, and maintain optimum levels of health. Consider an example of a ballplayer who must sit out due to injury during training or practice. In this scenario, the player's personal opportunity and their value to the team will plummet. This is mainly due to two things: **1** the injury itself; and **2** for every injured player, there are a handful of able-bodied replacements fighting for the open spot on the roster.

Injury-prone players, or those with less versatility, will not have the same opportunities year after year. For career longevity, an athlete must maximize their playing time to create the biggest impact on the team. Simply put, you can't make the club in the tub.

Further, training should always be for the purpose of improving baseball-playing ability. It is important to remember that baseball is a power sport that is played within a marathon season. We must not sacrifice the precious time it takes to learn how to backhand ground balls, improve feeds, long toss, practice blocking, or watch and absorb baseball only to set a new squat record at the gym or risk injury by maxing out on an Olympic lift. Baseball is a game of averages, rather than striving for personal bests or setting Olympic records. Using recommendations that follow, ensure your athlete's strength and conditioning workouts are improving baseball-related skills while decreasing risk of injury. This will build a better athlete.

Baseball success is largely determined by on the field production from a combination of a player's mental savvy, physical ability, and situational adaptability. The greatest players

Simply put, you can't make the club in the tub.

have the ability to make adjustments, remain healthy, and contribute situationally in a specific set of skills. Comparatively, sports such as football, powerlifting, or track and field rely more heavily on pure strength output or aerobic capacity. However, baseball success is dependent on refined skill paired with athletic measures that can be enhanced by strength and conditioning.

This is the reason that some of the most impressive looking players in a uniform never make it to the highest level. It is also why coaches, college scouts, and pro scouts must watch a player play the game before making a decision on their potential. Obviously, excellent physical appearance never hurts anyone; physical prowess always draws eyes and creates opportunity. Nevertheless, unique to skill sports based on statistics such as baseball, strength and conditioning is only a supplement to success on the field, rather than a guarantee. The most important takeaway is this: remember that strength training should be used as a tool, not relied on as the measuring stick for success on the field.

BASEBALL STRENGTH AND CONDITIONING

Strength and conditioning is the repetitive commitment to preparing the cardiovascular and muscular systems for increases in heart rate and power output, waste product eradication/metabolism, and movement demands of the sport through targeted exercise. Depending on your athlete's position or role on the team, strength and conditioning needs may vary in importance or specificity.

We reject the belief and practice that baseball players should be conditioned like cross country runners. Even though team practice requires athletes to be on their feet for extended periods of time (pitcher fielding practice "PFPs," pick-offs, run-downs, and other defensive work), baseball strength and conditioning should predominantly be improved by sprints and repeated explosive power-based activities, which will be covered in this chapter.

Although research has shown that periodic low intensity aerobic exercise of 20-30 minutes can increase oxygen and nutrient delivery to tissue; this type of training should be sparingly used for baseball athletes. The best way to describe the metabolic demands of a baseball athlete is a collection of power activities performed over a marathon season.

PROGRAM DESIGN

The goal of strength and conditioning programs is to improve and enhance specific abilities and career longevity. Unlike Olympic lifting or powerlifting, strength and conditioning for baseball is meant to improve results on the field and career longevity. A ballplayer's efforts should be dedicated to improving skeletal tissue quality and training explosive movements that improve every aspect of their game, while minimizing injury susceptibility.

There are three main considerations when designing a strength and conditioning program for your athlete:

1 MOVEMENT QUALITY AND TECHNICAL EFFICIENCY -

Movements must be performed properly and with the purpose of generating maximum power, with as little wasted effort or movement as possible. This will limit injury risk and promote strength gains.

2 CHRONOLOGICAL AGE AND TRAINING AGE - Chronological age is the age indicated by an athlete's birth certificate. Whereas, training age is how many years your athlete has strength trained, often, through lifting weights or other resistance, with proper coaching. It is unwise to blanket exercises or programs over athletes with the same chronological age simply because they appear equal on paper. When performing complex lifts or plyometric exercises, athletes differing in tissue quality, movement quality, and technical efficiency could have differing injury risks if they are not executed correctly.

3 RISK VS. REWARD - It is important to teach correct movements, understand the potential for injury, and evaluate which programs will elicit a positive response to move each individual athlete in the right direction. Because baseball success relies on in-game repetitions and timing, it is not beneficial to create a high-risk strength and conditioning program for an athlete who is required to perform 6-7 times per week for 6-plus months. Missing even 2 weeks of competition due to injury could cost a baseball player a large chunk of a competition season. An injury could also cost the player future playing opportunities and/or additional time to recover to previous overall performance levels.

Pre-testing each athlete before beginning a strength and conditioning training regimen provides baseline measurements for future improvement. It also allows for a head-to-toe movement assessment to determine areas of weakness, or where attention is most needed to improve movement quality. Further, this baseline testing provides a comparison to other baseball players and the correlation of their measurements on performance. This allows for effective program design for each individual athlete.[120]

While tailoring a program to an individual athlete's needs may be important, especially at advanced levels, custom programming may not be initially necessary. Mastering the foundational movements of pulling, pushing, and pressing in a safe manner, in as many planes as possible, is of primary importance. This is essential to building a more explosive and injury-resistant athlete.

Some athletes may be predisposed to injury because of a prior injury or genetic risk factors such as shoulder instability, an anatomical alignment issue, or biochemical makeup. In this case, modification of presses or other foundational strength exercises may be modified to reduce the risk of injury. Simplified, early baseball strength training can be similar to other General Physical Preparedness (GPP) programs, but with careful emphasis placed on avoiding injury risk for throwing athletes.

The best movements that translate from the weight room to the playing field are: squat, deadlift, pullup, single-arm dumbbell press, and rotational movements such as medicine ball scoop tosses. Variations of these are acceptable as long as focus remains on movement mastery, power generation, and mitigation of injury risk.

DIFFERING APPROACHES AT DIFFERENT LEVELS IN BASEBALL STRENGTH AND CONDITIONING

Aside from individually prescribed programs with your athlete's performance specialist, team strength and conditioning coaches are not necessarily concerned with individual gains in strength, speed, or overall fitness. Team coaches are not paid to develop individual players to put them on a roster at the next level or to prepare them for the MLB Draft. Instead, they are paid to facilitate workouts for a large group of athletes to win games. Their goal is to make their teams better with a mentally tough and well-conditioned body of athletes for the purpose of winning, which is what a coach's career depends on at all levels below professional baseball.

As a staff member of a professional baseball organization, training athletes becomes science-driven to protect athletes from injury risk and the organization from lawsuits. These considerations drive the justification for the type of training programs that are permitted by the organizations. This is especially true when teams are paying millions for public personalities and high-class performers for on the field performance and market reach. The teams must be conservative in their approach because it is detrimental to the organization, as a whole, for a player to be sidelined because of a staff member's careless oversight. The purpose in this realm of training is not to push the envelope, but to keep athletes healthy and strong to play the game.

As a result, many professional athletes employ performance specialists in the private sector to push and assist them in increasing their performance. These specialists must exercise many of the same cautions to decrease injury risk, while improving progress on the field and extending careers for better performance and more lucrative playing contracts. This topic leads us into some important considerations regarding injury prevention.

INJURY PREVENTION DURING STRENGTH AND CONDITIONING TRAINING

Injury is a speed bump that your ballplayer may face at some point in their career, yet many are preventable when the necessary precautions and training protocols are followed.

First, remember the goal of any strength and conditioning program for baseball is to enhance on-the-field performance and minimize injury risk. With training, the purpose is to mimic or simply improve performance, increase tendon and ligament integrity, and increase muscle size/neural drive for greater power output. Over time, as volume (repetitions) increases and tissue quality improves, athletes are better able to withstand the repeated demands of their sport. This is the basis for training to prevent injury.

On this note, it is important to distinguish hypertrophy from hyperplasia. Hypertrophy is the enlarging of muscle fibers, whereas hyperplasia is the increase in the total number of muscle fibers. Hyperplasia is physiologically improbable without banned substances such as growth hormone, steroids, or other substances that have the potential to create devastating long-term consequences to the body and result in penalties for violating the rules of the sport.[121] Hypertrophy should be your athlete's goal until the excess muscle mass and/or consequential weight gain becomes detrimental to the athlete' performance. We are always looking for the optimal rather than maximal amount of muscle tissue.

We will discuss specific baseball injuries in an upcoming chapter, but it is important to address two critical areas for injury prevention in throwers with regard to strength and conditioning programs. First, The Ulnar Collateral Ligament (UCL) of the elbow withstands up to three times the amount of force at maximal throwing effort that the same ligament can withstand in a laboratory setting. This resistance to injury is due to the surrounding muscles that stabilize, counterbalance, and slow down the forces put on the ligament during throwing. Do not neglect forearm and biceps exercises during training simply because your athlete is not in a beach body competition. Pull downs, rows, band curls, and other biceps lengthening and strengthening exercises can help protect the UCL.

Second, the shoulder's labrum and rotator cuff muscles must

be protected to avoid tears and throwing longevity. The rotator cuff muscles and tendons are seriously stressed while stabilizing, counterbalancing, and slowing down the arm during throwing. Overhead presses, band exercises, pushes, horizontal pulls, pulldowns, and pull apart movements all aid in strengthening the shoulder. People often ask when they should perform arm care exercises. The truth is, there is never a bad time to perform arm care exercises. Make it a year-round effort.

Active and static scapular positioning exercises are commonly utilized in arm care. Active scapular positioning can consist of tubing and "Kibler" exercises.[122] Static scapular repositioning can consist of exercises such as "6-backs," static holds, or "Y-T-I-W" position holds. Correct scapular positioning can improve breathing and increase subacromial space, which gives the supraspinatus, one of the rotator cuff muscles, room to move in the shoulder capsule without impingement. Again, there is no right or wrong time to perform these exercises, however, it is important to remember the goal when performing them. If your athlete can focus on correct postural positioning post-workout with these exercises repeatedly, they will be in a position for advances months and years down the road.

First, remember the goal of any strength and conditioning program for baseball is to enhance on-the-field performance and minimize injury risk.

Finally, your athlete's workouts must not neglect the abdominal core, which translates power and stability for many dynamic baseball movements. Abdominal training should be done in the direction of the muscle fibers and with the direction of the baseball sport movement. Examples include: "wood chopper" diagonal medicine ball movement, swinging and throwing trunk rotation, and flexion movements meant to mimic the contraction movements that occur during sport competition. These approaches to rotational abdominal strengthening will translate to improved swinging, throwing, and defensive movements.

Not all abdominal training should involve movement, however. In many instances, it's equally important to resist change or rotation, or "brace and breathe" during compound movements. Variations of the plank, Pallof presses, and single arm presses or pulls can train abdominal resistance to change or rotation. Whereas, "bracing and breathing" during squat and deadlift are excellent core isolation exercises.

🔻 **DEMMINK**: *When I was playing baseball at Clemson, I was invited to play summer ball in the New England Collegiate Baseball League and the Cape Cod Baseball League. Instead of bagging groceries as a summer job, I prepared for and passed my strength and conditioning certification exams. This allowed me to train other athletes and myself early each day before games at night.*

As I bridged the gap between anatomy and physiology textbooks and real-world application, my passion for strength and conditioning grew. I quickly understood the value and role it played in improving my performance on the field. My relentless pursuit of outworking and outperforming others acted as a live résumé as I graduated college and was drafted to play professional baseball.

Shortly thereafter, professional athletes would spend their off-seasons training with me in Clemson and Charlotte, where I was also training for my upcoming professional seasons. This is how 3D Performance Training began.

My best advice for readers of this book is this: strength and conditioning workouts are a tool to improve performance in baseball, but being great at fitness does not guarantee success in baseball. Use the weight room as a place to enhance performance and devote careful attention to the skills and fundamentals required to become a great baseball player.

HOW TO DO THE PALLOF PRESS

- Fasten an exercise band to a sturdy object at chest height.

- Interlace the fingers of both hands around the free end of the band and step back from the anchor point to create some tension on the band.

- Turn your body so it's perpendicular to the anchor point and band, hold your hands near the center of your chest, and assume an athletic stance: feet shoulder width and parallel, knees slightly bent, torso upright. This is your starting position.

- Without moving your torso, slowly reach both arms in front of your chest until they are straight.

- Hold this extended position for a five-count, then slowly return to the starting position. Repeat for reps.

- Turn and perform the same number of reps facing the other direction.[123]

COMMON MYTHS IN BASEBALL STRENGTH AND CONDITIONING

As explored in other places in this career guide, baseball tends to carry an "old school" mentality, despite physiological and psychological research that shows proven methods of training, performing, and recovering. We will address the top two baseball training myths that your athlete is sure to encounter, if they have not already.

MYTH #1 - Baseball players should not perform any overhead training.
    Generally speaking, overhead athletes have a tighter posterior shoulder capsule in the throwing or serving arm, and with a range

of motion that favors external rotation more than the non-throwing arm. The limited internal rotation can cause upward rotation and elevation of the throwing arm scapula. As upward rotation and elevation in the shoulder capsule exceeds normal ranges, the acromion process can limit the space needed for the supraspinatus in the rotator cuff to move correctly.

When there is a decrease in this space, the rotator cuff is more susceptible to fraying and impingement down the road. Maintaining shoulder integrity is crucial. Without it, additional stress can be placed on the elbow/UCL. All too often, this can lead to increased susceptibility to ligament tears or strains, ulnar nerve irritation, and other throwing injuries.

This is the reason for the perceived need to avoid overhead training activities. However, baseball is an overhead sport with high-velocity movements of throwing, diving, jumping, and holding the bat after a maximum effort swing with one arm. Rather than avoiding overhead strengthening movements that are viewed as dangerous to an athlete's throwing arm, your athlete should always train to strengthen the shoulder capsule to adapt to these movements and protect against injury.

Incorporation of proper overhead movements will provide balance, decrease injury risk, and protect the shoulder joint.

Many overhead exercise movements can be done safely. Without overhead strength training, an imbalance is created when a program is designed to do a high volume of vertical pulling, such as lat pulldown exercises, but has no balance with pushing movements overhead, such as a shoulder press, landmine press, or incline dumbbell press.

The movement quantity and force necessary during a workout should be determined by a player's position, or if the athlete has a predisposition to injury. Regardless, adjustments can and should be made to provide alternative movements that provide shoulder balance by incorporating exercises that push/press and raise weights head-high and above. Incorporation of proper overhead movements will provide balance, decrease injury risk, and protect the shoulder joint.

MYTH #2 - Pitchers should be extremely well conditioned, similar to a cross-country distance athlete.

This is a concept that is severely misunderstood, especially in baseball. Training as a distance runner immeasurably decreases the performance of baseball athletes. Baseball players perform power movements and then rest repeatedly over the extended duration of a game. Occasionally, an athlete benefits from a conditioning program that includes an aerobic training bout of up to a 5-kilometer run (20-30 minutes), but the majority of conditioning should incorporate repeated intervals and maximal power output sprints, with high intensity repeats.

With these 30-, 40-, 60-, or 100-yard interval repeats, the athlete learns to recruit fast twitch muscle fibers and increases the speed of recovery between bouts. In baseball, this type of training translates similarly to situations where the athlete must reach back for special focus to make the difficult defensive play, execute a crucial pitch, or make an adjustment to beat the opponent. Thus, comparing a baseball athlete to a cross-country runner and prescribing similar training is devoid of logic. The skills and body types required for success in long-distance running and baseball are inherently different.

If you had suspected the myths shared in this section were not the truth, or if you learned something completely new, our mission was accomplished. Debunking these myths not only improves the game, it allows us to transition to understand and incorporate which workouts *do* translate to enhancement of on-the-field baseball skills, injury prevention, and endurance needed for your athlete's specific position.

POSITION-SPECIFIC TRAINING CONSIDERATIONS

Many athletes turn the corner in their careers when they start training with high-level, baseball-specific training. We support the school of thought that designs training for athletes according to individual strengths and weaknesses, rather than a general program for each position or sport. While many exercises will transfer from athlete to athlete, ultimately the anatomical and training needs will vary as the athlete progresses based on various individual factors.

Remembering that success in this sport depends on overall averages and full-season statistics, it is best to stay away from the one-time risks for results, such as maxing out on weight lifting movements that could simultaneously end a career. If baseball was about throwing the hardest or hitting a ball the furthest only one time, we might train as if we were preparing to compete in a single championship event.

However, baseball is a marathon of short duration sprint movements over the course of an extremely long season. Our goal is for the athlete to repeat movements as consistently and as often as possible over an extended period of time. This will enhance the success measures of fielding percentages, batting averages, slugging percentages, and earned run averages over the long-haul.

One final word about body composition before analyzing training by position. Body composition can drastically affect performance. For example, body mass is highly correlated with throwing velocity for pitchers, and performance could be affected if a pitcher suddenly becomes lean and lightweight. Whereas, a centerfielder may benefit by a leaner and lighter frame to improve base stealing ability or by covering more ground. On the other hand, a corner outfielder might generate better offensive power numbers at the plate with more body mass and less defensive impact in the field. Training is all about the position and the goals needed on the field.

PITCHERS

A long-running joke among professional baseball players is that the best way for a pitcher to train for the season is to stand in brand new spikes in their front yard for 8-10 hours a day. While this is obviously not completely accurate, pitchers are on their feet and stagnant for much of the day. There is an element of standing that must be prepared for in advance to avoid shin splints and dead legs.

Nevertheless, there are considerations specific to the art and movements of pitching that should be considered when training. With the exception of training cycles that build physical endurance or mental capacities by running longer distances than the actual race distance or performing more repetitions in weight training than required for competition, it is no secret that, generally, sprinters sprint and bodybuilders lift heavy weights during the majority of their training regimens to coincide with the demands of their sports. This should be true of pitchers as well.

Let's review some concepts about the biomechanics of pitching to understand how your athlete needs to train. The goal of pitching is to throw a 5.9-ounce baseball 60 feet, 6 inches toward a target so that the batter for the other team will be unsuccessful in making solid contact. Generating as much velocity, spin, movement, deception, long-term arm stamina, and command (pitch control) are the dominant traits that produce a better outcome each day they are improved.

Improvement of these traits comes from utilizing the body's explosive fast twitch muscle fibers during a maximum effort pitch, and then resting 10-20 seconds until the next pitch. However, the common misconception is that pitchers should refrain from upper body weight lifting, condition mid- to long-distances, and avoid fast twitch movements. Yet, pitching is anything but slow. The majority of training should be focused on total body power output and transferring energy from the ground through the baseball. Focusing on each aspect of energy transfer will avoid a weak link to impede the energy transfer, or become fatigued before the rest of the body.

If your athlete is a starting pitcher, a high-volume training regimen built for both power and endurance is important. This is because starting pitchers perform a power activity and must generate as much velocity on the ball as possible while maintaining precision and location over multiple innings. Thus, the ability to repeat power activities over an extended period of time does demand moderate cardiovascular conditioning. Whereas, a setup or closer role typically requires as much power as possible for speed and velocity. Because the overall performance duration is far less than that of a starter, relievers require less cardiovascular conditioning.

CATCHERS

The name of the game for catchers is endurance and fortitude. Quick agility, lateral explosiveness, and flexibility are your catcher's bread and butter. Solid defensive skills and hitting for a batting average higher than their body weight (in pounds), with some pop, will ensure value behind the dish. That being said, catchers should train in such a way that creates an impenetrable, agile, mobile, quick, and reactive "wall" behind the plate.

As an extension of the pitcher to get batters out, catchers must stay comfortable to receive pitches and mentally manage the game from behind home plate. Due to a catcher's involvement in every pitch, they do not need an abundance of in-season volume in lower body training because they are constantly squatting and standing during games. Training for strength and power with limited volume is key to prevent further breakdown of their body than is already endured.

INFIELDERS AND OUTFIELDERS

Infielders and outfielders, which we will refer to as the "position players," are commonly grouped together as the "athletes" of the team. This is commonly accompanied by joking disagreement from the pitchers and catchers. While there are skills required of pitchers and catchers that some position players could never achieve, these 7 position players are typically evaluated as the most athletic, based on their raw athletic ability measures such as speed, strength, quickness, agility. These measures contribute to the five tools: speed, arm strength, fielding, hitting for average, and hitting for power.

What's your athlete's identity? No defensive play requires more than 60 yards of movement from a position. Therefore, training to be adaptive, explosive, and flexible in all directions is key. Whether it is the first quick step defensively, the ability to turn-and-burn to catch a ball, or hitting a missile in the gap, the athlete's training goals should be the same.

Additionally, outfielders must be most concerned with top velocity running for tracking down balls in the gap and explosive first steps toward the ball. Rotational work, along with powerful and explosive training regimens will translate to power at the plate for outfielders. Infielders, on the other hand, spend most of their time in a crouched position with their eyes low to the ground to read ground ball hops. Therefore, hip mobility and moving low and agile on a regular basis during training is most important for an infielder.

Regardless of the particular position, all position players must work on the ability to use their lower halves to generate rotational force at the plate, and train their obliques and abdominals in diagonal patterns to ensure that the weight room work translates to the field.

ARM CARE

No matter how hard your athlete trains, they could be ripe for disappointment if arm care is neglected. There are no positions where throwing is not required or when throwing well does not enhance your athlete's productivity, impact, and long-term value. Arm care training not only enhances an athlete's throwing ability but also protects from potential injury events. Examples include: maximum effort throws from the outfield or across the diamond, when they must adjust at full-speed, such as sliding headfirst into a base, breaking up a double play, or when a hand slips off the bat after a big swing at the plate. Shoulder stability maintains the integrity of the shoulder capsule during these adverse events, as well as strengthens the predictable throwing aspects of the game.

Athletes should approach arm care with dynamic and static warm up routines as a part of the athlete's strength and conditioning regimen in preparation for overhead movements. Prior to a lift session or practice, your athlete should use dynamic movements to allow for smooth transitions and for the joints to glide with ease through the desired ranges of motion.

After a lift session or practice, your athlete should stabilize with static position exercises that were previously mentioned to reinforce proper postural positioning. After completing static postural training, they will improve post-workout shoulder stability and be better able to maintain the correct posture and ideal standing or resting positions for longer periods of time, which eventually become second nature.

FLEXIBILITY

Similar to arm care, flexibility and adequate range of motion are essential pieces in maximizing your athlete's potential. Many injuries from a lack of adequate flexibility occur due to restricted ranges of motion in the joints. In biomechanics, these areas are referred to as force-generating and load-bearing junctions. However, do not confuse the need for flexibility with becoming a yogi. In this sport, ideal stiffness is important in our tendons and ligaments because excessive laxity can lead to instability and vulnerability.

Ultimately, our goal is to prime the muscles to stretch into desired biomechanical positions without compromising the muscle connective tissue during movement. This will allow your athlete to be in the correct positions for running speed, throwing velocity, and swinging force generation. It is also important to acknowledge the role of "activity-induced tissue stiffness." This is a degree of tissue rigidity that can allow for tissue to move throughout ideal ranges of motion while limiting excessive joint movement.

The two types of stretching, dynamic and static, both serve important purposes at the appropriate times.

1 Dynamic stretching, also known as active stretching, is generally part of a warm up routine to encourage quick muscle firing activities and range of motion movements to prime the body for higher amounts of power output.

2 Static stretching is typically used for downregulation and during the cooling off phase post-workout. This allows the nervous system to relax and transition into recovery. This is best accomplished by holding positions for the muscle fascia to stretch while still hot and warm from exercise.

Finally, it is important to remember that just because an athlete is unable to get into a certain position, it does not mean that they are too tight or inflexible. Anatomical differences exist that may give the illusion that a muscle is too tight or that the athlete has a poor range of motion in a specific area. When in fact, it may not be an issue with the connective tissues at all. This is why each individual athlete must improve their own unique traits and abilities.

For more on stretching, please visit: www.3dperformance-training.com/ to make a consultation appointment or send a DM through Instagram or Twitter @3d_performance.

RECOVERY

Recovery consists of proper rest, nutrition, and strength and conditioning practices to generate the healing and adaptive responses in the body. In this portion, we only address the aspects of recovery that are specific to strength and conditioning.

Generally speaking, recovery practices from any physical activity are the same. The goals are to increase blood flow, decrease inflammation, and deliver nutrients to the affected tissues to ultimately enhance and/or speed the recovery process. In baseball recovery, the athlete will target the specific muscles used. For pitchers, recovery will target lower body and arm care. These areas are heavily taxed during the explosive and repetitive movements required for pitching. Position players will most often target the lower body and the chronic, repetitive stresses of baseball movements from extended games and practices. In contrast, strength and conditioning training recovery will focus more on the entire body and which muscle groups were targeted in the previous training sessions.

Recovery is the athlete's ability to return to the original state or reach an improved physiological state. This is accomplished through stretching, active cool down, decreasing inflammation, rest, sleep, and nutrition. Stretching, while not a tissue repair mechanism, does allow the tissue to remain mobile while new muscle tissue is generated. Active cool down assists with flushing toxins and inflammatory properties generated during workouts and increasing blood flow to catalyze muscle and nutrient regeneration as quickly as possible.

Finally, rest and sleep, which are the two most overlooked areas when evaluating recovery quality and efficiency, are critical for tissue growth and regeneration from inactivity and growth hormone production. Eight to eleven hours of sleep can do more for recovery and subsequent performance than missing sleep to perform additional training and movement.

In the short-term, proper recovery provides the athlete a mental and physical edge for the next training session. In the long-term, proper recovery allows for an increase in total activity and decrease in inflammation after training based on adaptation. This allows the athlete to prevent many injuries, stay on the playing field, and train hard for continued improvement.

FINAL WORD

We can develop the perfect program or approach to training and find that each athlete requires individual adjustments with time or responds in different ways to the program or approach. Biology, physiology, and often psychology dictate the needs of each individual training session. Time, education, experience, and adjustment lead to long-term learning and adaptation for your athlete, just as learning how to hit a curveball or throw an effective 2-seam fastball takes time and repetition. No cue or technique is perfect for each individual.

Therefore, the athlete, along with their performance specialist or coach, must learn what works for their best outcome. The best training program combines it all: nutrition, flexibility, strength, conditioning, psychological training, and recovery.

OUR FAVORITE PERFORMANCE AND WELLNESS TOOLS

1   Polar fitness watches are a great resource for personalized training data for training, sleep, and other activities. Polar offers several options for cycling, running, fitness, and cross-training, and does not require a subscription membership to activate or continue services. Visit: www.polar.com/us-en for more information about the many useful products offered.

2   Whoop is designed specifically to "help you improve your exercise performance, recover better, get more sleep, and feel empowered about your health and fitness habits." Although it is subscription based and more expensive than other devices that provide tracking and analytical data, Whoop is Apple Watch compatible and reliable. Visit: www.whoop.com/ for more information about the products and subscriptions available.

3   Therabody's Theragun percussive therapy tool is excellent for recovery and soft tissue maintenance. Therabody also offers a line of effective performance enhancing products. For more information, visit: theragun.com.

4   Compex offers electrode stimulation and TENS (Trans-Cutaneous Electrical Nerve Stimulation) units that are portable, effective, and a helpful addition to an athlete's pre- and post-workout arsenal. For more information, visit: compex.com.

THE MENTAL PREPARATION EDGE

"More than anything, what differentiates people who live up to their potential from those who don't is their willingness to look at themselves and others objectively and understand the root causes standing in their way."

▼ RAY DALIO, BRIDGEWATER ASSOCIATES

INTRODUCTION

A player can have the ideal physical makeup and perfect scores in all five tools of the MLB scouting evaluation metric, yet still lack the mental acuity necessary for success between the foul lines. How are you or your athlete preparing off-the-field for the narrow window of opportunity? Are you paying attention to your athlete's overall mental wellbeing and its undeniable impact on reaching their goals? There are countless practices available that are just as advantageous and impactful as physical training and skill development, if not more so.

This chapter covers the most impactful mental practices, habits, and thought patterns that bring all of the segmented physical training together to complete the tools required to rise up as a well-armored competitor. The mental preparation edge will help your athlete to prepare, confront, and overcome any challenge.

Mental conditioning often separates good from great in the short-term, and the "haves" from the "never-weres" in the long-term.

Ironically, paying greater attention to this part of self-improvement enhances the physical aspects immeasurably and reduces the need to grind excessively in physical practice. The brain and body adapt and learn much more efficiently when primed for success.

PREPARATION AND PERFORMANCE

The cornerstone of maximizing mental fortitude and preparation is understanding what is necessary to give the athlete that mental edge, i.e., the awareness necessary to separate from the pack. Each athlete will prepare for competition differently. But the bottom line is that all who succeed prepare mentally as well as physically. While the discipline of mental preparation may seem taxing at first, it will become second nature as your athlete begins to sincerely believe in and prioritize their championship training mindset. It will noticeably pay dividends in every aspect of their life, even in personal relationships and learning unrelated to athletics. The discipline becomes easier, more fruitful, and welcomed once an athlete adopts the mindset of "this is simply the way it has to be and I am better for it."

How are you or your athlete preparing off-the-field for the narrow window of opportunity?

If an athlete struggles with competition anxiety and performs poorly in games after mastering a skill in practice, encourage them to focus on other tasks before the big game or encourage meditation or mindfulness practice. If an athlete benefits from visualizing success, schedule "quiet time" for focusing on the upcoming game. Some athletes vomit or lose sleep, while others simply need time to collect themselves and discover independently how to switch from training mode to performance mode. These are only a handful of ways players may attempt to assert mental control over the many challenging aspects of the game.

When channeled in appropriate and positive ways, these tactics can facilitate the mental fortitude necessary for success. The best way to help your athlete is to be honest about their specific needs. Encourage self-awareness by promoting personal discovery of mental strengths and weaknesses. In addition to promoting the mental stability necessary for specific skill development, this will also allow you, as a parent, to understand and empathize with your athlete's emotions. Let's put all the silly superstitions that ballplayers have concocted over time to rest. What matters are the skills your athlete develops to prepare and perform, not which dirty socks will lead to a base hit or a win for the team. Know thyself.

Successful baseball players are often very detail-oriented in the way that they approach the game. Many athletes perform best when concentrating on the specifics, viewing the season as a series of independent battles, instead of focusing on the overall war. Worrying about the season as a whole can be overwhelming. Understand that overcoming a challenge in this game of failures is dependent upon acute awareness of each specific moment, not an all-encompassing emphasis on the final outcome. This can only be achieved through a focused, pitch-by-pitch approach.

Statistically, as a hitter, an athlete will fail more than they succeed. Encourage your athlete to prioritize only those things they can control, such as hitting the ball on the screws instead of focusing on the audience or perceived difficulties in getting on base. MLB players rarely focus on hitting home runs. Resolve to attack specific pitches in specific zones that make success more likely and trust their trained abilities. Emphasize correct processes over desired outcomes, this will lead to long-term success.

Further, encourage your athlete to stick with a plan. Aborting the mission derails commitment and invalidates any possibility of success. If a plan needs adjustment, so be it. As humans, we often mistakenly rely upon the future to be predictable and stable, forgetting the many turns, compromises, and challenges we endure along the way to reach a desired outcome.

Have faith in preparation and trust the learning and refining process to deliver the results. By weathering the storm and trusting it to carry you through unanticipated or negative circumstances, the name of the game becomes execution, not paralysis by analysis. Unexpected changes or bumps in the road are no longer debilitating. This is all part of the growth process that mental conditioning enhances.

UTILIZE COACHES AS A BENEFIT

Another advantage that many athletes do not realize is how valuable a coach can be as a bridge to their goals. A challenging authority dynamic often arises when a coach restricts a player from opportunities based on lack of seniority or initial evaluation of the athlete. Yet, consistent performance within the windows of opportunity to build trust and reliability of performance, however small they may be, will improve the chances that the coach will stay out of the athlete's way and provide additional opportunities to succeed as time progresses.

In team sports, there are personnel decisions and roster-moves that are out of a player's control, which can result in tension between coaches and players. This is the difficult aspect about team sports with coaches and administrators that is different from individual sports where the winner always advances and is responsible for the outcome, as discussed in the introduction to Part I. Be aware of which coaches want to help your athlete and the ones they must find a way around.

Ultimately, the athlete spends years refining performance, relationships with teammates and coaches, and climbing the ladder to the next best level by devoting physical and emotional energy in an attempt to perfect the sport that is impossible to conquer! It is no wonder these players can be high strung or carry high expectations, great performers often are. Organized sports are inherently competitive. This is not P.E. class.

UMPIRES AS ALLIES

Umpires at any level will make mistakes because human error is inevitable. Umpiring is a thankless job that gets more difficult at the higher levels as the speed of the game increases. When stepping into the batter's box or on the rubber, players have the choice to make umpires allies or enemies. If a player complains constantly and shows up the umpire with poor body language when there is a borderline call, that borderline pitch will likely be called for the opposition. Maintaining composure and showing respect is the best way to gain an umpire's favor. At the higher levels, speaking to the umpire on a first-name basis, rather than calling them "blue" or "ump" will pay off in the short- and long-term. If your athlete is younger, teach them to address the umpire as "sir" or "ma'am" with a respectful tone.

> **Ultimately, umpires will make mistakes and it is up to the athlete to make an ally, and keep an at-bat out of the umpire's hands, whether at the plate or on the mound.**

Here's an example of how to engage an umpire during competition. If an athlete swings at a borderline pitch and is unsure whether it was a strike or not, teach them to turn and ask respectfully, "excuse me sir did you have that on or off the plate?" The umpire will usually respond, "No that was a ball off the plate," or "Yes, it was on the outside corner." This allows the umpire to define their strike zone, which provides information for later in the game. Engaging in these conversations will also make it less likely for the umpire to "ring" a hitter up on a borderline pitch, or miss a good pitch from a pitcher.

Ultimately, umpires will make mistakes and it is up to the athlete to make an ally, and keep an at-bat out of the umpire's hands, whether at the plate or on the mound. Otherwise, your athlete is playing against 10 players on the opposing side, instead of 9.

CLINICALLY PROVEN METHODS OF INTERNAL IMPROVEMENT

There are many foundational and under-utilized methods that are clinically proven to increase awareness, reduce anxiety, and improve an athlete's ability to focus through the highs and lows of their career. Elite performers worldwide utilize the following practices to enhance self-awareness, preparation, and adaptability to maximize potential and enhance their experience.

VISUALIZATION AND AFFIRMATIONS

Visualization is defined as "creating a mental image or intention of what you want to happen or feel in reality."[124] Rather than hoping that a desired goal comes to pass, by visualizing and affirming the precise outcome, the athlete takes the necessary action to produce the desired result. If the task is new or requires advanced skill development for consistent achievement, the athlete's mind will naturally prioritize the achievement of the result by solving problems as they arise, and through trial and error, discover the best methods to achieve the result. Visualizing and affirming the successful outcome declares commitment to the goal and raises the bar. In response, the mind trains to prepare to perform the task successfully.

The discovery of mirror neurons supports this truth. Mirror neurons are sensory motor cells that are activated when we perform an action or observe another performing an action.[125] Scientists believe that these neurons help humans learn new actions by watching actions performed, visualizing oneself performing them, or performing them in reality. As evidence, these neurons are activated on brain scans during observation, visualization, and performance.

As a practice, set goals with your athlete and help them to write and speak goals such as "I am confident that I will master this skill," visualize success in that skill, and witness the improvement as they raise the bar and grow in expertise. By devoting intention and will-power to goals with the end result in mind, your athlete will be better than yesterday!

MEDITATION

"...Breathing is the invisible bridge to performance, it is both mental and physical."

LANTZ WHEELER, NATIONALLY RECOGNIZED PITCHING INSTRUCTOR AND NCAA DIVISION I PITCHING COACH

Regardless of how one chooses to meditate or bring attention to the present, studies reveal that meditation targets and affects the brain's default mode network of the brain, referred to by many as the wandering or "monkey-mind."[126,127] Meditation practice, also known as mindful awareness, is comparable to a cardiovascular conditioning workout. Yet this workout is to build the skill of emotional control rather than aerobic capacity.

Increased emotional control is a valuable skill to have when you're a high performer in any field.[128] Meditation relieves anxiety, improves information absorption, and improves the efficiency of mental and emotional recovery, among many other benefits. While meditation techniques can be deeply personal and a matter of preference for each individual, Alan Jaeger, founder of Jaeger Sports and the famous "Jaeger Bands," has shared a mental practice exercise to assist athletes in bringing their awareness to the present moment. Here is the full article to add the practice to your athlete's routine: whosonfirstbook.com/jaegermental.

Tim Ferris, author of several best sellers, including The 4-Hour Work Week, and internationally respected host of the podcast, The Tim Ferriss Show, explains, "So meditation, or mindfulness practice, is about decreasing emotional reactivity so you can pro-actively create your day and create your life; versus, just being a walking reflex . . . ."[129]

Although meditation began in Asia as many as 7,000 years ago, the practice is now fully Westernized and people of all beliefs and backgrounds practice it. In fact, you and your athlete will likely notice positive changes in mood, contentment, and intuition rather quickly. Trust us on this one. Encourage your athlete to intentionally improve in this area, just as the athlete would with any skill practice or physical exercise.

We will leave the structure and method of a mindfulness practice to your athlete's discretion, but we recommend choosing from the most popular meditation and mindfulness apps on the market to assist your athlete in learning about the benefits of consistent practice. Here are a few suggestions to get you started:

- WAKING UP: Guided Meditation

- HEADSPACE: A Netflix series is also available called Headspace Guide to Meditation. The official trailer is available here: www.headspace.com/netflix

- CALM

SLEEP SCIENCE

We would be doing you and your athlete a disservice if we shared a comprehensive plan on how to maximize performance and wellness, but did not address the most important and necessary aspect for humans to survive and flourish: sleep. Healthy sleep directly results in a longer lifespan and quality of life, yet somehow institutions do not endorse the necessity of sleep. This could be out of fear of permitting laziness. Interestingly, the result of satisfactory sleep actually produces outcomes opposite of laziness. In particular, healthy sleep creates far more quantity and quality work output due to a rested mind.[130]

Our youth population, and adults for that matter, are in a harmful downward spiral in the current age, "with 15-year-olds sleeping, on average, 2 hours less per night than 15-year-olds 100 years ago." Without curbing this deficiency, we are knowingly stunting growth potential in the education and athletic endeavors of our youth. "Under slept [athletes] are less productive, less motivated, less happy, and more lazy."[131]

We are voluntarily setting the stage for negative thinking, poor motivation, and less satisfaction while we claim to be building young warriors on the field. With this knowledge, we must prioritize sleep in our athletes while we seek to improve with each practice, private lesson, and game. This is the most important performance and recovery variable in our control.

As a parent, it may be insightful to know that "employees have been found to be less ethical, more deviant, and more dishonest when sleeping 6 hours or less." This is hardly a healthy environment we are cultivating for positive behavior and team building in our athletes.[132] What was once misunderstood or incorrectly viewed as either a luxury or laziness, research is showing the absolute necessity of sleep in our overcaffeinated society. Athletes need between 7-9 hours of consistent sleep on a nightly basis.

The benefits of deep sleep for an athlete include reduction of the stress/fatigue state,[133] energy restoration, cell regeneration, cognitive processing, increased blood supply delivery to the muscles, growth and repair of tissues and bones, and strengthening of the immune system. With 6 hours or less of sleep per night, an athlete's time to physical exhaustion decreases by 30% compared to when fully rested. Further, there is a higher risk of injury, increased lactic acid accumulation, less efficiency in lung function for extricating carbon dioxide and receiving oxygen, and decreased jumping, sprinting, and overall muscular output peaks.[134] This overall decrease in performance and injury risk must be avoided to keep your athlete safe and give them the best outcomes in the short- and long-term.

Matthew Walker, Professor of Neuroscience and Psychology at the University of California, Berkeley, and founder and Director of the Center for Human Sleep Science, states that REM sleep is chiefly responsible for memory, learning, and mood.[135] Following the day, REM sleep consolidates, filters, and establishes what has been learned over the previous days, weeks, and months.

This is a nightly practice by the brain and happens in the late stages of sleep, in the late morning hours prior to waking. If an athlete, who normally goes to bed at midnight, is forced to wake two hours early for an early morning workout, as an example, rather than sleeping sufficiently, they are not losing only 25% of their sleep. Rather, by waking two hours early, an athlete would be losing 60-90% of total REM sleep, which specifically aids vital recovery, memory, learning, and mood. Restoration through sleep is not comparable to one continuous charging bar, as we see on our cell phones. In fact, "There is no such thing as burning the candle at both ends, or even at one end, and getting away with it."[136] This is especially true for athletes at any age who are competing at their highest level yet each day.

We recommend the most comprehensive book on sleep to date: Why We Sleep by Matthew Walker, Ph.D. You may access it here for audible and e-reader download, or standard print version: whosonfirstbook.com/sleep. This book will not only help educate and encourage your family to prioritize sleep but will also make for great conversation on the latest scientific understandings of sleep. Here are 12 tips for good sleep hygiene from the book to make sleep a priority for the athlete, beginning tonight. Don't hesitate to utilize these tips for your own mental and physical well-being to be a better parent and a better individual.

1. Establish and stick to a sleep schedule. This means go to bed and wake up at the same time each 24-hour period. Yes, oversleeping may harm the following evening's ability to sleep.

2. End exercise 2-3 hours prior to bed.

3. Avoid caffeine altogether but certainly after lunch. Caffeine can take up to 8 hours to wear off and imagine how a daily stimulant can affect long-term rest.

4 Avoid alcohol, which robs the body of REM sleep. Contrary to what you may believe, it does not help rest. Alcohol produces both stimulating and sedating effects in the body, causing tiredness but preventing the most restful stages of sleep.

5 Avoid large meals and too many fluids immediately before bed.

6 Be aware of medications that disrupt sleep, pay attention if this is currently an issue.

7 Do not nap after 3 pm because this can disrupt circadian rhythm.

8 Establish some form of relaxation before bed such as reading, listening to music, or meditating.

9 Take a warm bath before bed. This aids in the necessary 2-3 degree drop in body temperature required to drift off into sleep.

10 Establish a bedroom that promotes sleep. Cool, dark, quiet, and gadget free. Melatonin release is affected by the cool blue light wavelength, which is most of our technology in the current age. Inexpensive blue light filtering glasses are recommended for athletes. Also, many software devices now have settings to turn down the blue light displays in the evening.

11 Get outside in the day, especially in the morning. Natural sunlight aids a healthy circadian rhythm.

12 Do not lie in bed awake for more than 20-30 minutes. If there is trouble sleeping, get up and do a relaxing activity for a period of time.[137]

LIFE AFTER BASEBALL

When the competition days are over, some athletes lose their identities and sense of purpose. This transition can be more difficult for some because of the purposeful devotion and reward that accompanies success. New and improved athletes arrive on the scene, and the ex-athlete must develop new areas of expertise discover their future with a blank canvas.

While the uncertainty can generate intense depression or anxiety among the most accomplished former athletes, turning the page provides the freedom to create, rather than respond to circumstances. This psychological transition is as difficult as any goal achieved during the playing journey. Remember that the athlete has gained meaningful self-belief and grit that now translate beyond the game. The passing of time will help release the grip on previous attachments as they are introduced to new responsibilities and passions.

INJURIES, INJURY PREVENTION, AND INJURY RECOVERY

INTRODUCTION

Injury. A word that carries many meanings ranging from disappointment and endings, to overcoming challenges and new beginnings. The impact of injury on a career and the value of receiving proper care is the reason for this chapter. Informing you of the most common baseball injuries, the best surgical and non-surgical considerations, and the best current methods of rehab and recovery will provide the best protection if your athlete ever faces an injury that sidelines them for a period. The knowledge you and your athlete have at the time the decision must be made could determine the athlete's future.

> Although swinging produces a few common injuries in baseball, injuries most commonly occur during throwing.

BASEBALL INJURIES

Dr. J.P. Bramhall, M.D., who contributed the medical content of this chapter, has devoted his career to practicing sports medicine. He was the Director of Sports Medicine and Team Physician at Texas A&M University for over 30 years. He serves athletes of all ages by providing pre-game, in-game, post-game, and surgical care. Many of the athletes

Almost all athletes face an injury or need to rest at some point. During this down time of rest and rehab, the athlete should improve in areas that have been neglected. They can watch the game from a different perspective or learn new mental and physical conditioning exercises. This work will translate to improvements on the field when they return to play.

he cares for are among the highest profile names in collegiate and professional sports, past and present.

Injuries are common in any sport when maximum effort or a high volume of repetitions is required. Although swinging produces a few common injuries in baseball, injuries most commonly occur during throwing. The rotation of the throwing shoulder during the delivery of a pitch is one of the fastest motions performed by the human body.[140] Let's explore the most common baseball specific injuries.

SWINGING INJURIES

- Posterior Shoulder Subluxation and Posterior Labral Tear
- Medial Epicondylitis
- Distal Biceps Tendinitis and Distal Biceps Rupture
- Hook of the Hamate Fracture
- Oblique Muscle Strain and Oblique Muscle Tear

THROWING INJURIES OF THE SHOULDER

- Rotator Cuff injuries and tears
- Tendinitis

- Instability

- Internal Impingement

- Glenohumeral Internal Rotation Deformity (GIRD)

- Biceps Tendinitis

- Proximal Humeral Epiphysitis ("Little Leaguer's Shoulder")

- Labral Tears and SLAP (superior labrum tear from anterior to posterior) Tears

THROWING INJURIES OF THE ELBOW

- Medial Epicondylitis

- Little Leaguer's Elbow

- Medial Epicondylitis

- Flexor Pronator Tendinitis

- Avulsion Fracture of the Medial Epicondyle

- Ulnar Collateral Ligament Tears

- Ulnar Neuritis and Ulnar Subluxation

- Olecranon Stress Fractures

- Valgus Extension Overload

- Osteochondritis Dissecans

SWINGING INJURIES

POSTERIOR SHOULDER SUBLUXATION AND POSTERIOR LABRAL TEAR

Tears of the posterior labrum, which occur in the lead shoulder during swinging, are often overlooked during diagnosis. The initiation of the swing is a sudden and violent event. When the lead arm begins the swing, a maximum contraction of the posterior shoulder muscles occurs pulling the humeral head posteriorly. This repetitive action may result in laxity (looseness) of the posterior capsule or tearing of the posterior labrum over time. A loose or torn posterior labrum may cause the shoulder to sublux (come out of socket) or partially dislocate.

In individuals with hypermobility of the shoulder or mild laxity of the shoulder joint, the posterior shoulder subluxation may occur more easily. Particularly in females who demonstrate more flexibility than males, this injury may result from the initiation of the swing, or the sudden stopping of the swing, such as during a "check swing." Once this condition occurs, and the athlete experiences multiple subluxation episodes, a surgical procedure to stabilize the shoulder is frequently required to eliminate the instability of the shoulder.

Following surgical repair of the posterior labrum, return to hitting in non-throwing shoulders occurs at 3 months as long as rehabilitation, and strength and conditioning programs are completed. The success rate following posterior labral repair for an athlete to return to previous level of performance is approximately 95%.

MEDIAL EPICONDYLITIS

Medial Epicondylitis is a common overuse condition of the elbow that may result from swinging. Also known as "golfer's elbow," the medial aspect of the elbow in the dominant hand (right elbow in right-handed hitters) is subjected to repetitive stress during swinging. This is particularly true in athletes who are advanced in their baseball career and undergo high levels of training and high-volume repetitions. This condition may occur suddenly following a maximum effort swing on an inside pitch, or as a result of chronic overuse.

This condition has a good prognosis (prospect of recovery) with non-operative conservative management. Athletes who have previously undergone surgical reconstruction of the ulnar collateral ligament, may experience medial epicondylitis and tendinitis of the medial elbow when hitting and swinging on a repetitive basis after surgery. Duration of recovery from non-surgical rehabilitation or surgical repair is dependent on the athlete's playing position and time of year. Pitchers may require an extended recovery due to the demands on the throwing elbow. Non-pitchers will usually respond to conservative treatment and return to play without significant loss of time.

HOOK OF THE HAMATE FRACTURE

This injury is a fracture of the hook shaped protrusion of the hamate bone in the wrist. Pressure from the bat resting against the hypothenar eminence of the hand and repetitive swinging results in a stress fracture of this bone over time. The fracture begins as a stress fracture that has very little healing capabilities because of poor blood supply in the hamate bone. The complete fracture occurs when the stress fracture continues to be weakened from repetitive swinging. The injury often causes a sudden onset of pain or swelling, bruising, loss of range of motion, and weakness of grip. Surgical repair most commonly consists of removal of the small bone fracture fragment. This procedure is highly successful and results in return to play in 6 to 8 weeks following the operation, rehabilitation, and reconditioning of the injured area.

DISTAL BICEPS TENDINITIS AND DISTAL BICEPS RUPTURE

This less common injury occurs in the lead elbow during a violent swing as the lead arm is rotated during the follow-through phase of the swing. The athlete will usually have a history of biceps tendinitis or elbow pain prior to the rare event of an actual distal biceps rupture. Duration of recovery from non-surgical rehabilitation may be only days to a few weeks. Surgical repair will require 3 months of rehabilitation and reconditioning before beginning return to play protocols. Post-injury recovery rates, surgical or non-surgical, are excellent.

THROWING INJURIES

Unlike the few injuries that occur from swinging, throwing injuries are extremely common and likely what comes to mind when we think of a "baseball injury." Throwing injuries to the shoulder and elbow in competitive athletics are common due to the violent nature of the overhead throw. Injuries most commonly occur as a result of overuse, but may also occur as an acute injury or event. In the throwing shoulder and the throwing elbow, injuries occur as a result of repetitive microtrauma to the soft tissue and supporting structures. This repetitive microtrauma is additive during the course of a throwing athlete's career.

Throwing injuries to the elbow occur during the late cocking, early acceleration, and deceleration phases of throwing. The athlete may describe sudden onset or gradually developing injuries. Acute injuries may include a "pop." The athlete may report a decline in performance with decreased accuracy, velocity and/or stamina. Throwing injuries are commonly associated with difficulty recovering between innings or between outings, and the athlete may notice pain, soreness, tingling or burning in the shoulder and/or elbow.

> **Throwing injuries to the elbow occur during the late cocking, early acceleration, and deceleration phases of throwing.**

A review of the publications on biomechanical aspects of throwing provides understanding of the forces across the throwing shoulder and elbow during training and competition. We recommend the Biomechanics of Throwing by Glenn Fleisig, PhD from the American Sports Medicine Institute as an excellent resource for in-depth knowledge on the subject, available here: whosonfirstbook.com/fleisig.

SHOULDER INJURIES

The majority of athletes who have a painful shoulder during throwing respond to treatment using nonsteroidal anti-inflammatory medications and oral steroids for inflammation and pain control. Activity modification for up to 6 weeks is important. However, it is sometimes difficult to gain compliance from the athlete depending on the time of year and the athlete's desire to return to play as soon as possible. Rehabilitation of the shoulder, scapula, and core musculature is the key to a successful nonoperative regimen of treatment of throwing injuries to the shoulder.

The complexity of the shoulder anatomy, and the close proximity of the important structures of the shoulder that are at risk for injury are illustrated in the above diagram.

ROTATOR CUFF TENDINITIS AND BICEPS TENDINITIS

Rotator Cuff Tendinitis occurs as a strain of the rotator cuff musculature, or may occur from excessive repetitive throwing. The condition is common in both young developing athletes and experienced professionals. Fortunately, if recognized early and managed appropriately with rest, rehabilitation, and anti-inflammatory medications, complete healing and resolution of symptoms is expected. It is important to note that continued throwing with tendinitis without proper care may further injure the rotator cuff and/or surrounding structures such as the labrum or the biceps tendon.

Duration of recovery from non-surgical rehabilitation may be only a few days or weeks in pitchers, and is not likely to require extended recovery time in position players. Chances of returning to the previous level of performance are excellent.

The forces that occur across the biceps tendon during competitive throwing in overhead athletes is well documented. Inflammation and soreness in throwing athletes, called Biceps Tendinitis, is common. The biceps tendon rests in the bicipital groove on the anterior (front) aspect of the shoulder, and biceps tendinitis causes pain in this region. It is important to note that biceps tendinitis is rarely an isolated condition, and may indicate a more serious condition in the shoulder such as a labral tear, or shoulder instability.

Duration of recovery from non-surgical rehabilitation is variable depending on the underlying cause or etiology. In the event Biceps Tendinitis is a symptom of another more serious condition in the shoulder such as a labral tear or a SLAP tear, surgical repair of the biceps labral complex may be required. Rehabilitation and return to play is approximately 6-9 months, depending on the athlete's position.

Recovery statistics and chances of returning to previous level of performance is guarded in surgically treated shoulders. Return to pitching requires at least 9 months of post-operative rehabilitation and conditioning, and approximately 6 months for positions with lower throwing demand, such as a first base and corner outfield positions.

The oval-shaped glenoid labrum of the shoulder, which is the attachment site of the ligaments and biceps tendon to the socket of the shoulder, is subjected to extreme forces during both the acceleration phase and deceleration phases of the throwing motion. This commonly results in labral tears and/or SLAP tears, which is the next injury discussed. Extensive literature has been written on the subject of labral tears in the overhead and throwing athlete.

Importantly, protection measures are recommended for young developing athletes and more experienced throwing athletes advanced in their careers to prevent labral tears. Return to previous levels of performance is difficult following a labral tear, and especially difficult in the event surgical intervention is required.

SUPERIOR LABRUM TEAR FROM ANTERIOR TO POSTERIOR ("SLAP" TEAR)

The term "SLAP Tear" describes a specific tear of the glenoid labrum at the superior rim of the glenoid involving the attachment site of the biceps tendon. The term SLAP stands for superior labrum anterior to posterior. The attachment of the biceps is subject to rotational stresses resulting in the peeling of the labrum from the superior glenoid, which results in a SLAP tear. This injury was described by Dr. James Andrews in 1985, and further classified by Dr. S. Snyder in 1990. The glenoid labrum is a fibrocartilaginous tissue that surrounds the glenoid fossa or shoulder socket. The labrum serves as the anchor point of the biceps tendon in the shoulder and the attachment site of the ligamentous structures that support the arm and provide stability.

Injuries to the shoulder and labrum occur with normal activities of life. The challenge in diagnosing shoulder pain in a throwing athlete is to differentiate between the variations of minor labral wear and tear, versus injuries that create a significant disabling injury. A further challenge is to appropriately treat only those injuries that are clinically relevant i.e., good SLAP versus bad SLAP tears. Sports medicine literature in the study of SLAP tears has documented labral injury in up to 82.5% of all minor league baseball players.

> **Highly trained orthopaedic sports medicine physicians will exercise caution in treating baseball players with SLAP tears and will carefully treat non-operatively for as long as possible.**

SLAP tears occur due to the violent nature of throwing that creates repetitive traction on the biceps tendon and its attachment into the superior glenoid labrum. Tears may also result from falls on an outstretched arm creating shear forces on the biceps-labral complex.

Outcomes of return to play following repair of SLAP tears are guarded at best, with reported 84% return to play following an isolated SLAP tear. Of those athletes that were able to return, 26% required a position change and only 66% were able to return to their previous level of competition. 89% felt some pain, stiffness and tightness on their return. Pitchers have a much lower rate of return with multiple studies indicating a wide range of results from 30%-80% return to play.

Position players, as one would expect, demonstrate a much higher success rate of return to play, with 60-90% reporting good to excellent outcomes. Highly trained orthopaedic sports medicine physicians will exercise caution in treating baseball players with SLAP tears and will carefully treat non-operatively for as long as possible.

ROTATOR CUFF INJURIES AND TEARS

These injuries are the result of the repetitive violent forces on the throwing shoulder and rotator cuff. Mechanisms for rotator cuff tears, which usually occur in a more experienced throwing athlete, include tendon failure from eccentric overload or internal impingement of the rotator cuff on the posterior superior (upper back) labrum. Most likely, these mechanisms of injury overlap and are contributing factors.

INTERNAL SHOULDER IMPINGEMENT

The concept of internal impingement of the shoulder has developed as the understanding of the thrower's shoulder has evolved. Internal impingement occurs when the posterior rotator cuff repetitively contacts the posterior glenoid labrum during throwing. This repetitive contact results in partial thickness tears of the rotator cuff and posterior labral tears.

The condition of internal impingement of the rotator cuff occurs as a result of the acquired increased external rotation that highly trained throwing shoulders demonstrate. This increased external rotation develops gradually throughout a player's career, and is easily demonstrated when the dominant or throwing shoulder is compared to the non-throwing shoulder in an individual.

The throwing shoulder in developing players undergoes adaptive changes, one of which is increasing external rotation of the shoulder. Over the course of a young player's growth and maturity, the throwing shoulder will develop increasing external rotation with less internal rotation of the shoulder. Internal impingement occurs in most talented players and can be detected on MRI, but may or may not be symptomatic during the player's career.

Early in the process of these adaptive changes, and with the increased range of motion and laxity, the posterior aspect of the rotator cuff will impinge on the posterior labrum. Over a period of time, the posterior shoulder capsule becomes extremely tight, resulting in Glenohumeral Internal Rotation Deformity (GIRD). Recognition and treatment at an early stage with focused posterior capsular stretching under the direction of an athletic trainer or physical therapist will result in improvement and resolution of the symptoms.

In throwers or overhead athletes with symptomatic internal impingement, the goal of treatment is non-operative management. This involves a 4- to 6-week period of active rest and rehabilitation, followed by a gradual return to throwing before competitive throwing. Pitchers usually require 3 months of rehabilitation to return to their previous level of play. Most position players can shorten this recovery and treatment period due to less demands on their arms. It is difficult to estimate the numbers of athletes who eventually require surgical treatment for internal impingement, but the goal of the treating physician is non-operative care, provided the labrum and rotator cuff injuries are mild.

Once symptomatic internal impingement with a labral tear is detected, making the decision to proceed with surgical treatment in the athlete with internal impingement is a difficult one. Usually, the decision to proceed with surgery occurs only in the event the athlete fails at least 2 courses of conservative management. When the athlete and treating physician determine that surgical treatment is the best option, it is important to discuss lengthened return to play times, and less optimistic outcomes after surgical treatment. The return to competitive throwing in these cases approaches 9 months for pitchers, and between 4-6 months in a low demand position player.

Some studies will report only a 30-60% success rate of return to the previous level of competition for throwers treated surgically. However, the expectation in appropriate management is currently closer to 80% of athletes who experience good to excellent results.

PROXIMAL HUMERAL EPIPHYSITIS ("LITTLE LEAGUER'S SHOULDER")

This throwing injury is the result of inflammation of the epiphysis or "growth plate" of the humerus. Little Leaguer's Shoulder occurs in youth and adolescent athletes who are in the active growth stages of skeletal maturity. Pain is located in the upper arm or shoulder and will completely recover but requires cessation of throwing for an extended period of time. Symptoms usually resolve with appropriate treatment in 3 weeks, but more severe cases have been noted to take as long as 3 months to return to throwing activities. No long-term consequences or injury results from this condition.

ELBOW INJURIES

Throwing injuries to the elbow most commonly occurs in the 5 structures on the medial aspect of the elbow, and are in close proximity to one another. These 5 structures are:

1. Medial Epicondyle
2. Flexor Pronator Tendon
3. Ulnar Collateral Ligament
4. Ulnar Nerve
5. Olecranon Process

The correct diagnosis in a painful throwing elbow remains a difficult task. The spectrum of injury ranges from a mild strain injury of the medial soft tissues to a more severe soft tissue and bony injury. The throwing elbow in a competitive thrower is subject to repetitive stresses that accumulate up over the career of the athlete, which places the elbow at various stages of the spectrum of injury.

Youth and adolescent athletes usually have injuries that are less advanced along the spectrum of injury. The different diagnoses of a throwing injury all occur with a similar mechanism of injury, which is medial elbow stress during competitive throwing. The complexity of reaching the appropriate diagnosis lies in the proximity of the 5 important structures on the medial aspect of the elbow. The resulting injuries of these 5 structures are discussed below.

MEDIAL EPICONDYLITIS

Medial Epicondylitis, or Elbow Tendinitis, is the inflammation of the attachment site of the flexor tendon on the bony prominence of the medial epicondyle. The flexor tendon attaches to a small area on the medial epicondyle, which results in higher strain forces at the tendon attachment site. It is very similar to flexor pronator tendinitis, which is inflammation of the flexor pronator tendon attachment, in its response to treatment.

The condition has a short duration of symptoms lasting from a few days to a few weeks, and X-rays will not show any skeletal changes. This condition frequently occurs in younger athletes with advancing baseball skills as they place more demand on their elbows. Conservative management of rest, ice, and anti-inflammatory medication resolves the condition.

FLEXOR PRONATOR TENDINITIS

This condition is due to inflammation of the flexor pronator tendon attachment. The condition has a short duration of symptoms that last a few days to a few weeks, and X-rays will not show any skeletal changes. This condition frequently occurs in younger athletes with advancing baseball skills as they place more demand on their elbows. Conservative management of rest, ice, and anti-inflammatory medication results in resolution of the condition.

LITTLE LEAGUER'S ELBOW

Little Leaguer's Elbow is similar to Medial Epicondylitis, except this condition occurs in an athlete with open epiphyseal plates (growth plates). This condition is also caused from inflammation or tendinitis of the attachment site of the flexor tendon on the bony prominence of the medial epicondyle. However, it may involve inflammation or injury to the growth plate or medial epicondylar apophysis.

Little Leaguer's Elbow presents symptoms of medial elbow pain in skeletally immature athletes who are in the rapid growing phase of their skeletal development. The pain originates from traction on the apophysis or "growth plate." In a growing child, the growth plate is weaker during periods of growth and has less strength to resist traction forces. Onset of pain in this region in youth and adolescent athletes is of concern. There is a significant risk of injury to the growth plate, and possible fracture of the growth plate, which would require surgery.

As a result of repetitive throwing or ignoring the signs of Little Leaguer's Elbow, there are increased forces placed across the growth plate, which risks an avulsion fracture of the medial epicondyle. In the event that an avulsion fracture occurs, surgery is required for fixation and repair of the fracture. On x-ray exam, there is noted to be open apophysis of the medial aspect of the elbow. The athlete will notice a gradual onset of pain with throwing activities, with pain isolated to the medial epicondyle.

It is important to immediately discontinue throwing once an athlete develops medial epicondyle pain because of the high risk of medial epicondyle avulsion fracture requiring surgical fixation. Early recognition of Little Leaguer's Elbow results in improvement and recovery in 3-6 weeks.

The athlete must completely eliminate any throwing activities or activities that cause pain in the elbow. If surgical treatment is required, the post-surgical healing time is usually 6 weeks. This period is followed by a prescribed return to throwing program that progresses over an additional 6 weeks, for a total recovery of 3 months. Excellent outcomes are seen with these injuries, both surgical and non-surgical, and these conditions usually resolve without long-term consequences or disabilities.

AVULSION FRACTURE OF THE MEDIAL EPICONDYLE

In the event of an avulsion fracture of the medial epicondyle, when the tendon comes away from the bone and can take a piece of the bone with it, surgery is required for fixation and healing. Before the fracture occurs, the athlete will notice a gradual onset of pain with throwing activities, with pain isolated to the medial epicondyle. It is important to immediately discontinue throwing once an athlete develops medial epicondyle pain because there is a high risk of fracture if competitive throwing or pitching is not discontinued.

Recovery time in the thrower with pain and symptoms prior to avulsion fracture or separation is usually 3-6 weeks. The athlete must completely eliminate any throwing activities or activities that cause pain in the elbow. If surgical treatment is required, the post-surgical healing time is usually 6 weeks, followed by a prescribed return to throwing program. Excellent outcomes are seen with these injuries, both surgical and non-surgical, without long-term consequences or disabilities.

ULNAR COLLATERAL LIGAMENT TEARS OR SPRAINS

Ulnar collateral ligament injuries are the result of recurrent stress and demand on the UCL during competitive throwing. The injury to the UCL most commonly occurs over the course of a player's career. Rarely are the tears acute, but usually result from the repetitive microtrauma that occurs to the throwing elbow of an athlete during the course of their career. Tears of the UCL of the elbow are the most common throwing injury that occurs on the medial aspect of the elbow.

The strength of the UCL is only 1/3 of the forces that are created in the elbow with maximum effort throwing. The term "repetitive microtrauma," is important to consider in evaluating UCL injuries. The talented thrower who becomes a pitcher will have more repetitions during the course of their playing career than the position player.

With the development of youth and select baseball moving from seasonal to year-round participation over the past 30 years, the incidence of UCL injuries continues to climb at the same injury rate as the increase in the number of games and months of play. The athlete with an injury to the UCL has pain symptoms on the medial aspect of the elbow. In injuries that progress, the athlete will report a declining performance with a decrease in velocity and loss of control. In younger athletes, the early recognition of elbow pain and UCL injury may be treated conservatively with rest and rehabilitation.

Other treatment options in the early stage of UCL injury include biologic treatment such as Platelet Rich Plasma injections. Over the past 12-15 years, treatment of partial UCL injuries with biologic therapy, such as Platelet Rich Plasma (PRP), has reported good outcomes in return to play, and avoiding surgery in younger athletes.

With the development of youth and select baseball moving from seasonal to year-round participation over the past 30 years, the incidence of UCL injuries continues to climb at the same injury rate as the increase in the number of games and months of play.

In athletes who require surgical treatment, returning to play for position players may be possible 6-9 months after operation. Pitchers, on occasion, may return to competitive pitching as early as 9 months postoperatively due to the demand on their arms. However, in more advanced throwers, 12-15 months to return to competition is more common.

Chances of a successful outcome are extremely high. In a study performed by the American Journal of Sports Medicine, "A total of 179 pitchers with UCL tears who underwent reconstruction met the inclusion criteria and were analyzed. Of these, 148 pitchers (83%) were able to [return to play] in the MLB, and 174 pitchers were able to [return to play] in the MLB and minor league combined (97.2%), while only 5 pitchers (2.8%) were never able to RTP in either the MLB or minor league."[141]

In athletes with acute tears of the UCL from the attachment site of the UCL, direct repair of the UCL provides an excellent option to athletes. The option of direct repair of the UCL may be the most beneficial course of treatment for position players, or athletes in whom formal UCL reconstruction may be too much of an operation, such as a youth or adolescent athlete. This method allows for earlier healing, shorter rehabilitation time, and faster return to play. The treating surgeon will make this determination on an individual patient basis. It is of utmost importance that the treating surgeon has extensive experience in treating all levels of throwing athletes from youth to professional baseball. There is extensive literature and educational information available for ulnar collateral ligament injuries. These resources are highly recommended for further exploration of the subject.

ULNAR NEURITIS AND ULNAR NERVE SUBLUXATION

Ulnar Neuritis and Ulnar Nerve Subluxation is a condition that occurs on the medial aspect of the throwing elbow. The condition occurs for two reasons:

1 when inflammation of the ulnar nerve develops as a result of repetitive elbow stress during throwing, or

2 due to increased mobility of the ulnar nerve, causing the nerve to move in and out of its groove.

The ulnar nerve location is just behind or posterior to the medial epicondyle in the ulnar groove. Due to its location, the ulnar nerve is subject to the same stresses as the other structures on the medial aspect of the elbow. On occasion, injury to the ulnar nerve may be isolated, but the majority of ulnar nerve conditions occur in combination with other medial elbow injuries. Inflammation of the nerve may exist as an isolated entity or may occur when there is ulnar nerve subluxation. The athlete will describe and complain of pain in the nerve with occasional tingling or shooting pain into the ring and little fingers during throwing.

Most commonly, Ulnar Neuritis or ulnar nerve pain is secondary to underlying instability of the elbow, which may indicate a UCL injury. If the symptoms of ulnar neuritis are isolated, recovery is most often successful in a period of 3-6 weeks. Modified throwing and medications such as non-steroidal anti-inflammatory or a short course of oral steroids are often prescribed for resolution of symptoms.

In the event conservative management fails and surgery is indicated, an ulnar nerve transposition is performed. This surgical procedure involves moving the nerve to a different location, which removes the stresses on the nerve during throwing. This procedure also shortens the course of the nerve as it crosses the elbow. Recovery time following an ulnar nerve transposition procedure is approximately 6 weeks in postoperative recovery and rehabilitation, followed by a progressive throwing program and return to play at 3 months.

OLECRANON STRESS FRACTURES

Olecranon stress fractures occur in the olecranon process, which is the large bone on the posterior aspect of the elbow. As the elbow extends, the olecranon fits into the olecranon fossa. With the violent nature of the throwing motion, the repetition of the olecranon impacting the olecranon fossa can create a stress fracture in the olecranon. These fractures occur with the same mechanics as those seen in a valgus extension overload injury.

Two fracture patterns are identified. One pattern is a transverse (complete) fracture due to traction forces created by the triceps tendon. In youth and adolescent athletes, this traction on the unfused olecranon growth plate creates an avulsion stress fracture. In the more mature athlete, oblique (angled) fracture patterns occur with the repetitive valgus force of the olecranon shearing in the olecranon fossa. Olecranon stress fractures, if recognized early, will usually heal with appropriate rest and time. Those fractures that do not heal are best treated surgically and have excellent outcomes of returning to play.

In addition, the same biomechanics can result in a condition known as valgus extension overload.

VALGUS EXTENSION OVERLOAD

This condition results in pain and the development of osteophytes or "bone spurs," which are abnormal bone growths, on the tip of the olecranon. Overhead throwing creates valgus and extension forces across the elbow. If these forces are not well-controlled by the ligaments supporting the elbow, or the dynamic stabilizers (muscle strength), the condition of valgus extension overload occurs.

Repetitive throwing results in shearing of the olecranon process in the olecranon fossa on the posterior aspect (back) of the elbow. This condition describes the abnormal mechanics that occur in the elbow during the violent nature of throwing. Pitchers, in particular, are subject to this condition and will report elbow pain during the release and deceleration phases of throwing. Degeneration and osteophyte formation may occur, requiring excision (surgical removal) of the bone spurs to return to competition.

Recovery time from surgery is shorter than most surgical treatment of the elbow. Following appropriate rehabilitation and conditioning, the athlete is encouraged to begin the return to throwing protocol at 6 weeks postoperatively. In the event the injured athlete does not have an additional injury in their throwing career, recovery statistics and chances of returning to previous level of performance is excellent. In athletes with valgus extension overload with osteophytes, non-operative management is always pursued with good results. It is imperative to confirm that another secondary underlying condition is not present in those athletes with osteophyte (spur) formation.

OSTEOCHONDRITIS DISSECANS

This condition is a challenging problem in the adolescent overhead athlete. It occurs as a result of the loss of blood supply to the bone and cartilage of the capitellum or humerus on the lateral aspect of the elbow. The segment of cartilage and bone then separates from the normal bone creating pain, catching, locking, and loss of motion in the elbow. This condition is commonly seen in youth and adolescent throwers and gymnasts, and occurs due to the repetitive impact of the humerus or capitellum on the lateral aspect of the elbow.

The treatment and recovery time are dependent on the grade or stage of the condition. In the earlier stages, conservative treatment with rest, elimination of throwing, and time (up to 3 months) will result in a healed lesion and return to throwing. However, most cases in advanced stages of the condition require surgery. The best outcomes of treatment occur with surgical fixation of the loose fragment, or replacement of the loose fragment with an osteochondral allograft to restore the joint surface with normal cartilage. Surgical outcomes result in 94% of athletes returning to throw competitively at approximately 3 months postoperatively.

MANAGEMENT OF BASEBALL INJURIES

The discipline of Sports Medicine involves the knowledge and understanding of the demands of each sport, and the demands of each position in that sport. Overhead athletes that place increased demands on the shoulder and elbow compete in sports such as baseball, softball, volleyball and swimming.

The decision-making process in the treatment of athletic injuries requires consideration of many factors affecting the athlete, including but not limited to: the time of year, current eligibility status, and real-

The decision-making process in the treatment of athletic injuries requires consideration of many factors affecting the athlete, including but not limited to: the time of year, current eligibility status, and realistic outcomes of the treatment of the injury or condition.

istic outcomes of the treatment of the injury or condition. Once an athlete enters a university or college, the NCAA allows student-athletes 5 years to complete 4 years of eligibility. This additional year allows for recovery from injury or for other circumstances which may have prevented the athlete from competition during a particular season. The time constraints on the athlete at the collegiate and professional levels are extremely demanding.

Currently, athletes at these levels train year-round, with little to no off-season, and have high expectations in practice and game competition. Other factors that create psychological demands on the athlete are parental involvement, expectations of peers, families and coaches, and previous success. In the event that an injury is the first significant injury for the athlete, the pressure of recovery, while teammates continue to progress and advance, creates additional psychological stress and pressure to return to competition.

Nevertheless, treatment and recovery protocol should be specific to each injury and needs of the athlete based on the severity of the injury and age of the athlete. While rest will always be the best mode of recovery and future injury prevention, active recovery methods and physical therapy, paired with cryotherapy (ice, cryo chambers, and ice baths) reduce inflammation and swelling, tissue damage, blood clot formation, and pain. Cryotherapy related treatments also aid in the removal of metabolites (waste products) and promote healing of the injured area.

If you would like access to additional resources regarding sports injuries, the American Orthopaedic Society for Sports Medicine

(AOSSM) initiated the Sports Trauma and Overuse Prevention (STOP) program in 2007, available here: stopsportsinjuries.org. STOP provides injury prevention resources that are both sport and injury specific, a sports medicine specialist locator to provide access for physicians who are exposed to and specifically treat sports injuries as a part of their medical practices, and a blog that covers a wide array of topics.

🗨 **BRAMHALL:** *There were two medical mishaps that detrimentally affected my career, which I will share for two reasons. First, we often only hear of the success stories in medicine, unless a major media company covers a story to educate the public on a specific danger. Medical failures are often either forgotten, buried in court documents and settlement agreements, or never fully understood. My experience taught me that it is important to approach major decisions conservatively, weighing all treatment options and possibilities to make the most informed decision. This protects against hindsight regret and allows time for the old adage "measure twice, cut once."*

The second reason is to emphasize the importance of paying careful attention when decisions by others are hastily or unwisely made, before any long-lasting mistakes take place. Sometimes there is no going back. Whether these insights help your athlete directly, or inform an acquaintance on the ballfield, the value of preventing irreparable harm is priceless.

GET THE FACTS, WEIGH THE POTENTIAL SIDE-EFFECTS AND RISKS

Before my first week at Rice University as a two-way scholarship baseball student-athlete, I underwent LASIK eye surgery to correct my vision and eliminate contacts and glasses altogether. After all, LASIK gave Tiger Woods 20/15 vision, therefore, I would have the same result to better my career. I would enter a top 5 nationally ranked NCAA Division I baseball program as a freshman with my best foot forward.

Unbeknownst to me, I was actually not a candidate for the procedure, and the probability of a beneficial outcome was very slim. This was well-known in ophthalmology.[138] My surgery resulted in double vision, inability to track fly balls, spots, intense dryness, difficulty wearing contacts, and poor depth perception.

After returning from summer ball in Cape Cod, a surgical expert at the Baylor College of Medicine reluctantly agreed to "re-lift the flap" and perform a second LASIK surgery. Thankfully, the surgery was successful in fixing some of the vision issues and I was able to continue my career playing a different position. I now remain extremely cautious of hurried decisions that don't have an "undo" function. The experience serves as a humbling reminder to make informed decisions and empathize with others who have had experiences that they too, will forever carry.

TRUST YOUR GUT, IT IS YOUR CAREER

During my first full-season in professional baseball, I beat out the future 2016 Cy Young Award winner, Rick Porcello, to earn the Hi-A Florida State League ERA Title. Entering my second season, I was a top 50 prospect and rated the "Best Changeup" in the Milwaukee Brewers system by Baseball America.

Unfortunately, like many professional pitchers, I partially tore my UCL early in my AA season as a starting pitcher. The Milwaukee Brewers minor league system policy allowed only one specific doctor to perform the surgeries. In fact, the head minor league trainer said that I would be "blackballed" by the system if I did not use their chosen physician.

Within hours after the surgery, I knew something was wrong. My elbow had no range of motion where it was supposed to be flexible, and dropped to full extension immediately when changing my bandages. This was the beginning of a trying and futile year of rehabilitation.

After consulting other orthopaedic surgeons (at my family's expense) it was *determined that the surgery had not been properly performed and the best option was to tear out the reconstructed ligament and undergo a second reconstruction. Given this information, I decided to have a second Tommy John surgery with world renowned orthopaedic surgeon Dr. Andrews. The decision led to weeks of meetings by the Brewers and their legal advisors, and the ultimate release of my contract because I chose to go outside of the system to have the second surgery. This was despite another player who suffered a career-ending blowout after having the same procedure by the same doctor only months before me.*

This destroyed the equity and accomplishments I had earned as one of their top pitchers. The second surgery, however, was a success. Unfortunately, I had lost my prospect status with the team that drafted and invested in me and I would be forced to start over as a free agent.

Thanks to David Crowson, the long-time professional baseball scout and administrator, the Miami Marlins gave me an opportunity only 12 months after the second reconstruction. I entered Spring Training only months into my rehab throwing program and had the best season of my career, one that as a prospect may have landed me on a Major League roster. That season, I had a 20-plus inning scoreless streak in AA and earned my first AAA promotion. Our manager called me "Seabiscuit."[139]

CONCLUSION

Understanding the different types of injuries and the appropriate treatment options will inform your decisions if they occur. Remember to seek care from competent physicians who practice sports medicine. As you have learned, there are physicians and medical personnel that don't provide accurate information or proper care, which can be the difference in good outcomes and long-term consequences. It is your athlete's career and you have every right to ask questions, do the research, and advocate for the best medical care at any age or level.

PERFORMANCE AIDES AND EVALUATION TECHNOLOGY

INTRODUCTION

Familiarizing yourself with the latest and most useful technology and tools in the baseball industry will educate you and your athlete on the usefulness of the products available. We eliminated products from consideration that may have a "gimmick" reputation or fail to provide accurate and reliable data. The primary goal is to use reliable tools to foster improvement. However, the list is not exhaustive as technology continues to improve and new products are developed.

While many of the products covered are outside the means of the average family to own, as is true with most state-of-the-art technology, many data driven training facilities have invested in them and use them regularly. This provides affordable avenues to benefit from the tools and track the measurements during the athlete's developmental progression through lessons or rental of a diagnostic and evaluation tool. Additionally, prices will likely decrease as the product supply increases or becomes widely recognized, or as other competitors enter the market to contribute to similar areas of improving performance.

> **The primary goal is to use reliable tools to foster improvement.**

The value of a tool depends on: 1 how often the athlete will use it and 2 whether the athlete understands the information and benefits provided for their career. Not all tools are a quick fix or useful to each and every individual. Becoming a ballplayer who wins and produces results will trump any standardized measurement of performance. As you consider the options, evaluate the specific purpose of each and whether that purpose will elevate your athlete's game. Using any product as a band-aid for a major mechanical issue can be counterproductive to your athlete's career. However, there are a number of products that allow an athlete to measure and evaluate the progression of their development.

LAUNCH MONITORS AND OTHER MONITORS

"Launch monitors" or other ball tracking units all share similar Doppler Radar technology. Each of the units listed provide hitting post-contact information, detailed batted ball path and spin analytics, and pitching analytics. The HitTrax unit also includes a catching module.

- Hit Trax - www.hittrax.com
- Trackman - trackmanbaseball.com
- Flight Scope - flightscope.com
- Rapsodo - rapsodo.com
- PitchTracker Smart Ball by Diamond Kinetics - diamondkinetics.com/pitchtracker/
- Yakkertech - yakkertech.com

HITTING MONITORS OFTEN PROVIDE:

- Launch angle (LA)
- Exit velocity
- Ball flight distance
- Point of impact
- Strike zone analytics

- Batted-ball outcome projection
- Hard-hit ball average (The percentage of hard-hit balls over a period of time).
- Line drive percentage
- Ball flight time

Some hitting monitors provide more detailed analytics

PITCHING AND CATCHING MONITORS OFTEN PROVIDE:

- Pitch velocity
- Pitch location
- late break measurement (when the break occurs in the ball's flight path)
- strike percentage
- Opposing team batting statistics
- Pitch type
- Spin axis
- Ball release height
- Ball release point
- Horizontal break
- Vertical break
- Ball movement at 40 feet
- Acceleration rate at 50 feet
- Spin rate
- Spin efficiency
- Pitch location
- Video

CATCHING MONITORS OFTEN PROVIDE:

- Throw velocity
- Pop time
- Transfer time
- Throw accuracy (vertical and horizontal)
- Reaction time
- Caught stealing percentage
- Video analysis

ADDITIONAL STATE-OF-THE-ART TECHNOLOGY USED IN BASEBALL

K-MOTION KVEST: K-MOTION.COM/K-COACH/K-BASEBALL

K-Motion's product includes wearable sensors that are designed to analyze biomechanical sequencing, acceleration and deceleration patterns throughout the athlete's movements in real-time for measurements, evaluation, coaching, and training. Some of the most useful data gathered by the tool are: peak speed sequence throughout the movement, peak speeds for specific body parts, time to contact, rotation degree around the spinal axis, and bend posture.

GROUND FORCE PLATES

Ground force plates measure ground reaction forces, providing information about ground force produced during movements in real time. The plates provide information about weight and energy transfer to improve efficiency in pitching and swinging movements.

EDGERTRONIC CAMERAS: EDGERTRONIC.COM

Edgertronic offers high-speed cameras for frame-by-frame evaluation from multiple angles. These cameras provide players and coaches precise movements during swing and pitching mechanics, or of the ball during flight. When paired with a launch angle device, a comprehensive picture of the movement and result provides proper coaching and answers to any question.

NEUROTRAINER: NEUROTRAINER.COM AND WIN REALITY: WINREALITY.COM

These virtual reality video systems provide neurological conditioning, virtual repetitions for practice sessions, and fine tuning prior to in-game competition. Neurotrainer trains the athlete to improve decision making; switch between tasks; expand field of vision and situational awareness; and improve and build mental focus and endurance by conditioning the same reflexes and cognitive processes that an athlete faces in live competition. Win Reality, provides tools for pitch recognition, and velocity and pitch preference training for workouts without physical expenditure. It also allows the hitter to connect the controller to the bat and swing at a virtual reality pitch.

COACH'S EYE: COACHSEYE.COM

HUDL TECHNIQUE: HUDL.COM/PRODUCTS/ TECHNIQUE

These apps are the two most common and user-friendly slow-motion video analysis tools that are accessible from any smartphone or tablet. Both apps provide tools such as: slow motion analysis (forward and reverse), drawing lines, shapes, and angles, side-by-side video comparison, voice over recording, and sharing video to other devices (to send to coaches, parents, scouts, or athletes). The free versions offered are sufficient for most athletes, but upgrade options provide advanced features for low monthly or annual costs.

SMART BAT TECHNOLOGY

BLAST MOTION SWING ANALYZER: BLASTMOTION. COM AND DIAMOND KINETICS SWINGTRACKER: DIAMONDKINETICS.COM/SMART-BATS

Distinguished from the launch monitors discussed above that provide post-contact point information, these cost-effective bat sensors provide pre-contact measurements such as:

- On-plane efficiency

- Rotational acceleration

- Early connection

- Connection at impact

- Bat speed at impact

- Angle of attack/contact

- Vertical bat angle

- Time to contact

- Peak hand speed

- Power

These measurements provide hitters a general overall swing score. Each product allows the athlete to use their smartphone or tablet as the launch monitor and provides pre-contact data. The Blast Motion Sensor and Diamond Kinetics sensor provide very similar information. Terminology is the biggest difference between the two. Additionally, the products are used by MLB organizations to provide in-depth metrics for evaluation and development purposes.

POCKET RADAR: WWW.POCKETRADAR.COM

The Pocket Radar is a compact sized radar gun that measures pitched or batted velocity from in front or behind the athlete. This user-friendly, cost-effective, and highly accurate tool is a good substitute for the more expensive radar gun options.

USEFUL TRAINING TOOLS AND PROGRAMS

ALWAYS GRIND: ALWAYSGRIND365.COM, @ALWAYSGRIND365

Always Grind provides notebooks and game logs for coaches, pitchers, catchers, and hitters to track and record game results on a game by game, weekly, monthly, or annual basis. They are excellent for post-competition review of successes and failures. Many seemingly poor performances are the result of only a couple of pitches or plays in the field. By evaluating pitch sequencing or preparation for quality at bats, or understanding the precise moment a pitcher makes a mistake, the athlete can reinforce successes or learn from missed opportunities in a constructive manner.

WEIGHTED THROWING PROGRAMS (OVERLOAD/UNDERLOAD)

PHANTOM WEIGHTS: PHANTOMWEIGHTS.COM

DRIVELINE WEIGHTED LEATHER BASEBALLS PLYO BALLS: PLUS.DRIVELINEBASEBALL.COM/ PRODUCT/DRIVELINE-LEATHER-WEIGHTED-BASEBALLS

Velocity enhancement throwing programs are designed to strengthen athletes throwing muscles and sequencing for increased velocity output, strength, mobility, and injury prevention. These programs incorporate a series of weighted balls or weighted sleeves for training. Proper throwing mechanics and strength and mobility screening are crucial prior to beginning a weighted throwing training regimen to prevent injury.

Weighted programs such as Driveline or Phantom Weights are proven to improve an athlete's arm when performed properly at the appropriate age. Prior to pursuing a weighted throwing program, focusing on proper throwing mechanics with a long-toss program and improving overall strength with weight training. This may be the safest and most efficient route before an athlete matures in body composition and skill.

JAEGER BANDS: WWW.JAEGERSPORTS.COM

These easy-to-use exercise bands are used for strength and warm-up routines before or after practice or competition. With a unique design made with rubber tubing and velcro wrist straps, Jaeger Bands are a safe and effective tool, easily packable, and low cost.

WEIGHTED BAT TRAINING (OVERLOAD/UNDERLOAD)

PRO VELOCITY BAT: PROVELOCITYBAT.COM
SUPERSPEED SLUGGER: SUPERSPEEDSLUGGER.COM

DRIVELINE AXE BAT: WWW.DRIVELINEBASEBALL.COM/AXE-BAT

Similar to the design of the weighted ball programs, weighted bat training programs use overloaded and underloaded bats with weights at the handle or the end of the bat. Some of the programs also incorporate hitting weighted plyo balls. Programs range from 10-12 weeks and require 60-180 swings each day for 3-4 days per week. Not only do these programs help players generate more bat speed and increase exit velocity, but training with the varying weighted bats and plyo balls builds sequencing, barrel accuracy, and control for hitters.

Weighted bats are also effective for on-deck preparation.

To create a DIY weighted bat, wrap the barrel with double-sided adhesive athletic tape and place nickels or pennies in rows covering the barrel. Next, wrap athletic tape over the coins. This homemade option can create any chosen weight and is durable enough to swing with tee or front toss drills.

It is important to use common sense when determining the appropriate bat weight for your athlete because an unmanageable bat weight will create improper habits. For athletes who are younger than high school age, we recommend an oversized bat of no more than 20% of their game bat weight. Athletes at the high school, collegiate, or professional levels may be able to properly manage and produce positive results by swinging a bat above 20% of their game bat weight.

LONG AND SHORT BAT TRAINERS

Long bat trainers are longer in length than a standard game bat, such as a standard fungo or Axebat's Long Bat Trainer. Long bat trainers can be useful for developing more compact swings and tighter turns, especially on pitch locations on the inner third of the plate. Lengthy swings or inefficient movement patterns are exposed when using a bat significantly longer than a game bat. Weighted long bat trainers also increase the difficulty level and incorporate a strength development aspect.

Short bat trainers are shorter than a standard game bat. These bats are ideal for single arm training drills, focusing on barrel path and directional issues, and isolating individual arms for specific body awareness. Short bat trainers are available in regular game weights to train opposite field barrel path and timing. The shorter length exposes improper path or when hitters swing too early on away pitches and run out of barrel.

CONCLUSION

As with any performance enhancement aid or device, the key is understanding how and when to incorporate them into training for the player's benefit. The players who succeed are those who have learned to properly utilize the aids and devices that work for them to improve their ability and transfer it on the field for in-game results.

THE LAST OUT

In this book, we've endeavored to provide a realistic and informative guide for the many decisions you will face and the knowledge you will need as a parent or guardian of a ballplayer. We are hopeful that for Part I, the answers to questions that were not available to us in advance throughout our career journeys were clearly explained for you. Our goal is for those answers to serve as a preview and reference for each playing level and that your athlete's experiences will be more fulfilled as a result. For Part II, our goal was to point you in the right direction as it relates to failure, adaptation, and overspecialization as your athlete builds their athletic foundation. The access to proper hitting and pitching instruction, and resources we've provided, will prove worthwhile if you choose to incorporate them. We shared the best in the business. Part III's purpose was to share performance and wellness insights that would be difficult to obtain even with a vast network, hours of research, consultations, and field experience. For the first time, for your benefit, the best information by the experts in each critical area is in one place. As your athlete moves through their career, refer back to specific chapters when you need a refresher.

POST-GAME:
LIFE AFTER BASEBALL

As difficult as it may seem for you and your athlete, there will be a day when it all ends. It is difficult to realize that this enjoyable period is temporary and will radically change at the completion of the journey. Appreciate each pursuit, but do not let the outcomes create a boundary for who your athlete can be in the future. The investment of emotion, energy, money, and time will fade into memories of an incredible passion and pursuit that shaped a large portion of their identity.

We struggle to comprehend that everything is temporary and ever-changing, which means we must be grateful for the present moment and taste the nectar in the journey. World renowned author and endurance running enthusiast Malcolm Gladwell said, "To say I ran as fast as I possibly could have run is more important than to say I won a gold medal or I set a world record . . . To say I got to 99 percent of my ability is huge."[142]

While you may have many other ventures and responsibilities as a parent and working professional, your athlete will need to uncover a new identity and new ways of creating an impact after their baseball career. Perhaps, this could be accomplished by giving back to the game in some way or using what they learned while playing to make a difference elsewhere. In forming this new identity, you both will have the opportunity to seek new hobbies and take the positive lessons and experiences gained from practices, games, diet, travel, reflection, and politics to other areas of your lives. No experience is ever wasted.

Be understanding with your athlete during this time as they find a new arena to use their passions. Whether it is apparent or not, a great deal of meaning comes from the influence and recognition as an athlete in a society that worships athletics, whether that journey ends in high school, college, or professionally. This transition may be a struggle for some and easier for others. In Alex's Rodriguez's TV series: Back in the Game, "A-Rod" describes an athlete as having two deaths in their lifetime. The first is the death of the playing career, a death that can spiral into bankruptcy, family trouble, and addiction for many well-known superstars. The second death is the end of life that we will all face.[143]

Simply because the audience has changed does not mean the degree of influence must change. Starting over is healthy and essential. While one life may end in the 7th or 9th inning of the athlete's last game, an entirely new one will begin. Allow the skills your athlete learned in their playing career pivot for a new career to unfold. They could stay in sports, pursue a new field of study, or learn a new trade, rather than dwelling on a past that no longer serves them. Whatever you and your athlete decide for the next step, remember to always make your moves from a position of strength, confidence, and fearlessness.

We look forward to serving you and your athlete before, during, and after the many phases of this baseball journey. Thank you for spending time with us, we look forward to hearing from you! info@whosonfirstbook.com.

"To be prepared is half the victory."

◆ MIGUEL DE CERVANTES

KEY CONTRIBUTORS

🔻 **HERMAN DEMMINK** *is a former NCAA Division I and professional athlete. He is the owner of 3D Performance Training (www.3dperformancetraining.com) and holds his Master's degree in Biomechanics from the University of Tennessee. As a former TEAM USA Sports Performance Director (Baseball), he also holds a Registered Strength and Conditioning Coach with 15-year Distinction (RSCC*D) honor as one of the premier performance coaches in the country.*

Herman has compiled almost 30 years of coaching experience with clients ranging from a 5-year-old gymnast to a 90-year-old patient suffering from Parkinson's Disease. Herman was a 4-year Clemson University baseball letterman and 2006 team captain, 2004 National Strength Athlete of the Year Award winner (NSCA), and he competed in the 2006 College World Series. He was drafted by the Philadelphia Phillies in the 2006 MLB Draft, and played professionally from 2006–2009.

What separates Herman from other baseball strength and conditioning coaches is that he was a starting infielder on the 2006 Clemson Tigers College World Series team and played professionally before transitioning to training athletes at the collegiate and professional levels. There are few strength and conditioning coaches who compete at the highest level before training athletes, especially in baseball.

After his professional athletic career, Herman joined the strength and conditioning staff at the University of Tennessee where he produced All-Americans in baseball and tennis, and assisted the track and field program with athlete preparation. In Herman's coaching career, he has trained athletes in: Major League Baseball, the National Football League, the PGA Tour, Association of Tennis Professionals (ATP), Major League Soccer, Association of Volleyball Professionals (AVP), Olympic Track and Field, and triathletes around the world.

DR. JP BRAMHALL *has devoted his career to practicing sports medicine. He was the Director of Sports Medicine and Team Physician at Texas A&M University for over 30 years. He serves athletes of all ages by providing pre-game, in-game, post-game, and surgical care. Many of the athletes he cares for are among the highest profile names in collegiate and professional sports, past and present.*

Dr. Bramhall completed medical school at the Texas A&M College of Medicine in 1985 and completed his Orthopedic Surgery residency in Fort Worth in 1990. He was then selected for the prestigious Orthopedic Sports Medicine Fellowship with James Andrews, MD, in Birmingham, Alabama. He provides supervision for the medical care of the student athletes and is the medical director of the Texas A&M Sports Medicine and Physical Therapy Clinic.

Dr. Bramhall continues to serve on the Advisory Boards for the Huffines Institute of Sports Medicine and Human Performance and the Exercise Sports and Nutrition Lab. He is an active member of the SEC Team Physicians, the American Orthopedic Society of Sports Medicine, and is an active Fellow of the American Academy of Orthopedic Surgeons. He also serves as a statutory member of the Texas A&M Lettermen's Board. In 2013, he was inducted into the Texas High School Football Hall of Fame for his medical contributions to Texas High School Football, and he was the SEC Team Physician of the Year in 2019.

◆ **TAYLOR STOLT** *is a former Texas A&M University Track & Field athlete who now practices as a Functional Medicine Dietician and owns her own private practice. Taylor empowers her clients with timeless truths about how the human body was designed to process and utilize nutrients. She uses a comprehensive, whole-body approach by combining laboratory analysis with individualized nutrition, supplements, and lifestyle recommendations to help her clients feel their best. In addition to sports nutrition, Taylor specializes in gut health, inflammation and hormone balance. She sees clients both in-person and virtually, and shares free nutrition tips and recipes on her social media channels and on her website: plateandcanvas.com.*

◆ **JENNA WATERS** *is a Registered Dietitian who practices functional nutrition at the University of Tennessee Medical Center. Jenna helps enlighten and unleash the body's ability to function flawlessly when nourished correctly. In her "pre-mom" days, Jenna spent several years as the Assistant Sports Dietitian for the University of Tennessee Athletics Department. She worked with various teams and individual athletes, using the science of nutrition to help athletes perform, recover, sleep, and feel their best. Jenna's other clients have included the Nashville Predators (NHL), Syracuse University Football, and several Minor League and Major League Baseball players throughout their off-season training. With simplified nutrition for real life in mind, Jenna has created multitudes of nutrition tools, resources, and recipes that can all be found on her website: JennaWaters.com.*

ACKNOWLEDGEMENTS

We would like to thank the following individuals for helping us turn this dream into a reality. This book would not be complete without you. Whether you offered a quote or helped contribute your knowledge and subject matter expertise to a chapter, we are grateful for your time and dedication to seeing this project to completion. We wish you success in all your endeavors. Clare Zutz, Ph.D., Ariana Mansolino, Esq., Taylor Stolt, RDN, LD, CLT, Jenna Waters, MS, RD, J.P. Bramhall, M.D, Chase Headley, Matt Langwell, Zach Neal, Joe Savery, Jonathan Maurer, Lance Zawadski, and Brian Krumm, Esq.

⬣ **BRAMHALL:** *To Tim Ferriss - Thank you for showing me the way to discover truth and purpose in so many areas of my life over the past six years.*

REFERENCES

1. Adam Grant, THE MOST MEANINGFUL WAY TO SUCCEED, https://trendyquotes.com/the-most-meaningful-way-to-succeed/ (last visited November 30, 2020).

2. "What are the chances a Little League baseball player gets to the Major Leagues someday?", Spreadsheet Solving (last visited Apr. 10, 2020), https://spreadsheetsolving.com/little-league/., "Probability of Playing College and Professional Baseball," High School Baseball Web (last visited Apr. 10, 2020), http://www.hsbaseballweb.com/probability.htm., "Estimated probability of competing in professional athletics," NCAA.org (last visited Apr. 10, 2020), http://www.ncaa.org/about/resources/research/estimated-probability-competing-professional-athletics., "Estimated probability of competing in college athletics," NCAA.org, (last visited Apr. 10, 2020), http://www.ncaa.org/about/resources/research/estimated-probability-competing-college-athletics., J.J. Cooper, "How Many MLB Draftees Make It To The Majors," Baseball America (May 17, 2019), https://www.google.com/amp/s/www.baseballamerica.com/stories/how-many-mlb-draftees-make-it-to-the-majors/%3Famphtml.

3. Alan Webber, "Red Auerbach on Management," Harvard Business Review (March 1987), https://hbr.org/1987/03/red-auerbach-on-management.

4. Charles Duhigg, "What Google Learned From Its Quest to Build the Perfect Team," The New York Times Magazine (February 25, 2016), https://www.nytimes.com/2016/02/28/magazine/what-google-learned-from-its-quest-to-build-the-perfect-team.html.

5. Here is a great resource from one of the game's top players, Justin Verlander. In this video, he demonstrates proper warm-up techniques for baseball players of any age. Visit: www.stack.com/a/the-perfect-baseball-warm-up.

6.   "Big Fish/Small Pond: "David and Goliath" by Malcolm Gladwell," Achieve Admissions, https://www.achieveadmissions.com/single-post/2016-1-3-big-fishsmall-pond-david-and-goliath-by-malcolm-gladwell.

7.   Mark T. Williams, "An analysis of nearly 4 million pitches shows just how many mistakes umpires make," The Conversation (Apr. 8, 2019). https://theconversation.com/an-analysis-of-nearly-4-million-pitches-shows-just-how-many-mistakes-umpires-make-114874?mod=article_inline.

8.   Id.

9.   Herman Demmink of 3D Performance offers a class called "How to Run the 60." Demmink is the nation's leading expert on the sixty yard dash. For more on 3D Performance, visit: www.3dperformancetraining.com.

10.   "Rating the Physical Tools of a Potential Major League Player," High School Baseball Web (last visited, Nov. 30, 2020), http://www.hsbaseball-web.com/pro-scouting/rating_system.htm.

11.   "Baseball Recruiting 101," Go Big Recruiting (last visited Dec. 3, 2020), http://gobigrecruiting.com/recruiting101/baseball/positional_guidelines/middle_infielder.

12.   "Rating the Physical Tools of a Potential Major League Player," High School Baseball Web (last visited, Nov. 30, 2020), http://www.hsbaseball-web.com/pro-scouting/rating_system.htm.

13.   "Rating the Physical Tools of a Potential Major League Player," High School Baseball Web (last visited, Nov. 30, 2020), http://www.hsbaseball-web.com/pro-scouting/rating_system.htm.

14.   Baseball Factory (last visited December 4, 2020), https://www.baseball-factory.com/player-development/all-america-game/.

15.   Area Code Baseball (last visited December 4, 2020), https://www.areacodebaseball.com/area-code-games.

16.   East Coast Pro (last visited December 4, 2020), http://www.eastcoastpro.org/.

17.   Jeff Dahn, "The Classic: By The Numbers, Perfect Game" (Aug. 31, 2020), https://www.perfectgame.org/Articles/View.aspx?article=17430

18.   High School Baseball Web (last visited Dec. 3, 2020), www.highschool-baseballweb.com.

19.   "Baseball Recruiting 101," Go Big Recruiting (last visited Dec 4, 2020),

https://www.gobigrecruiting.com/recruiting101/baseball/recruiting_timeline/baseball_recruiting_timeline.

20. Lynn O'Shaughnessy, "The Odds of Playing College Sports," CBS News (Apr. 4, 2011, 12:49PM), https://www.cbsnews.com/news/the-odds-of-playing-college-sports/.

21. Malinda Zellman, "Salary for a High School Baseball Coach," Career Trend (Sept. 26, 2017), www.careertrend.com/salary-for-a-high-school-baseball-coach-13658470.html.

22. "Early Signing Period," Baseball Factory (last visited Dec. 4, 2020), https://www.baseballfactory.com/early-signing-period/.

23. https://www.ncsasports.org/recruiting/managing-recruiting-process/national-signing-day

24. In Tennessee, the Tennessee Promise Scholarship provides a tuition scholarship to any community or technical college for all Tennessee residents. Whether the athlete receives an athletic scholarship or not, they may not be responsible for tuition based on similar state-funded education initiatives. For more information: https://www.tn.gov/college-pays/money-for-college/state-of-tennessee-programs/tennessee-promise-scholarship.html.

25. http://www.ncaa.org/governance/committees/division-ii-student-athlete-do-you-know

26. Our Three Divisions, NCAA.org (last visited Dec. 4, 2020), http://www.ncaa.org/about/resources/media-center/ncaa-101/our-three-divisions.

27. Actual and necessary expenses are permitted and limited to: meals; (b) lodging; (c) apparel, equipment and supplies; (d) coaching and instruction; (e) health/medical insurance; (f) transportation (expenses to and from practice and competition, cost of transportation from home to training/practice site at the beginning of the season/preparation for an event and from training/practice/event site to home at the end of season/ event); (g) medical treatment and physical therapy; 4/19/20 61 (h) facility usage; (i) entry fees; and (j) other reasonable expenses.

28. NCAA 2020-2021 Division I Manual, Amateur Status 12.1.2 (Dec. 4, 2020), https://web3.ncaa.org/lsdbi/reports/getReport/90008.

29. "Want to Play College Sports?" NCAA Eligibility Center (last visited Dec. 4, 2020), https://web3.ncaa.org/ecwr3/.

30. "NCAA Clearinghouse Basics," San Clemente Tritons (last visited Dec. 4, 2020). https://www.sanclementeathletics.com/ncaaclearinghouse.

31. "Test Scores," NCAA.org (last visited Dec. 4, 2020), http://www.ncaa.org/student-athletes/future/test-scores

32. A maximum of 4 hours in one day may be used for practice and other team activities. 20 Hour Rule Document, NCAA, (last visited Dec. 4, 2020). https://www.ncaa.org/sites/default/files/20-Hour-Rule-Document.pdf.

33. College Rating Percentage Index (RPI), The Baseball Cube (last visited Dec. 4, 2020), http://thebaseballcube.com/college/rpi/.

34. There are 8 national seeds who are guaranteed to host each round of the playoffs prior to the College World Series in Omaha, NE, unless they are eliminated by another team.

35. In 2003, Rice University won the National Championship in the first year of its current form of the two bracket winners facing off in a 3-game final championship series.

36. "Summer College Leagues," Collegiate Baseball Newspaper (last visited Dec 4. 2020), http://baseballnews.com/summer-collegiate-leagues/.

37. Michael Lewis was the first journalist to dig into this phenomenon in Moneyball. After interviewing Billy Bean, GM of the Oakland Athletics (A's), he discovered that the A's were looking for underappreciated baseball players as a business model for success just as an investor looks for underappreciated stocks. Lewis, and the A's, have found that between two players with similar stats, the player appearing more physically fit is usually paid more, which creates the opportunity to sign an equally productive but undervalued player. "It became a very universal story about the mistakes we make when we look at another person [and determine their value]." The Tim Ferriss Show: "Michael Lewis - Inside the Mind of an Iconic Writer" (May 1, 2020) (downloaded using Apple Podcasts).

38. Maury Brown, "Minor League Ballplayers Would Lose Minimum Wage Rights As Part Of $1.3 Trillion Spending Bill," Forbes (Mar. 22, 2018, 12:13am), https://www.google.com/amp/s/www.forbes.com/sites/maury-brown/2018/03/22/minor-league-ballplayers-will-lose-minimum-wage-rights-as-part-of-1-3-trillion-spending-bill/amp/.

39. Richard, T. Karcher, "The Chances of a Drafted Baseball Player Making the Major Leagues: A Quantitative Study," Society for American Baseball

Research (Spring 2017),

40. "Service time" is time spent on a 25-man roster or the MLB Injured List.

41. Joe Rivera, "What is MLB arbitration? Explaining the rules, eligibility & how the process works," Sporting News (Jan. 13, 2020), https://www.sportingnews.com/us/mlb/news/what-is-arbitration-mlb-what-does-it-mean-baseball-eligibility-process/1atg6py-cmf69o1x5yy2v31o03w#:~:text=What%20is%20MLB%20arbitration%3F%20Arbitration%20is%20what%20happens,the%20club%20and%20the%20player%2C%20which%20is%20

42. The age of social media has created a unique opportunity for athlete and agent self-marketing by tagging and including organizations and other businesses or individuals in posts about an athlete's achievements and impact. It is no longer up to fate to decide whether a great moment, game, season, or stat line is recognized by the general public or an organization's front office staff.

43. AP, "MLB minimum salary rises $8,500 to $563,500 next season," USA Today (Nov. 13, 2019, 8:14PM),

44. "Baseball: Use of Agents Versus Advisors," NC State University Professional Sports Counseling Panel, (Sept. 18, 2021), https://sportspanel.wordpress.ncsu.edu/athletes-and-parents/baseball-use-of-agents-versus-advisors/.

45. There are specific exceptions in different sports across the NCAA. If the athlete is considering opportunities in sports besides baseball, please refer to the most current NCAA Manual for rules and regulations pertaining to athletes in a particular sport. The manual can be downloaded for free at: https://web3.ncaa.org/lsdbi/reports/getReport/90008

46. DI NCAA Manual, NCAA 2020-2021 Use of Agents 12.3.1.1 Exception -- Baseball and Men's Ice Hockey -- Prior to Full-Time Collegiate Enrollment (Dec. 4, 2020), https://web3.ncaa.org/lsdbi/reports/getReport/90008.

47. Agents (last visited Dec. 4, 2020). https://static.lsusports.net/custompages/assets/docs/ad/compliance/pdf/agents.pdf

48. Bryce Pruitt, Memorandum: Division I Baseball Student-Athletes with Remaining Eligibility, NCAA (May 31, 2019), https://ncaaorg.s3.amazonaws.com/enforcement/2019ENF_MLBEducationalMemo.pdf.

49. Id.

50. DI NCAA Manual, 11.1.3.1 Exception – Professional Sports Counseling Panel and Head Coach, NCAA 2020-2021 (Dec. 4, 2020), web3.ncaa.org/lsdbi/reports/getReport/90008.

51. "Agents and Amateurism," NCAA.org (accessed 12 February 2021), https://www.ncaa.org/enforcement/agents-and-amateurism#:~:text=The%20UAAA%20is%20an%20important%20tool%20in%20regulating,improper%20and%20illegal%20conduct%20of%20some%20athlete%20agents.

52. MLBPA Agent Certification FAQ, MLBPA (last visited Dec. 4, 2020), https://registration.mlbpa.org/FAQ.aspx.

53. Id.

54. Jim Callis, "Here are the 2019 Draft pools and bonus values," MLB.com (Jun. 3, 2019),

55. Jim Callis, "Here are the 2019 Draft pools and bonus values," MLB.com (Jun. 3, 2019),

56. "Official Rules, First-Year Player Draft," MLB.com (last visited Dec 5, 2020). available at: http://mlb.mlb.com/mlb/draftday/rules.jsp.

57. "Minor League Contracts & Roster Rules," The Cub Reporter (last visited Dec.5, 2020),

58. Interview with Lance Zawadzki, Former MLB player, Boston Red Sox Coach (April 10, 2020).

59. George Strait Lyrics, "A Showman's Life," AZLyrics.com (last visited May 14, 2020), https://www.azlyrics.com/lyrics/georgestrait/ashowmanslife.html.

60. No Stupid Questions Podcast: "How Does When You are Born Affect Who You Are?" (Mar. 7, 2021) (downloaded using Apple Podcasts).

61. At the minor league level, organizations often require community service in the mornings or on off days by the players without compensation, in addition to the time demands of a full season.

62. From 2007-2011, and likely in the years that followed, the breakfast provided by the Milwaukee Brewers at Spring Training: frozen waffles and bagels made available in plastic storage bins with peanut butter and cream

cheese. Hard-boiled eggs were cooked for over 4 hours by the clubhouse manager in a giant pot. The yolks were a burnt blueish purple color and gave intestinal issues to everyone who ate them. Players were forced to peel the whites off the "blackened" yolks because the resulting burn in the colon was so severe. This breakfast was deemed satisfactory for professional athletes before a 10-hour training day.

63. Associated Press, "Minor Leagues Get a Reset With 120-Team Regional Alignment" (February 12, 2021), https://www.si.com/mlb/2021/02/12/minor-league-baseball-realignment-regional-divisions.

64. "Many fans of the game openly pine for a return for "the good old days," when players played for the love of the game. It should be recognized, however, that the game has always been a business. All that has changed has been the amount of money at stake and how it is divided among the employers and their employees." Michael J. Haupert, "The Economic History of Major League Baseball," EH.net (last visited May 15, 2020), https://eh.net/encyclopedia/the-economic-history-of-major-league-baseball/.

65. Federal Minimum Wage for 2020-2021, Minimum-Wage.org, https://www.minimum-wage.org/federal.

66. Patrick Pinack, "Minor League Baseball Players Earn Less Than School Janitors," Fan Buzz (May 15, 2020), https://fanbuzz.com/mlb/minor-league-baseball-salary/.

67. Craig Calcaterra, "Major League Baseball sets new revenue record: $10.7 billion," NBC Sports (Dec 22, 2019, 7:17 AM), https://mlb.nbcsports.com/2019/12/22/major-league-baseball-sets-new-revenue-record-10-7-billion.

68. The "Save America's Pastime Act" MLB's Dirty Secret, Gaslamp Ball (Aug. 1, 2018, 3:29pm),

69. Ronald Blum, "MLB average salary at around $4.4M for 5th year in row, AP study says," The Associated Press (May 5, 2020 at 7:16 a.m.), https://www.denverpost.com/2020/05/05/mlb-average-salary-study/.

70. Michael Baumann, "The Disgrace of Minor League Baseball," The Ringer (Apr. 20, 2018, 5:50am), https://www.theringer.com/mlb/2018/4/20/17259846/minor-league-baseball-anti-labor-ronald-acuna-scott-kingery.

71. John D. Rockefeller's Standard Oil Company is an example of a monop-

oly that in 1911 the Supreme Court decided was a business involved in interstate commerce that had monopolized the petroleum industry and created an unreasonable restraint to trade through a series of "abusive and anti-competitive actions." This decision led to the dissolution of the Standard Oil empire and increased competition in the market that was previously excessively concentrated in Standard Oil's economic power. The Editors of the Encyclopedia Brittannica, "Standard Oil," Britannica (last visited Oct. 2, 2021), https://www.britannica.com/topic/Standard-Oil, Standard Oil Co. of New Jersey v. United States, 221 U.S. 1 (1911), Standard Oil Co. of New Jersey v. United States, Wikipedia (last accessed Oct. 2, 2021), https://en.wikipedia.org/wiki/Standard_Oil_Co._of_New_Jersey_v._United_States#:~:text=Sherman%20Antitrust%20Act.%20 Standard%20Oil%20Co.%20of%20New,through%20a%20series%20 of%20abusive%20and%20anticompetitive%20actions.

72. Commerce Clause, The Free Dictionary By Farlex (last visited Dec. 5, 2020), https://legal-dictionary.thefreedictionary.com/Commerce+Clause.

73. The 1953 ruling was again challenged in 1972 and 1998. The subsequent ruling narrowed the exemption and gave many rights to the players through the ability to collectively bargain agreements with Major League Baseball through labor union representation, The Major League Baseball Players Association (MLBPA). However, the minor league exemption remains unchanged.

74. Paul Kasabian, "Report: MLB Negotiating Proposal That Would Eliminate 40 Minor League Teams," Bleacher Report (Oct. 18, 2019). https://bleacherreport.com/articles/2858746-report-mlb-negotiating-proposal-that-would-eliminate-40-minor-league-teams#:~:text=%22The%20 %27Save%20America%E2%80%99s%20Pastime%20Act%27%20 was%20the%20result,Fair%20Labor%20Standards%20Act%20of%20 1938%2C%22%20Waldon%20wrote.

75. H.R. 5580 - Save America's Pastime Act, 114th Congress (Introduced Jun. 24, 2016), https://www.congress.gov/bill/114th-congress/house-bill/5580/text?format=txt.

76. "This section does not create, permit, or imply a cause of action by which to challenge under the antitrust laws, or otherwise apply the antitrust laws to. . . any conduct, acts, practices, or agreements of persons engaging in, conducting or participating in the business of organized professional baseball relating to or affecting employment to play baseball at the minor

league level, any organized professional baseball amateur or first-year player draft, or any reserve clause as applied to minor league players; . . .." Curt Flood Act of 1998 §15 USC 27(a)(1), 112 Stat. 2825 (Oct. 27, 1998), https://www.congress.gov/105/plaws/publ297/PLAW-105publ297.pdf.

77. H.R. 5580 - Save America's Pastime Act, 114th Congress (Introduced Jun. 24, 2016), https://www.congress.gov/bill/114th-congress/house-bill/5580/text?format=txt.

78. Michael McCann, "MLB Faces Tough Legal Road to Restructure Minor League Baseball," Sports Illustrated (Nov. 19, 2019), https://www.si.com/mlb/2019/11/19/minor-league-baseball-lawsuit.

79. Id.

80. "The "Save America's Pastime Act" MLB's Dirty Secret," Gaslamp Ball (Aug. 1, 2018, 3:29pm), https://www.gaslampball.com/2018/8/1/17640894/the-save-americas-pastime-act-mlbs-dirty-secret.

81. Mike Axisa, "Cubs win Kris Bryant service time case: Bryant will become free agent after 2021, per report," CBS Sports (Jan. 30, 2020 12:39PM), https://www.cbssports.com/mlb/news/cubs-win-kris-bryant-service-time-case-bryant-will-become-free-agent-after-2021-per-report/

82. MLB Team Payroll Tracker, Spotrac (last visited Dec. 5, 2020), https://www.spotrac.com/mlb/payroll/2019/.

83. NBA Team Salary Cap Tracker, Spotrac (last visited Dec. 5, 2020), https://www.spotrac.com/nba/cap/2018/.

84. Sung Min Kim, "Asia is No Longer a Last Stop for Major Leaguers," Fan Graphs (Feb. 21, 2018), https://blogs.fangraphs.com/asia-is-no-longer-a-last-stop-for-major-leaguers/.

85. September Call-Ups occur when the active rosters expand from 25 players to up to 40 players. September call-ups, while exciting, are not always beneficial for team dynamics as there may be several new inexperienced players in the clubhouse, and the opposing teams do not have detailed scouting reports on the players. This can be challenging for established players finishing their seasons and potentially competing for playoff spots.

86. "Scott Kelly – Lessons Learned from 500+ Days in Space, Life-Changing Books, and The Art of Making Hard Choices" (#478), The Tim Ferriss Show (Nov. 5, 2020) (downloaded using Apple Podcasts).

87. Ray Dalio, Principles, Chapter 3 (2020) (downloaded using Audible.com).

88. Richard Koch, Unreasonable Success and How to Achieve It, Thrive on Setbacks (2020) (downloaded using Audible.com).

89. Nasim Nicholas Talib, Antifragile: Things That Gain from Disorder (quoted in Richard Koch, Unreasonable Success and How to Achieve It, 2020).

90. Andrew Sergeyev, "3 Powerful Lessons from The Chinese Bamboo" (Timewiser.com, 2020), https://timewiser.com/blog/powerful-life-lessons-chinese-bamboo-story/.

91. Richard Mott Gummere, Seneca's Letters from a Stoic, On Groundless Fears (Dover Publications, 2016).

92. Leah Fessler, THE NITTY GRITTY: "you're no genius: Her father's shutdowns made Angela Duckworth a world expert on grit" (March 26, 2018), https://qz.com/work/1233940/angela-duckworth-explains-grit-is-the-key-to-success-and-self-confidence/.

93. Angela Duckworth FAQ: "What is Grit?", https://angeladuckworth.com/qa/ (last visited May 13, 2020).

94. TED Talks Education: "Grit: The Power of Passion and Perseverance" (TED Conference Speaker May 2013, available at: https://www.ted.com/talks/angela_lee_duckworth_grit_the_power_of_passion_and_perseverance/transcript).

95. Richard D Ginsburg, et al., "Patterns of Specialization in Professional Baseball Players," Journal of Clinical Sport Psychology, Sept. 2014, Vol. 8 Issue 3, at 261.

96. Tom House is a former MLB pitcher, baseball psychology professor and therapist, and professional baseball pitching coach. Information from live discussion with Tom House, Founder, Rod Dedeaux Research and Baseball Institute (RDRBI) (Jan. 2012).

97. Id.

98. This phrase is used as a figure of speech and is not meant to be disrespectful. We are aware that many, if not all, natives prefer to be referred to as "Native American" or "Native" rather than "Indian."

99. Many parents who have an athlete who prefers a composite bat will purchase a new or used alloy bat for cold weather.

100. "Position of the American Dietetic Association, Dietitians of Canada, and the American College of Sports Medicine: Nutrition and athletic perfor-

mance," J. Am. Diet. Assoc., 509 (2000).

101. Schoenfeld and Aragon, "How much protein can the body use in a single meal for muscle-building? Implications for daily protein distribution," Journal of the International Society of Sports Nutrition (Feb. 27, 2018), https://jissn.biomedcentral.com/articles/10.1186/s12970-018-0215-1. This assumes that athletes will spread consumption across four meals each day to meet the minimum requirement of 1.6g per kilogram of body weight, per day, for building lean muscle mass.

102. Example: An athlete weighing 200 lbs: 200/2.2 = 90.91 x 1.6 = 145.46 grams per protein needed each day for anabolism.

103. Nancy Rodriguez, Nancy DiMarco, Susie Langley, "Position of the American Dietetic Association, Dietitians of Canada, and the American College of Sports Medicine: Nutrition and Athletic Performance," Journal of The American Dietetic Association, 510 (March 2009), https://pubmed.ncbi.nlm.nih.gov/19278045/. Example: an athlete weighing 200 lbs would.: 200/2.2 = 90.91 x 6 to 10 = need 545 to 900 grams of carbohydrate per day.

104. "Omega fatty acids are fats that are not naturally produced, and thus, must be consumed. The three most important types of Omega-3 fatty acids are ALA (alpha-linolenic acid), DHA (docosahexaenoic acid), and EPA (eicosapentaenoic acid). ALA is mainly found in plants, while DHA and EPA occur mostly in animal foods and algae." Kris Gunnars,"What Are Omega-3 Fatty Acids? Explained in Simple Terms" (May 23, 2019), https://www.healthline.com/nutrition/what-are-omega-3-fatty-acids.

105. Caution on MCT Oil ingestion! The liver requires gradual adaptation to MCT Oil, and consuming too much initially may result in gastrointestinal distress and diarrhea.

106. Heaton, et al., "Selected In-Season Nutritional Strategies to Enhance Recovery for Team Sport Athletes, A Practical Overview," Sports Medicine, 2202 (July 2017).

107. Dr. Sears Zone, Evidence-Based Wellness (accessed Feb. 28, 2021), https://zonediet.com/the-zone-diet/.

108. Yvette Brazier, "The Zone diet: all you need to know," Medical News Today (Jan. 29, 2020), https://www.medicalnewstoday.com/articles/7382#what-is-it.

109. Kris Gunnars, BSc, "The 8 Most Popular Ways to Do a Low-Carb Diet,"

Healthline (Mar. 7, 2019), https://www.healthline.com/nutrition/8-popular-ways-to-do-low-carb.

110. "Keto Diet," U.S. News (accessed Feb 28, 2021), https://health.usnews.com/best-diet/keto-diet.

111. Jeff S, Volek, PhD, RD, Stephen D. Phinney, MD, PhD, The Art and Science of Low Carbohydrate Performance, pp. 30-34 (2012).

112. Rudy Mawer, MSc, CISSN, "The Ketogenic Diet: A Detailed Beginner's Guide to Keto," Healthline, (October 22, 2020), https://www.healthline.com/nutrition/ketogenic-diet-101#bottom-line.

113. Yvette Brazier, "How many calories do you need?," Medical News Today (Dec. 13, 2017), https://www.medicalnewstoday.com/articles/263028#empty-calories.

114. "Top 5 Body Composition Tests," Fitnescity (Sept. 24, 2018), https://www.fitnescity.com/blog/how-to-measure-body-fat.

115. Id.

116. Id.

117. Id.

118. Ronald J. Maughan, et al., "IOC consensus statement: dietary supplements and the high-performance athlete," Br. J. Sports Med. Vol. 52 Iss. 7, 439–455 (Apr. 2018). 10.1136/bjsports-2018-099027.

119. protein, carbohydrate, or fat

120. One example of beneficial pre-testing and evaluation is for a pitcher with restricted hip mobility. Hip mobility restriction limits range of motion, which limits their ability to generate maximum force from the ground through their hips. In turn, the restriction limits the total output force that the arm can generate to put maximum velocity on the baseball.

121. In the research of highly trained athletes, a degree of hyperplasia has been documented in rare instances when a muscle fiber splits into two fibers.

122. Dr. Benjamin Kibler established The Shoulder Center of Kentucky and was at the forefront of comprehensive shoulder rehabilitation and repair for most of his career. Dr. Kiber announced his retirement from Lexington Clinic in 2020. "Dr. Ben Kibler Retires from Lexington Clinic," Lexington Clinic (Jun. 1, 2020), https://www.lexingtonclinic.com/news/news/dr--ben-kibler-retires-from-lexington-clinic.

123. Andrew Heffernan, CSCS, GCFP, "How to Do the Pallof Press," OpenFit.com (Aug. 19, 2019), https://www.openfit.com/pallof-press-exercise.

124. Elizabeth Quinn, "Visualization Techniques for Athletes" (July 27, 2020), https://www.verywellfit.com/visualization-techniques-for-athletes-3119438#:~:text=Using%20Visualization%20Techniques%20for%20Better%20Sports%20Performance%20.,you%20want%20to%20happen%20or%20feel%20in%20reality.

125. Natalie Sebanz, "Mirror Neuron," Brittanica.com (May 28, 2014), https://www.britannica.com/science/mirror-neuron.

126. Areas of the brain in the default mode network (DMN) include: the medial prefrontal cortex; the posterior cingulate cortex; the hippocampus; and the amygdala, as well as parts of the inferior parietal lobe. Edward Hallowell, M.D., "ADHD's Secret Demon - and How to Tame It," Additude Inside the ADHD Mind (Nov. 6, 2019), https://www.additudemag.com/default-mode-network-adhd-brain/.

127. Meditation has a tangible positive effect on the amygdala, the part of the brain responsible for emotions, fight or flight responses, and memory. Richard Feloni, "After interviewing 140 people at the top of their fields, Tim Ferriss realized almost all of them share the same habit," Business Insider (Nov. 23, 2017), https://www.businessinsider.com/tim-ferriss-meditation-mindfulness-2017-11.

128. Meditation helps to "turn off" the DMN and keep us in the present, focused on the task at hand, and increasing awareness and filtering of many aspects that come into consideration. Buckner RL, "Know your Brain: Default Mode Network," Neuroscientifically Challenged (June 16, 2015), https://www.neuroscientificallychallenged.com/blog/know-your-brain-default-mode-network

129. Richard Feloni, "After interviewing 140 people at the top of their fields, Tim Ferriss realized almost all of them share the same habit," Business Insider (Nov. 23, 2017), https://www.businessinsider.com/tim-ferriss-meditation-mindfulness-2017-11.

130. Matthew Walker, Why We Sleep, Chapter 16 (Oct. 3, 2017).

131. Harvard Health Publishing, "Sleep and mental health" (Mar. 18, 2019), https://www.health.harvard.edu/newsletter_article/Sleep-and-mental-health.

132. Matthew Walker, Why We Sleep, Chapter 15 (Oct. 3, 2017).

133. tephen Bird, "Sleep, Recovery, and Athletic Performance: A Brief Review and Recommendations," Strength and Conditioning Journal (Oct. 2013).

134. The Joe Rogan Experience: "Sleep Expert and Neuroscientist Dr. Matthew Walker" (April 29, 2018) https://podcastnotes.org/joe-rogan-experience/why-we-sleep/.

135. Matthew P. Walker, Berkeley Psychology (last visited August 1, 2020), https://psychology.berkeley.edu/people/matthew-p-walker

136. Matthew Walker, Why We Sleep, Chapter 3 (Oct. 3, 2017).

137. Matthew Walker, Why We Sleep, Appendix: "Twelve Tips for Healthy Sleep" (Oct. 3, 2017).

138. There are more LASIK complications and dangers than are publicized. Do your own research because you only get two eyes. https://www.lasikcomplications.com/.

139. Andy Barkett is a former Pittsburgh Pirates MLB player and former Boston Red Sox Hitting Coach. An excellent game manager and on-the-field player advocate.

140. Shane Seroyer, et al., "The kinetic chain in overhand pitching: its potential role for performance enhancement and injury prevention" Sports Health: A Multidisciplinary Approach, 135-46 (Mar. 1, 2010), https://pubmed.ncbi.nlm.nih.gov/23015931/.

141. Brandon Erickson, et. al, "Rate of Return to Pitching and Performance After Tommy John Surgery in Major League Baseball Pitchers," The American Journal of Sports Medicine (Dec. 18, 2013), https://journals.sagepub.com/doi/abs/10.1177/0363546513510890.

142. The Tim Ferriss Show: "Malcolm Gladwell - Dissecting the Success of Malcolm Gladwell" (Jun. 1, 2018) (downloaded using Apple Podcasts).

143. Alex Rodriguez, "BACK IN THE GAME" (CNBC 2019).

CPSIA information can be obtained
at www.ICGtesting.com
Printed in the USA
BVHW041226260722
643031BV00009B/613